LOCATING THE MOVING IMAGE

THE SPATIAL HUMANITIES

David J. Bodenhamer, John Corrigan, and Trevor M. Harris, editors

The spatial humanities is a new interdisciplinary field resulting from the recent surge of scholarly interest in space. It prospects a ground upon which humanities scholars can collaborate with investigators engaged in scientific and quantitatively-oriented research. This spatial turn invites an initiative focused on geographic and conceptual space and is poised to exploit an assortment of technologies, especially in the area of the digital humanities. Framed by perspectives drawn from Geographic Information Science, and attentive to cutting-edge developments in data mining, the geo-semantic Web, and the visual display of cultural data, the agenda of the spatial humanities includes the pursuit of theory, methods, case studies, applied technology, broad narratives, persuasive strategies, and the bridging of research fields. The series is intended to bring the best scholarship in spatial humanities to academic and lay audiences, in both introductory and advanced forms, and in connection with Web-based electronic supplements to and extensions of book publication.

LOCATING THE MOVING IMAGE

NEW APPROACHES TO FILM AND PLACE

EDITED BY JULIA HALLAM AND LES ROBERTS

INDIANA UNIVERSITY PRESS

Bloomington & Indianapolis

This book is a publication of

INDIANA UNIVERSITY PRESS
Office of Scholarly Publishing
Herman B Wells Library 350
1320 East 10th Street
Bloomington, Indiana 47405 USA

iupress.indiana.edu

Telephone orders 800-842-6796
Fax orders 812-855-7931

⊖The paper used in this publication
meets the minimum requirements of the
American National Standard for
Information Sciences–Permanence of
Paper for Printed Library Materials,
ANSI Z39.48–1992.

*Manufactured in the
United States of America*

*Library of Congress
Cataloging-in-Publication Data*

Locating the moving image : new
approaches to film and place / edited by
Julia Hallam and Les Roberts.
   pages cm. — (The spatial humanities)
   Includes bibliographical references and
index.
   ISBN 978-0-253-01097-1 (cl : alk. paper) —
ISBN 978-0-253-01105-3 (pb : alk. paper) —
ISBN 978-0-253-01112-1 1. Motion picture
industry. 2. Film criticism—Philosophy.
3. Motion pictures—Production and
direction. 4. Motion pictures—Social
aspects 5. Arts and geography. 6. Motion
picture audiences. 7. Spatial analysis
(Statistics) I. Hallam, Julia, [date]- editor
of compilation. II. Roberts, Les, [date]-
editor of compilation.
   PN1995.L56 2013
   791.43'62—dc23
                              2013024341

1 2 3 4 5   19 18 17 16 15 14

Contents

Acknowledgments

This collection of essays explores the methodologies that are being used by film scholars to develop a new area of inquiry, one we have termed in our concluding comments "a spatial history" of the moving image. The contributors are interested in exploring film production, distribution, and consumption as spatial phenomena, using empirical data and maps to create detailed knowledge of the ways transportation and communication systems shape local and national film practices and pleasures. Some of them are pioneers in what Richard Maltby has termed "the new cinema history," and they presented their work at the Mapping, Memory and the City conference at Liverpool University in February 2010. The conference was the culmination of a two-year project, Mapping the City in Film, funded by the UK Arts and Humanities Research Council (AHRC). We are indebted to the contributors, to the amateur cine societies on Merseyside, and collector and filmmaker Angus Tilston for enthusiastic support for the project, Marion Hewitt at North West Film Archive, and Janet Dugdale, Julia Bryan, and their colleagues at the Museum of Liverpool for helping to ensure that the moving image record of Merseyside is archived for the use and pleasure of future generations.

A networking scheme funded by British Telecom and the AHRC enabled Julia Hallam (Liverpool University UK) and Ian Gregory (Lancaster University UK) to bring together internationally renowned scholars from a diverse range of disciplines with digital artists and museum curators. The workshops generated a number of new projects and publications (including this one) and stimulated the development of new collaborations in this emergent area. We are particularly indebted to David Bodenhamer (Indiana University–Purdue University at Indianapolis), who commissioned this collection as part of his Spatial Humanities series for Indiana University Press; David's support and encouragement for this new area of work has been invaluable and we are most grateful to him. We would like to thank Taylor and Francis for permission to reprint an article by Robert C. Allen (2010) "Getting to Going to the Show," New Review of Film and Television Studies 8(3), 264–76, the British Film Institute for permission to use an image of Patrick Keiller's exhibition City of the Future at BFI Southbank (2007–08), and the Museum of Liverpool for providing images of the interactive map in the History Detectives Gallery. Les Roberts designed the cover for this collection and has overseen both the development of the Mapping the City in Film website and the GIS resource that supports it; Julia would like to extend particular thanks to him for his careful stewardship and creative input.

Finally we would like to thank staff and students in the Department of Communication and Media and the School of Architecture at Liverpool University for their ongoing support for the project and the AHRC for funding the projects that have enabled this new body of work in film and the spatial humanities to develop and thrive.

JULIA HALLAM and LES ROBERTS

LOCATING THE MOVING IMAGE

ONE

Film and Spatiality: Outline of a New Empiricism

LES ROBERTS AND JULIA HALLAM

SPATIAL (RE)ORIENTATIONS: INTERDISCIPLINARY EXCURSIONS

Metaphor is never innocent. It orients research and fixes results.

—JACQUES DERRIDA

In recent years ideas of the spatial and the cinematic have come together in an irresolute fashion, each fumbling hesitantly toward the other without appearing entirely sure of how or indeed if the other might respond. Discussions and debates around themes of, for example, cinematic geography, cartographic cinema, cinematic cartography, cinematic urbanism, urban cinematics, urban projections, movie mapping, cinetecture, city in film, cinematic city, geography of film, cinematic countrysides, and so on,[1] while testament to a rich and ever more expansive discourse on film, space, and place (albeit one with a disproportionate skew toward the urban), may also be seen as a jumble of discursive waypoints that confound as much as guide our way through a critical landscape that at times resembles an interdisciplinary quagmire.

Spatiality may be the common currency, but, much like the volatile euro, it struggles to hold together an otherwise fractured union that, in disciplinary terms at least, is just as likely to entrench as dissolve its internal borders. Part of the problem lies in the way specific film/space neologisms lay claim to a specificity of meaning and practice that is all too rarely self-evident. It is always therefore necessary to dig deeper around the terms to excavate a fuller understanding of how they are being theorized, what epistemological foundations they are built upon, who is advancing the arguments, and what disciplinary background he or she is coming from. As the briefest of surveys of recent literature makes plain, what might be meant by, say, the geography of film is open to any number of competing and overlapping claims. Take cartographic cinema and cinematic cartography, for example. Just how navigable is the pathway that leads us from Tom Conley's elaboration of the former to that of Sébastien Caquard or Les Roberts,[2] each of whom have deployed the term "cinematic cartography" in ways that are not only different from each other, but which are both markedly different from Conley's ideas on cartographic cinema or Giuliana Bruno's writings on film, cartography, and the psychogeographies of (e)motion?[3] Although it is certainly navigable, it is by no means as straightforward a journey as the terms themselves might lead us to believe. A widespread and seemingly contagious spread of metaphors of mapping across social and cultural fields of study further complicates attempts to nail down the conceptual parameters by which ideas of cartography in relation to film might be generically understood. As Conley himself notes, "[t]he field of cultural studies is riddled with the idea of 'mapping.'"[4] Indeed, a search on Google Scholar for the social sciences, arts, and humanities reveals nearly forty thousand academic texts with the word "mapping" in the title. "Locating" the moving image is, therefore, in the first instance a process of "mapping" the meanings that have variously clustered around discussions of space and place in recent studies on film history and practice.

Wittingly or otherwise, the essays in this book all represent more hands-on responses to the metaphorization of space and cartography that has overshadowed the development of more practice-oriented approaches to cultural mappings.[5] While, on the one hand, they may be cited as evidence of a spatial turn[6] in the humanities and social sciences (and in film studies research more particularly), they also—and perhaps more persuasively—may be seen as examples of a shift *away* from a self-regarding *rhetoric* of space that has, in the words of Henri Lefebvre, "become the locus of a 'theoretical practice' which is separated from social practice and which sets itself up as the axis, pivot or central reference point of Knowledge."[7] Each of the contributions therefore proceeds from the premise that spatial methods and analyses are not ends in themselves (a meta-theoretical foray into the innate spatialities or cartographic properties of the cinematic medium) but are more productively deployed as tools and apparatuses for exploring the social, cultural, and economic geographies surrounding different forms of film practice and consumption. Mapping as mapping, in other words, as analytical engagement with, on the one hand, *maps* and *mapping practices* as a means to explore new approaches and understandings of film and spatiality, and, on the other, with digital mapping and geospatial technologies that scholars are increasingly turning to as further explorations in this field continue to gather pace.

One of the chief aims of this book is to demonstrate the ways in which spatial methodologies are reinvigorating film scholarship by charting new pathways (figuratively and geographically) through the multilayered landscapes of film production, distribution, exhibition, and consumption. In this respect the contributions each serve to amply illustrate Franco Moretti's observation that maps function "as analytical tools [that bring] to light relations that would otherwise remain hidden."[8] These new approaches to film, space, and place thus expand understandings of the spatial histories and spatial geographies of the moving image by allowing fine-grained analysis of relations and correlations that would offer themselves up less readily by other means. In this regard, as well as probing questions of spatiality and exploring the methodological advantages of GIS (geographical information systems) and other spatial analytic software, the common factor that binds the chapters in this book together is that they all represent significant advances toward the development of a new empiricism in film studies research, one that is concerned with moving away from interpretive studies of cinema texts to embrace different forms of film production and consumption,[9] as well as refocusing on cinema as a site of social, cultural, and economic exchange.[10] It is important to stress that this need not be read as the sign of a positivistic backlash against the detailed interpretive work that has paid close attention to the formal and ideological properties of the film medium as a signifying system.[11] Rather, it is more instructive to look upon these methodological shifts in film studies as a restless desire to venture further outside the confines of more traditional approaches that have centered on the study of feature films to embrace perspectives that engage wholeheartedly with the social, economic, and cultural aspects of filmmaking and viewing in its many and varied forms. The scholars whose work is presented in this volume come from a diversity of interdisciplinary backgrounds and with that diversity bring new approaches to the study of film that embrace the heterogeneity and complexity of film's sociality.

Dismissive of the theoretical paint-by-numbers approach he sees as a dominant trend in current film discourse, filmmaker Allan Siegel argues that "present discursive practices surrounding the medium of film tend to exaggerate the decoding, deconstructing, and dissecting of the film text at the expense of those quotidian media creating experiences that elucidate and alter social space."[12] Siegel is by no means the first to voice exasperation at a critical default setting that has it that if you are doing film studies you are in the business of doing textual analysis, and that if you are doing textual analysis you will perforce be in the business of doing theory. Robert Allen notes that at the 2008 Society for Cinema and Media Studies (SCMS) conference in Philadelphia, three out of three hundred panels were focused on the sociality of cinema and that two-thirds of the one thousand papers presented involved readings of films. For Allen, this brought to the fore the need to redefine what his object of study is[13] (see also Allen, this volume) and to press the case for a re-evaluation of the role of empirical methods in a discipline hitherto characterized by "its suspicion of the empirical and [its] tendency to confuse intellectual engagement with the empirical world outside the film text with empiricism."[14]

If the SCMS example may be read as an indicator of a general ambivalence toward the empirical, not to mention an apparently deep-seated conservatism, then it is one that also brings with it the recognition that exploring other avenues of research (such as those that have drawn film scholars further into the domains of geography and history) demands intellectual engagement and dialogue that ventures beyond fixed disciplinary boundaries. This may also engender a degree of suspicion or anxiety inasmuch as it entails straying into less familiar territory, and hence it brings with it the need (or, as might also be the case, reluctance) to chart more uncertain terrain. In his masterful study of film noir and urban space, Ed Dimendberg notes that film scholars all too rarely "travel to the extra-cinematic precincts of geography, city planning, architectural theory, and urban and cultural history."[15] If we apply this formula to Charlotte Brunsdon's *London in Cinema*, which by the author's own admission makes only "fleeting reference to significant aspects of London's cultural history and geography,"[16] then we obtain a clearer picture of the way what is meant by "cinematic geography" in any given context is shaped with a particular constituency in mind, in this latter instance a film studies readership for whom the films, rather than the city, come first. Yet, as Dimendberg observes, "[t]reating the city as expression of some underlying myth, theme, or vision has tended to stifle the study of spatiality in film," that is, as a historical subject matter that is "as significant as [film's] more commonly studied formal and narrative features."[17]

Shifts in film scholarship that fall under the banner of what may be described as a new empiricism represent not so much a disavowal of theory, nor a post-theory battle line drawn in the sand, but are characterized instead by a methodological pragmatism in which the extra-cinematic precincts to which Dimendberg refers are seen as productive terrain for the cultivation of new research questions and for the development of different critical and theoretical approaches and perspectives. Insofar as these precincts play host to a coy exchange of interdisciplinary gestures, they stake out a space of potentiality that may take the form of "empty meeting grounds"—"characterized by bad faith and petty suspicion on both sides,"[18] but may equally flourish as contact zones: dialogic spaces of encounter, negotiation, and reciprocal exchange.[19]

On a practical level, for film researchers venturing into the world of geospatial computing, one of the most important issues to contend with is, of course, the difficulties faced in getting to grips with what, for the initiate, may seem like baffling and intimidating technology. In the early stages of the research this is often compounded by the researcher not necessarily being fully abreast of the full range of functionalities that GIS technologies can deliver. This brings with it the problem that a certain level of experimentation may be necessary before the scope and detail of the research questions and objectives become fully apparent. Given the steep learning curve demanded by software such as ArcGIS, those with no more than an approximate notion of where this geospatial dalliance may potentially lead them might well be disinclined to fully take the plunge, or might simply not have the time or resources to do the groundwork necessary to flesh out a viable project proposal.[20] On the other hand, it might be the case that a clear set of research questions has been formulated, in which case the challenge is to determine in what ways the technology can be harnessed to inform the research process and, as with the examples presented in this collection, to successfully deliver the project objectives. Such a scenario would in all likelihood entail the film researcher venturing across campus to seek advice from, or pitch a collaborative idea to, colleagues in the geography, computing, architecture, or civic design departments. This is where things can often get interesting, where the rhetoric of interdisciplinarity gets put to the test.

The hesitance of some in the film studies community to breach the interdisciplinary divide is certainly understandable insofar as an impression is cultivated that to do so risks entanglement with positivistic frameworks of analysis that fly in the face of the more critical, interpretive, and qualitative epistemologies more typically associated with film studies research. Although such an impression certainly downplays the extent to which film has long been of interest to geographers, urbanists, architects, and others working in so-called spatial disciplines, there nevertheless remains the attendant perception of wandering into an interdisciplinary zone of ontological insecurity in which the familiar landmarks and intellectual habitus that discursively locate the film scholar are thrown into flux.

Similarly, for those working in the geospatial sciences and computing, whose perspectives are more likely to be shaped by quantitative and statistical modes of analysis, measurement and survey, urban design, or land management, the more fuzzy humanistic language of film and cultural studies might also induce a certain level of insecurity to the extent that an alliance with the more interpretive paradigms routinely employed by film scholars might be seen in some way to compromise their reputation as "hard" scientists engaged in rigorous empirical research. Playing or performing their respective language games—a concept developed by the philosopher Ludwig Wittgenstein to "bring into prominence the fact that the *speaking* [and use] of a language is part of an activity, or of a form of life"[21]—scholars from across disciplines are to a certain extent only able to meaningfully converse by acquiescence to a process of what the anthropologist Tanya Luhrmann refers to as "interpretative drift." This refers to the slow shift in interpretation whereby "ideas about the world become persuasive as a by-product of a practice."[22] Given that the practice of interdisciplinarity as a process of interpretive drift entails a certain investment in terms of the utility and application that scholars might wish to benefit from in the longer term, then this too represents a factor that might militate against the otherwise enthusiastic consummation of an interdisciplinary marriage. In instances where the union is, let's say, more transactional, that is, wedded to short-term benefits without the expectation of longer-term commitment, the nature of the collaboration may take the form of an instrumental stitching together of two disciplinary perspectives that in all other respects have remained unyielding to the advances of the other.

The point we are making, therefore, is that the more "spatial" the spatial turn in film studies becomes, the more that questions surrounding the negotiation, management, and sustainability of interdisciplinary research into film and spatiality warrant critical attention. Accordingly, one of the aims of this introduction is to reflexively observe the research process, basing our discussion on the example of the University of Liverpool's Mapping the City in Film project, which formed part of a wider interdisciplinary research program conducted between the departments of architecture and communication and media in 2006–2010. Presented alongside the chapters in this collection, the purpose of this discussion is to provide an insight into the ways spatial methodologies have been used in recent research on film, foreground some of the issues and questions that have been raised along the way, and reflect on the interdisciplinary aspect of the research process. Taken as a whole, *Locating the Moving Image* represents the first collection of its kind that exclusively draws together research being conducted in this subject area, and as such will hopefully prove a useful resource and stimulus to others interested in exploring the potential of GIS and spatial databases in film studies research.

CINEMATIC CARTOGRAPHY: NAVIGATING THE FIELD

Before moving on to discuss the Mapping the City in Film case study, first it is necessary to consider in greater detail what exactly talk of a spatial turn in film studies actually means in practice. As we have already suggested, as a generic marker of a theoretical reorientation toward questions of spatiality in film, the idea of a spatial turn has arguably become too sprawling and imprecise to effectively signpost the critical pathways through an increasingly interdisciplinary terrain. Accordingly, there is "a need to draw out and refine further the specificities and coalescent features"[23] that have shaped the theoretical landscapes of film, space, and place in recent debates. One way of breaking down the otherwise unwieldy category of the spatial in relation to new theoretical perspectives is to acknowledge the specifically cartographic basis of these spatial (re)orientations. Adapting a typology previously set out elsewhere,[24] we identify below five thematic areas that constitute what in broad terms may be provisionally defined as "cinematic cartography." These are: (1) maps and mapping in films; (2) mapping of film production and consumption; (3) movie mapping and place marketing; (4) cognitive and emotional mapping; and (5) film as spatial critique. This loosely defined five-point typology is related in turn to three overarching critical frameworks or orientations that serve to delineate theoretical and methodological perspectives pertaining to the spatial turn in recent film studies.

The first of these is *spatial historiography*. The use of spatial methods to explore the historical geographies of film production and exhibition represents by far the most developed area of GIS and film. Indeed, all but two of the chapters in this volume fall under this category. What is instructive in these examples is consideration of the historiographical import of geospatial methods. What specifically can GIS tools offer the film historian that cannot be achieved by other means? What does bringing a spatial awareness to historical phenomena make explicit that would otherwise remain hidden? In what ways might the use of GIS in historical research on film and place illuminate understandings of social and cultural memory? Or of the affective and emotional geographies that attach themselves to landscapes? How might these and other spatial methods provide insights into the social and historical geographies of moviegoing? Or the geohistorical patterns of film exhibition and distribution? Or the macro-geographies of film industry practice? How might the introduction of spatial methods positively enhance forms of archival film practice or enable the refinement or rearticulation of what Catherine Russell describes as "an historiography of radical memory"?[25] These are all questions that contributions to this book variously address, thereby demonstrating the extent to which developments in the field of historical GIS,[26] which have hitherto largely proved hesitant in turning their attention to the production and consumption of cultural texts and practices, have begun to make significant inroads into historical research on film.

The second, though closely related critical framework, relates to film as various forms of *spatial practice*. This orientation places emphasis on film and filmmaking as socially and spatially embedded forms of practice. In methodological terms it thus reflects more qualitative and ethnographic perspectives on film, space, and place and is focused on the ways film and film practices are imbricated in wider social, cultural, and economic processes of spatial production and consumption. This anthropological approach draws critical attention to issues of agency and performativity: to what extent can film function as a form of spatial critique? What role do moving images play in the social and political production of space? What are the spatial dialectics of film? In what ways can film practices challenge and contest the territorialization of hegemonic spatial formations? Conversely, in what ways are moving images complicit in the cinematization or spectacularization of everyday landscapes?[27] The growth in film-related tourism and the convergence of the film, tourism, and place-marketing industries—a trend well-encapsulated in sociologist Rodanthi Tzanelli's designation of the "global sign industries"—represent some of the ways in which the spatial performativities of moving images are harnessed and exploited in the branding of cities and other landscapes as spaces of spectacle and consumption.[28] Reframing film practices as *spatial practices* opens up the socially embedded spatialities of film to closer critical scrutiny and thereby invites broader consideration of the way cinematic geographies are constitutive elements in the social production and consumption of space and place.

The third critical orientation relating to the spatial turn in film is *spatial ontology*. Given the more practice-based and historiographical focus to *Locating the Moving Image*, this is an area that has less immediate bearing on the discussions that unfold throughout this book. One of the foremost areas of analysis that falls under the rubric of spatial ontology are questions as to the specifically cartographic properties of the cinematic medium. To what extent can film itself be regarded as a map? Under what circumstances might filmmaking also be understood as mapmaking or cartography? As forms of "locational imaging,"[29] what affinities does cinema have with cartography in terms of locating the self (or other) in space, be it real or imagined? Or, following Conley's observation that "[w]hen we position ourselves in relation to the effects of plotting in cinema we quickly discern that ontology is a function of geography,"[30] to what extent do cinematic cartographies—accepting that these are wide and diverse and contextually informed by local cultural and geographical specificities—"plot" ideas or structures of being and subjectivity? Another area of spatial ontology, one that has direct relevance to this book, draws on conceptual understandings linked not so much to philosophy as to information systems analysis. In this usage, ontology is understood as a complete and internally logical system, such as a classificatory system represented in, for example, a database. In GIScience, a spatial ontology is "a unique statement of logic, a way of describing spatial entities from one perspective or knowledge system."[31] For GIS-informed spatial analyses of film, questions of spatial ontology are therefore closely bound up with database design and infrastructure, algorithmic logic, semantic data modeling, querying of attribute data, and so on (see Verhoeven and Arrowsmith's chapter in this volume for a good illustration of applied spatial ontology in relation to GIS). The distinctions and contradictions that inform conceptual understandings of what a spatial ontology is or speaks to underline some of the practical difficulties we have drawn attention to in the previous section in respect of interdisciplinary dialogues on spatiality and film. It is not our intention to suggest that these difficulties are in some way intractable or insurmountable, nor is it to peddle a spurious argument along the lines of "film scholars are from Mars, GIScientists are from Venus." Rather, reflecting on our own experiences as researchers working in an explicitly interdisciplinary field of study, it is to highlight areas where conceptual language can sometimes hit the buffers of interpretive meaning, where assumptions as to what is or might be meant by terms such as, say, "spatial ontology" can overlook the extent to which there are multiple and overlapping meanings being traded, and that being alert to these is itself a part of what doing cinematic cartography inevitably entails.

In the remainder of this section we examine in closer detail some of the different areas of scholarship that have clustered around ideas and practices of cinematic cartography. By ascribing the term "cinematic cartography" to these clusters of theory and practice, as Roberts has elsewhere noted, our aim "is not to mould or corral them into a unified framework of analysis but rather to explore the different ways the representational spaces of film and those of maps have found (or sought) convergence [and the ways that] film maps and film mapping might be understood as geographical productions of knowledge."[32]

MAPS AND MAPPING IN FILMS

Analyses that fall within the first thematic strand of research on cinematic cartography focus on the representation of maps that appear within the diegetic spaces of the medium. Tom Conley points out that "[s]ince the advent of narrative in cinema—which is to say, from its very beginnings—maps are inserted in the field of the image to indicate where action 'takes place.'"[33] Conley's work focuses primarily on examples from postwar cinema.[34] His approach to what he terms "cartographic cinema" can be defined in terms of, on the one hand, a focus on the geographic and representational cartographies contained with the film's diegesis and, on the other hand, psychoanalytical and affective forms of mapping that are mobilized between film and viewer in terms of his or her subjectivity and psychic positionality. Conley argues that many commercial films, similar to cartography, "share in the design of what one critic long ago called 'strategies of containment.'" Yet these fears can be displaced by alternative uses of "the cartographies the medium mantles to establish its hold on perception."[35] The forms of deterritorialization that Conley, per Deleuze, maps out in his book *Cartographic Cinema* are examples of films that have the potential to reorient the spectator through activating the imagination to negotiate different subject positions and places "in the area between the cartography of the film, as it is seen, and the imagination as it moves about and deciphers the film."[36] By way of contrast, from a cartographer's perspective, Sébastien Caquard, in his discussion of cinematic maps—or cinemaps—argues that early animated maps in films such as Fritz Lang's *M* (1931) predated many of the future functions of modern digital cartography such as the use of sound, shifts in perspective, and the combination of realistic images and cartographic symbols. Caquard suggests that professional cartographers can learn much from the study of cinematic techniques used by Lang and other filmmakers in terms of their status as cinematic precursors to modern forms and media of cartography, "[exploring] more systematically and more deeply the potential influence cinema could have on cartography."[37]

MAPPING OF FILM PRODUCTION AND CONSUMPTION

The second category of research on cinematic cartography focuses on geographies of film production and consumption. As noted previously, this is also the area in which some of the more substantive developments in historical GIS techniques have been deployed and developed in recent film studies research. It is also the focus of many of the contributions to *Locating the Moving Image*. Robert C. Allen and the members of the HOMER[38] network have pioneered research on the early days of cinemagoing, using historical maps to retrace film distribution networks and sites of exhibition. This has been part of a historical project that focuses on cinema as a social experience, conditioned by factors such as transportation networks, ethnicity, and social group as well as cinema architecture, ticket prices, and the changing patterns of work and leisure. In his discussion of his approach included in this volume, Allen points out that "understanding the experience of cinema at any one point in any place in the past also entails understanding the spatiality of the experience of cinema." Using Sanborn fire insurance maps, traces of early cinema sites in forty-five towns and cities in North Carolina were found; an online searchable database illuminates these sites with a range of other historical documentation, ranging from information about specific venues such as photographs and postcards to newspaper clippings, architectural drawings, and commentaries.[39] Going to the Show is one of the most extensive collections of material on the experience of early moviegoing in the United States and is being replicated elsewhere, such as in the Early Cinema in Scotland 1896–1927 project funded by the UK's Arts and Humanities Research Council.

In a similar vein, Jeffrey Klenotic is using historical GIS methods to visualize contexts for early moviegoing in New Hampshire. In an earlier article, Klenotic distinguishes between what he calls little "g" GIS and big "g" GIS, where even the modest scope and relatively piecemeal nature of little "g" GIS has the potential to radically alter how a researcher assesses received historical knowledge and analyzes historical evidence. Klenotic emphasizes an open, multiple, and fluid approach to GIS that chimes with a view of cinema history as a study aligned with people's history, "resulting in a bottom-up history of people, places and the manifold relations and flows between them."[40] In this volume, Klenotic explores a history of exhibition in a small New Hampshire town and focuses on the spatial determinants that help shape human agency—the entrepreneurial activities of a female venue proprietor. Using information gleaned in part from GIS visualization of population density and social demography in the 1910s alongside maps of existing and planned transportation networks, he sketches some of "the contours, pathways and networks that gave definition to the experience of small town life during the 1910s to suggest ways in which place and space mattered, not only as features of community identity but as forces shaping the uneven development of film exhibition amidst a time of pronounced urbanization, an expanding women's movement, and the emergence of a mass market for movies." Saliently, Klenotic also highlights the difficulties inherent in translating the open, iterative analyses offered by GIS technologies into the "tidy linearity of printed, published work." As he observes, "the 'zoom and pan' functions of GIS produce insights gleaned through multiple layers of data visualization that are difficult to capture in words."[41]

Adopting a more quantitative approach, Daniel Biltereyst and Philippe Meers's "Enlightened City" project has several research strands, including a longitudinal database of film exhibition structures, a large-scale database on film programming in various cities and towns, and an oral history project on cinema experiences.[42] In their chapter for this collection, the researchers focus on exploring the relationship between the geographical spread of cinemas throughout the state of Flanders, Belgium, demographic data on population density and the spread of cinemas in each of the five Flanders provinces over an extended period (1920–1990), demonstrating the ways in which visualizing existing sources of information such as census data can provide vital material for cinema historians. By way of contrast, Deb Verhoeven and Colin Arrowsmith combine the skills of cultural analysis with those of geospatial science to analyze changes and developments in cinema venues and distribution circuits in Melbourne between 1946 and 1986. Here the use of GIS extends beyond the use of existing big "g" GIS databases such as census data to using statistical visualization tools such as Markov chain analysis to examine patterns of spatial distribution and the use of clustering and proximity analysis "to identify which variables might explain the survival of cinemas in particular locations." Verhoeven and Arrowsmith are working within the context of an Australian Research Council (ARC)

Discovery funded interdisciplinary project, Mapping the Movies, "that is attempting to account for the ways in which cinema industries responded to demographic, social and cultural changes in the three decades after broadcast television became available throughout Australia." Embedded within their research inquiry is the question of how time can be managed within what for them remains an otherwise static technology, namely geographical information systems (GIS).

In her mapping of film production in Italy, Elisa Ravazzoli seeks to spatially analyze the contemporary film industry, with its interconnected network of small business practitioners, as a cultural and social process, exploring the association between the two. Her analysis draws on a different academic discourse from that of Allen, Klenotic, or Biltereyst and Meers, one that foregrounds the contribution of economic geography to contemporary understandings of cultural and industrial development in what is often loosely termed the "cultural industries" sector of the post-industrial economy.[43] Sébastien Caquard, Daniel Naud, and Benjamin Wright are similarly concerned with contemporary film production in Canada, national cinema, and issues of identity and representation. The Cybercartographic Atlas of Canadian Cinema maps the territories of Canadian cinema including production and postproduction locations, distribution networks, and venue locations and narrative content.[44] Their work seeks to understand how contemporary Canadian filmmakers are contributing to a reshaping of national identity away from understandings of national identity fixed to a territorial landscape into a postnational ethnic plurality. In their chapter for this collection, a geography of the audience for contemporary Canadian films is mapped "in order to better understand how cinematographic territories and audiences overlap and how films associated with places and communities can reach diverse audiences and contribute to the development of a collective multicultural identity."

MOVIE MAPPING AND CINEMATOGRAPHIC TOURISM

The third thematic area in the field of cinematic cartography is one that has received little in the way of scholarly attention to date. In recent years the role of film, or rather film *locations,* in the marketing and consumption of cities and rural destinations has become an increasingly important feature of place-marketing strategies aimed at tourists and other consumers. Film tourism has brought with it growing convergence between the film and tourism industries, with each providing mutually reinforcing promotional tie-ins and brand awareness, designed to stimulate both the consumption of place (the economic imperative of the tourism, leisure, and heritage industries) as well as the consumption of film and television productions. As we have already noted, responding to these processes of convergence, Tzanelli, in her book *The Cinematic Tourist*, deploys the term "global sign industries"[45] to draw together the different modes of production and consumption operative across the film, media, and tourist industries. In so doing, she provides a productive framework by which to examine the range of film-related tourism practices, critical discussion of which has hitherto been largely dominated by industry- and marketing-based perspectives.

The production of printed and web-based maps has become one of the principal marketing tools employed by both screen agencies and destination marketing organizations (DMOs). As a tool for urban regeneration, the role of film location sites in the economic revival of post-industrial cities such as, for example, Liverpool is now recognized by many local authorities as an important source of revenue and sustainable inward investment (although exactly *how* sustainable is open to debate). The result of a growing synergy between local film offices and screen agencies on the one hand and DMOs on the other, the production of tourist maps of film locations represents therefore a materialization of this ever-closer relationship.[46]

If, as a post-tourist[47] phenomenon, part of the appeal of movie maps is that they offer a knowingly inauthentic or pseudo[48] navigation of a region's landmarks and locations (both a real and vicarious engagement with a place's on-screen identity), then it is perhaps the very immaterial geographies that are constructed from these and other virtual landscapes that are best equipped to adapt to the shifting demands of the global consumer economy. Yet despite the economic benefits film-related tourism activities may bring to post-industrial cities and regions, there is, as Tzanelli argues, "a danger that tourist consumption of simulatory landscape and cultures will overwrite specific histories of actual places and cultures."[49] There is, then, an important sociopolitical dimension to developments surrounding tourist-related cinematic cartography that provides the critical rationale for the fifth category of cinematic mapping, discussed below: film as spatial critique.

COGNITIVE AND EMOTIONAL MAPPING

Among the proponents of the fourth category of cinematic cartography, cognitive and emotional mapping, are Giuliana Bruno and Tom Conley, each of whom provide a detailed theoretical exposition of the ways in which the affective properties of the cinematic medium can play host to psychic and emotional mappings of self and subjectivity. For Bruno, the affective geometries and mobilities that are unleashed by film and other forms of moving image culture prompt renewed understanding of not only the ways we might read or map the spaces of film, but also how these immaterial geographies might shape renewed understandings and engagements with landscapes more generally:

> Mapping is the shared terrain in which the architectural-filmic bond resides —a terrain that can be fleshed out by rethinking practices of cartography for travelling cultures, with an awareness of the inscription of emotion within this motion. Indeed, by way of filmic representation, geography itself is being transformed and (e)mobilized. . . . A frame for cultural mappings, film is *modern cartography*.[50]

Conley's writing on cartographic cinema treads theoretical ground similar to Bruno, noting that even if a film does not feature a map as part of its narrative, "by nature [film] bears an implicit relation with cartography . . . films *are* maps insofar as each medium can be defined as a form of what cartographers call 'locational media.'"[51]

As *cognitive* forms of mapping and cartography, the type of filmic practice and analysis to which these and other authors draw critical attention owes some degree of debt to the work of Kevin Lynch, whose ideas, while more recently criticized in geography, planning, and contemporary cognitive theory, have nevertheless remained influential in fields such as film studies, urban communication, and architecture.[52] Historicizing the development of these more humanistic and anthropological approaches to the urban environment, the critical cartographer Denis Wood highlights similarities between the work of theorists such as Lynch and David Stea, and that of Guy Debord and Situationist/Marxist psychogeography: "both elaborated methods that ensured reproducible results and a remarkable degree of objectivity. And both . . . accepted, in fact celebrated, the *necessity of using human beings to measure salient dimensions of the environment.*"[53]

Lynch's notational system of "edges," "nodes," "landmarks," "districts," and "paths" has been highly influential in understanding the ways people construct mental images (or cognitive maps) of urban environments and learn to navigate these spaces and places.[54] Jean-Pierre Melville's 1967 film *Le Samourai* provides a pre-eminent example of a film whose main protagonist, and the journey he undertakes through neo-noirish spaces of 1960s Paris, engages with an urban notational system that cements a certain imaginary of place in the consciousness of the viewer. "From the ruins of film noir," Bruno notes, "a story about mapping emerges. Ultimately, *Le Samourai* tells no other story than that of the subway map of Paris. By way of tours and detours, it shows how a transportation chart can function to map and remap a city."[55] Richard Misek extends this idea further in his study of the films of Eric Rohmer. In response to Benjamin's speculations as to the possibilities of producing a film map of Paris,[56] Misek explores the cinematic geographies of Rohmer's Paris as mapped in and across a number of films the director shot in the city between the 1950s and the 2000s. The journeys undertaken by the characters in Rohmer's films typically move through spatially contiguous locations, the action remaining consistent with the actual geography of Paris. Tracing pathways across time and space, the spatial continuity of the films is offset by the temporal discontinuities of action and milieu tied to specific points in time spanning more than fifty years. Misek's journey through the psychogeography of Rohmer's Paris itself creates new spatiotemporal mappings, new ways of understanding and navigating the cinematic and historical geographies of urban landscapes.[57]

One further application of what could be characterized as cognitive forms of cinematic cartography is in Teresa Castro's discussion of the mapping impulse.[58] Echoing Conley's description of moving images as locational media, for Castro the notion of the mapping impulse refers to a visual regime, a way of seeing the world that has cartographic affinities. Cinematic cartography here refers less to the presence of maps per se in films than to the cultural, perceptual, and cognitive processes that inform understandings of place and space. Focusing on what she describes as cartographic shapes, Castro shows how panoramas (point views shaping synoptic and spatially coherent landscapes and vistas), atlases (visual archives and spatiovisual assemblies), and aerial views (god's-eye or bird's-eye perspectives from planes or hot-air balloons) define a cinematic topography in which the mapping impulse is a central cognitive element. Drawing attention to the broad and complex theoretical terrain within which mapping and cartographic practices are embedded, Castro notes that "mapping can therefore refer to a multitude of processes, from the cognitive operations implied in the structuring of spatial knowledge to the discursive implications of a particular visual regime."[59] Following this line of argument, Hallam argues that the use of GIS visualization methods in partnership with traditional film analysis and historical contextual information can begin to map an affective architecture of place. In her chapter for this volume, she develops ideas about the similarities between cartography and filmmaking as two kinds of visual practice that share a number of similarities in the ways they describe the surface of an area or territory. The use of maps as a way of analyzing the visual dynamics of filmic space evolved from the spatial concerns of the Mapping the City in Film project, which has created an extensive database of more than 1,700 film and video items that depict a provincial city and its urban environment from the earliest known footage to the present day; the films range across early actualities and travelogues, newsreel footage, amateur and independent productions, promotional material, and campaign videos.[60] Focusing in particular on the period between 1930 and the mid-1980s, when newsreels, documentaries, and amateur films were the most popular genres recording local scenes, the chapter explores the ways these genres have depicted Liverpool's urban landscape, with a view to examining in greater depth both the cross-generic imaginary of depictions of place and the spatial dynamics of the representation of place at particular times in the city's history.

FILM AS SPATIAL CRITIQUE

The last in our five-point typology of cinematic cartography is what the artist and filmmaker Patrick Keiller has dubbed "film as spatial critique."[61] To date the most productive resource for research in this area has been archival film materials from the early days of film (1890s–1910s) and the postwar period (1950s–1970s). In the case of the latter, the example of Liv-

FIGURE 1.1. Patrick Keiller, City of the Future Exhibition,
BFI Southbank, 2007–2008. (Courtesy of BFI)

erpool has shown how a spatial reading of urban cinematic geographies
can expose some of the contradictory spatialities that were emerging
during this period as a result of large-scale and controversial modernist
urban planning, which left its destructive stamp on many cities during
the 1960s and 1970s (see below).[62]

Keiller's installation, City of the Future, draws from a database of approximately two thousand early actuality films held by the British Film
Institute (BFI) National Film and Television Archive. An interactive
map of topographic film footage, the installation was exhibited at the
BFI Southbank in London between November 2007 and February 2008.
A selection of sixty-eight items filmed between 1896 and 1909, showing
street scenes and "phantom ride" views filmed from trams and trains, was
viewable (navigable) across a number of screens on which historical maps
were also projected. Organized spatially and geographically, the footage
could be accessed by clicking on points on the maps, allowing users to
move back and forth between cartographic and cinematographic render-
ings of the same landscapes and topographies (see figure 1.1).

As Keiller points out, many early films allow the viewer's gaze to wander throughout their representational spaces, and as such are less likely to direct their attention to a single subject in the frame.[63] Unlike the montage aesthetics of the modernist "city symphony," early actuality films can often document the historic urban landscape in ways that provide ethnographic insights into the rhythms, mobilities, and lived spaces of urban environments. "In enabling us to see so much of this landscape," Keiller argues, "these early films are truly extraordinary, as they offer the most extensive views of the landscape of another time at or just before the moment of that landscape's transformation."[64]

Insofar as the early actuality material Keiller discusses may be described as "topographic films," they bear many comparisons with much of the footage of cities shot by amateur filmmakers in the postwar period. This has formed the basis of extensive ethnographic and cartographic research into amateur film practice in Liverpool and Merseyside from the 1950s to the present day. Alongside City of the Future, the University of Liverpool's Mapping the City in Film project, to which we turn in the next section, represents the most substantive exploration of urban cinematic cartography using archival film practices as forms of spatial critique.

MAPPING THE CITY IN FILM: REFLEXIVE INTERDISCIPLINARITY

With hindsight, it is perhaps by accident rather than design that Mapping the City in Film can be said to demonstrate ways in which "archival film practices [can] articulate an historiography of radical memory."[65] From its inception the project has been more notably focused around questions of urbanism and landscape, as might be expected with an interdisciplinary project initially developed in partnership with architects and with technical assistance from GIS specialists working in the fields of geography and civic design. As the research process unfolded, however, and as the architectural instrumentality that underpinned some of the earlier project aims lost much of its momentum, it quickly became apparent that issues of urbanism and spatiality were closely bound up with those of time and historicity, and that using filmic representations of urban landscapes as forms of spatial critique ipso facto meant engagement with questions of spatial historiography and deep memory. In other words, experimentation with GIS methods of analysis had begun to shape a form of cinematic cartography that for all intents and purposes constituted a critical *archaeology* of the moving image.

Also germane to reflections on cinematic cartography as an archaeological framework of spatial critique is the importance of qualitative modes of geohistorical analysis. From an architectural perspective this allows consideration of the more intangible and experiential properties of past urban environments. As Robert Kronenburg has suggested, "historic filmic evidence . . . provides powerful imagery of a vibrant past that can be regained, imagery which might be invaluable in convincing those who might place efficiency or expediency above richness and complexity in city design."[66] The positivistic undertones inherent in exploiting urban imagery as historical evidence sit uneasily alongside a more dialectical understanding of past and present spatialities of the image. This more critical approach throws light on the contradictions, or what Benjamin refers to as the "flash" of the dialectical image: "It's not that what is past casts its light on what is present, or what is present its light on what has past; rather, [the dialectical] image is that wherein what has been comes together in a flash with the now to form a constellation."[67] The idea of reading moving images dialectically in relation to archival film practices has been taken up by film theorists such as Russell, who suggests that film criticism that is attuned to its dialectical potential "as a form of critical exegesis" might inform processes of historical activism.[68]

The qualitative dimension to Mapping the City in Film—the geospatial embedding of archive film imagery in a GIS map; the georeferencing of place-specific film data drawn from extensive archival research on a wide range of film genres; the "constellation" of past and present geographies of film; interviews and ethnographic research with amateur filmmakers and others involved in film production in Liverpool and Merseyside (as discussed by Shand in his chapter for this collection); site-specific fieldwork conducted in key film locations; the use of video and still photography as visual research methods—all provide the foundations for a far richer and more complex navigation of the historical geographies of Liverpool's urban landscape that extend far beyond mere instrumental applications of cinematic cartography as the basis of contemporary urban design practices suggested by Kronenburg. If anything, as a method of spatial critique, the GIS model of archival film practice that resulted from the Mapping the City in Film research proved efficacious in mobilizing psychogeographic understandings of urban spatiality, in that the contestations and contradictions between lived spaces of urban memory and the abstract spatialities of the architect and planner are brought to the fore.[69] This Lefebvrean approach to film and spatiality—archival film practice as a critical methodology for exploring the dynamic imbrications of space, visuality, and everyday habitus—reflects more anthropological understandings of the relationship between urban landscapes and the moving image. The gravitational pull exerted by these practice-oriented perspectives defines an object of study—the city in film—that has kept in tight orbit the lived, symbolic, and affective constellations of everyday spatiality that operate in dialectical counterpoint to the disembodied abstractions of architectural (and filmic) form.

In this regard, Mapping the City in Film opens up a wider set of questions than those just relating to Liverpool's urban landscape and the moving image. As a collaborative interdisciplinary project, it (a) brought together researchers from the fields of architecture, film and communication studies, and social anthropology; (b) established a critical forum where different epistemological understandings of space, landscape, and the urban (and the place of the moving image therein) were brought into dialogue; (c) posited *spatiality* as a point or zone of theoretical intersection; and (d) developed links and networks with scholars from a range of other cognate (and non-cognate) disciplines, including human geography, digital humanities, history, and literary and cultural studies. Viewed from this more expansive locus of interdisciplinary exchange, the spatial ontologies that constellate around ideas and practices of the "city in film" map out an oft-times dissonant landscape where the object of study—the spatiality of film—remains intractably difficult to pin down. But insofar as spatiality, as Doreen Massey contends,[70] is by definition processual and relational, then this very intractability offers itself up as an object of study in its own right. This processual understanding shifts attention away from, say, the spatiality of film toward ideas of space as a performative and temporal praxis, or what David Crouch refers to as spacing. "Spacing," he suggests, "occurs in the gaps of energies amongst and between things: in their commingling."[71] In the commingling of disciplinary perspectives on space, landscape, visuality, and memory, the spatialities of the moving image and archival film practices more generally, play host

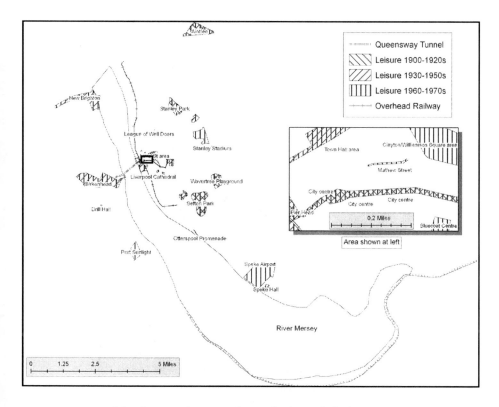

FIGURE 1.2. Map showing changes and growth of areas linked to festivals and parades in films of Liverpool (1900s–1970s).

to broader discussions and visualizations surrounding the representation and practice of space and place; as well as, more pointedly, the place of visual methodologies such as film in historiographical research.

On the one hand, therefore, the use of GIS in historiographical studies into film and urban landscapes leads to new and hitherto untapped insights into the spatial histories and geographies surrounding the production and consumption of film texts and practices. In the case of Mapping the City in Film, users can navigate spatial film data by decade, genre, film gauge (16 mm, 9.5 mm, 8 mm, etc.), building and location, spatial function (the architectural characterization of landscapes in each film), spatial use (the ethnographic and social forms of onscreen engagement with the city's spaces—see figure 1.2), or by plotting film geographies on and across layered historical maps dating back to the 1890s (year zero in cinematic

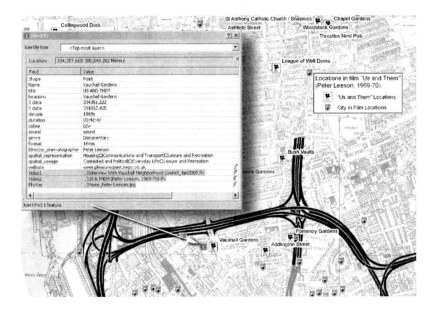

FIGURE 1.3. Map showing locations featured in the film *Us and Them*. The map shows part of a proposed (and subsequently abandoned) elevated motorway (expressway) scheme planned for the city in the 1960s. The map also shows the ArcGIS identify tool box from which users can access a video of the film, interviews, and other contextual materials linked to the specific locations queried.

geography terms).[72] They can follow routes and communications, whether journeys mapped on film around particular city locations,[73] historic tram and ferry routes, mobility networks linked to amateur film activity in Merseyside, films shot on or around bridge crossings or the road tunnels underneath the River Mersey.[74] They can query attribute data relating to more than 1,700 filmic items to map correlations between, for example, film genre (e.g., amateur, newsreel, promotional, municipal, documentary, etc.) and topographic categories of spatial function (e.g., industrial and commercial, housing, public spaces, leisure and recreation) or spatial use (everyday life, contested and political, festivals and parades, and so on). Users can also pull up georeferenced planners maps, such as the 1962 Liverpool Corporation map showing the proposed location of an elevated inner-city motorway (or expressway) system. While the expressway was (mercifully) never built, the ability to relate film data to the map of the proposed scheme provides a further layer of spatial contextualization with which to examine films inspired by road developments in parts of Liverpool, such as the amateur production *Us and Them* (Peter Leeson, 1969–70), or the documentary *Homes Not Roads* (Vauxhall Neighbourhood Council, 1978) (see figure 1.3).[75] In addition, the attachment of hyperlinks to location point data offers the user the opportunity to view spatially embedded film clips, videos of interviews, and photographs of sites of all former cinemas in Liverpool and the surrounding region, alongside related contextual information.

The Mapping the City in Film GIS map is, then, first and foremost a geospatial compendium of multimedia information relating to more than a century of filmmaking and film practice in Liverpool and Merseyside. Alongside its instrumental function as a geohistorical research tool, as an interdisciplinary hub of geospatial and historiographical engagement, the GIS map marshals together a range of spatial forms and practices that, deracinated from their otherwise localized constituencies, are rendered contingent and partial. In this regard they may be considered as interventions or interpolations in a wider process of spacing: the critical and epistemological *mobilization* of space as a form of urban bricolage. To the extent that GIS (contrary to form) might be harnessed to provide productive insights into the qualitative or affective dimensionalities of everyday urban life, past and present, it brings with it the need for more rigorous examination of the constitutive relationships that are being forged between those forms of locational media that are developing around film and visual cultures and those that are shaping new directions in GIScience and geospatial humanities. What is needed, in other words, is a critical mapping of the multifarious spatialities of film on the one hand, and the expressly visual cultures of geography and cartography on the other. Advancing new and more empirically based approaches to film, space, and place, *Locating the Moving Image* charts some of the interdisciplinary (re)orientations that have characterized trends in historical film studies research in recent years.

In our coda chapter at the end of the book we revisit some of the themes and perspectives outlined in this introduction, and we move the discussion toward consideration of the dissemination and knowledge-exchange possibilities that arise from the development of digital mapping resources that explore the spatial histories of film. In particular, we need to focus on the design of research that, as Kate Bowles states in her contribution to this collection, "is open to the collection of stories, and we need to think more carefully about the way these stories are told, and the best formats in which they can contribute to our research." With film scholars increasingly working in partnership with museum and gallery curators, archivists, or national film bodies such as the BFI,[76] the scope for cinematic geographies to reach out and engage interest beyond the academy is increasingly being recognized and built upon as research in this area gains a surer foothold in an ever more productive interdisciplinary terrain.

NOTES

Epigraph: Jacques Derrida, *Writing and Difference,* trans. A. Bass (London: Routledge, 2001), 17.

1. Stuart C. Aitken and Leo E. Zonn, eds., *Place, Power, Situation and Spectacle: A Geography of Film* (Lanham, Md.: Rowman & Littlefield, 1994); Chris Lukinbeal, "The Map that Precedes the Territory: An Introduction to Essays in Cinematic Geography," *GeoJournal* 59(4) (2004): 247–51; Chris Lukinbeal and Stefan Zimmermann, *The Geography of Cinema—A Cinematic World* (Stuttgart: Franz Steiner Verlag, 2004); Les Roberts, *Film, Mobility and Urban Space: A Cinematic Geography of Liverpool* (Liverpool: Liverpool University Press, 2012); Tom Conley, *Cartographic Cinema* (Minneapolis: University of Minnesota Press, 2007); Sébastien Caquard and D. R. Fraser Taylor, eds., "Cinematic Cartography," Special Issue of *The Cartographic Journal* 46(1) (2009); Les Roberts, "Cinematic Cartography: Projecting Place through Film," in *Mapping Cultures: Place, Practice, Performance,* ed. Les Roberts (Basingstoke: Palgrave, 2012); Nezar AlSayyad, *Cinematic Urbanism: A History of the Modern From Reel to Real* (London: Routledge, 2006); Francois Penz and Andong Lu, eds., *Urban Cinematics: Understanding Urban Phenomena Through the Moving Image* (Bristol: Intellect, 2011); Richard Koeck and Les Roberts, eds., *The City and the Moving Image: Urban Projections* (Basingstoke: Palgrave Macmillan, 2010); Stephen Barber, *Projected Cities: Cinema and Urban Space* (London: Reaktion, 2002); Julia Hallam, "Film, Space and Place: Researching a City in Film," *New Review of Film and Television Studies* 8(3) (2010): 277–96; Julia Hallam and Les Roberts, "Mapping, Memory and the City: Archives, Databases and Film Historiography," *European Journal of Cultural Studies* 14(3) (2011): 355–72; Julia Hallam and Les Roberts, "Mapping the City in Film," in *Toward Spatial Humanities: Historical GIS and Spatial History,* eds. Ian Gregory and Alastair Geddes (Bloomington: Indiana University Press, 2014); David B. Clarke, ed. *The Cinematic City* (London: Routledge, 1997); Teresa Castro, "Mapping the City Through Film: From 'Topophilia' to Urban Mapscapes," in *The City and the Moving Image: Urban Projections,* ed. Richard Koeck and Les Roberts (Basingstoke: Palgrave Macmillan, 2010); Charlotte Brunsdon, *London in Cinema: The Cinematic City Since 1945* (London: BFI, 2007); Robert Fish, *Cinematic Countrysides* (Manchester: Manchester University Press, 2007).

2. Conley, *Cartographic Cinema;* Sébastien Caquard, "Foreshadowing Contemporary Digital Cartography: A Historical Review of Cinematic Maps in Films," *The Carto-*

graphic Journal 46(1) (2009): 46–55; Roberts, "Cinematic Cartography: Projecting Place through Film."

3. Giuliana Bruno, *Atlas of Emotion: Journeys in Art, Architecture and Film* (New York: Verso, 2002).

4. Tom Conley, "*The 39 Steps* and the Mental Map of Classical Cinema," in *Rethinking Maps: New Frontiers in Cartographic Theory,* ed. Martin Dodge, Rob Kitchen, and Chris Perkins, 131 (London: Routledge, 2009).

5. Les Roberts, ed., *Mapping Cultures: Place, Practice, Performance* (Basingstoke: Palgrave, 2012).

6. Barney Warf and Santa Arias, eds., *The Spatial Turn: Interdisciplinary Perspectives* (London: Routledge, 2008); Jörg Döring and Tristan Thielmann, eds., *The Spatial Turn: Paradigms of Space in the Cultural and Social Sciences* (Bielefeld: Transcript, 2008); Jesper Falkheimer and Andre Jansson, eds., *Geographies of Communication: The Spatial Turn in Media Studies* (Göteborg: Nordicom, 2006).

7. Henri Lefebvre, *The Production of Space* (Oxford: Blackwell, 1991), 6.

8. Franco Moretti, *Atlas of the European Novel 1800–1900* (London: Verso, 1998), 3.

9. See, for example, Scott Anthony and James G. Mansell, *The Projection of Britain: A History of the GPO Film Unit* (London: BFI Publishing, 2011); Ian Craven, ed., *Movies on Home Ground: Explorations in Amateur Cinema* (Cambridge: Cambridge Scholars Press, 2009); Elizabeth Lebas, *Forgotten Futures: British Municipal Cinema 1920–1980* (London: Black Dog Publishing, 2011); Patrick Russell and James Taylor, eds., *Shadows of Progress: Documentary Film in Post-war Britain* (London: BFI Publishing, 2010).

10. See, for example, Annette Kuhn, *An Everyday Magic: Cinema and Cultural Memory* (London: I. B. Taurus, 2002); Richard Maltby, Melvyn Stokes, and Robert C. Allen, eds., *Going to the Movies: Hollywood and the Social Experience of Cinema* (Exeter: University of Exeter Press, 2007); Daniel Biltereyst, Richard Maltby, and Philippe Meers, eds., *Cinema Audiences and Modernity: New Perspectives on European Cinema History* (London: Routledge, 2011); and Richard Maltby, Daniel Biltereyst, and Philippe Meers, *Explorations in New Cinema History* (Oxford: Wiley-Blackwell, 2011).

11. By "new empiricism" we are not in any way advocating the resurgence or reclaiming of empiricism in the sense of a back-to-basics epistemology that sets itself up in opposition to more theoretically informed approaches to film and spatiality. Rather, the concept is presented in the terms succinctly outlined by the sociologist Nicholas Gane, who, in a discussion of the new empiricism of Gilles Deleuze, attributes it to critical approaches "in which concepts are not simply abstractions or tools that are to be used to explain concrete phenomena, but are themselves drawn out of a confrontation with the pre-conceptual realm of the empirical—a process which poses problems to thought and forces it to account for itself." Nicholas Gane, "Concepts and the 'New' Empiricism," *European Journal of Social Theory* 12(1) (2009): 83–97.

12. Alan Siegel, "After the Sixties. Changing Paradigms in the Representation of Urban Space," in *Screening the City,* ed. Mark Shiel and Tony Fitzmaurice, 141 (London: Verso, 2003).

13. Robert C. Allen, "'Going to the Show': Representing the Spatiality of Film History," paper given at Centre for Critical and Cultural Studies Seminar, the University of Queensland, March 11, 2008.

14. Robert C. Allen, "Relocating American Film History," *Cultural Studies* 20(1) (2006): 48–88, cited here at p. 49.

15. Ed Dimendberg, *Film Noir and the Spaces of Modernity* (London: Harvard University Press, 2004), 9.

16. Brunsdon, *London in Cinema*, 6.

17. Dimendberg, *Film Noir and the Spaces of Modernity*, 9.

18. Dean MacCannell, *Empty Meeting Grounds: The Tourist Papers* (London: Routledge, 1992).

19. Marie Louise Pratt, *Imperial Eyes: Travel Writing and Transculturation* (London: Routledge, 1992).

20. For an excellent account of the ways GIS can develop as a heuristic tool that encourages continual analysis and reanalysis of research materials, see Jeffrey Klenotic, "Putting Cinema History on the Map: Using GIS to Explore the Spatiality of Cinema," in Maltby, Biltereyst, and Meers, *Explorations in New Cinema History*, 58–84.

21. Ludwig Wittgenstein, *Philosophical Investigations* (Oxford: Basil Blackwell, 1953), I 23 (p. 11), emphasis in original.

22. Tanya Luhrmann, *Persuasions of the Witch's Craft: Ritual Magic in Contemporary England* (Cambridge, Mass.: Harvard University Press, 1991), 321.

23. Richard Koeck and Les Roberts, "Introduction: Projecting the Urban" in Koeck and Roberts, *The City and the Moving Image*, 7.

24. Roberts, "Cinematic Cartography: Projecting Place through Film."

25. Catherine Russell, *Experimental Ethnography: The Work of Film in the Age of Video* (Durham, N.C., and London: Duke University Press, 1999), xv.

26. Anne Kelly Knowles, ed., *Past Time, Past Place: GIS for History* (Redlands: ESRI, 2002); Ian Gregory and Paul S. Ell, *Historical GIS: Technologies, Methodologies, and Scholarship* (Cambridge: Cambridge University Press, 2007); Ian Gregory and Richard G. Healey, "Historical GIS: Structuring, Mapping and Analyzing Geographies of the Past," *Progress in Human Geography* 3(5) (2007): 638–53.

27. Akbar Abbas, *Hong Kong: Culture and the Politics of Disappearance* (Minneapolis: University of Minnesota Press, 1997), 41; Roberts, *Film, Mobility and Urban Space*, 51–61.

28. Rodanthi Tzanelli, *The Cinematic Tourist: Explorations in Globalization, Culture and Resistance* (London: Routledge, 2007).

29. Conley, *Cartographic Cinema*, 211.

30. Conley, *Cartographic Cinema*, 3.

31. Nadine Schuurman, "Spatial Ontologies," in *International Encyclopedia of Human Geography*, vol. 1, ed. Rob Kitchin and Nigel Thrift, 377–83, cited here at p. 377 (Oxford: Elsevier, 2009).

32. Roberts, "Cinematic Cartography: Projecting Place through Film," 69.

33. Conley, "*The 39 Steps* and the Mental Map of Classical Cinema," 132.

34. Conley, *Cartographic Cinema*; Conley, "*The 39 Steps* and the Mental Map of Classical Cinema"; Tom Conley, "Locations in Film Noir," *The Cartographic Journal* 46(1) (2009): 16–23.

35. Conley, *Cartographic Cinema*, 212.

36. Conley, *Cartographic Cinema*, 212.

37. Caquard, "Foreshadowing Contemporary Digital Cartography," 54.

38. HOMER (History of Moviegoing, Exhibition and Reception); for a full list of members and associates see http://homerproject.blogs.wm.edu/members/, accessed December 30, 2011.

39. Going to the Show, http://docsouth.unc.edu/gtts/index.html, accessed December 30, 2011.

40. Klenotic, "Putting History on the Map," 60.

41. Jeffrey Klenotic, personal communication, July 2012.

42. Daniel Biltereyst, Philippe Meers, and Lies Van de Vijver, "Social Class, Experiences of Distinction and Cinema in Postwar Ghent," in Maltby, Biltereyst, and Meers, *Explorations in New Cinema History*, 102.

43. For other approaches that adopt a cultural geography perspective see, for example, Clarke, *The Cinematic City*, Tim Cresswell and Deborah Dixon, *Engaging Film: Geographies of Mobility and Identity* (Lanham, Md.: Rowman & Littlefield, 2002), Lukinbeal and Zimmermann, *The Geography of Cinema*.

44. Canadian Cinematographic Territories, http://www.atlascine.org/iWeb/Site/e/index.html, accessed December 30, 2011.

45. Tzanelli, *The Cinematic Tourist*.

46. For a fuller discussion of movie mapping and cinematographic tourism, see Roberts, *Film, Mobility and Urban Space*, 128–61; Les Roberts, "Projecting Place: Location Mapping, Consumption, and Cinematographic Tourism," in Koeck and Roberts, *The City and the Moving Image*, 183–207.

47. John Urry, *The Tourist Gaze: Leisure and Travel in Contemporary Societies* (London: Sage, 1990), 100.

48. Daniel Boorstin, *The Image: A Guide to Pseudo-Events in America* (New York: Vintage Books, 1992 [1961]).

49. Rodanthi Tzanelli, "Constructing the 'Cinematic Tourist': The 'sign industry' of *The Lord of the Rings*," *Tourist Studies* 4(1) (2004): 21–42, cited here at p. 38.

50. Bruno, *Atlas of Emotion*.

51. Conley, *Cartographic Cinema*, 1–2.

52. Kevin Lynch, *The Image of the City* (Cambridge, Mass.: The MIT Press, 1960).

53. Denis Wood, "Lynch Debord: About Two Psychogeographies," *Cartographica* 45(3) (2010): 185–200, emphasis added. See also Roberts, *Film, Mobility and Urban Space*, 57–61.

54. In fact, as Stephen Cairns has observed regarding the concept of urban "imageability," Lynch's ideas have been so influential in terms of the cultural economy of contemporary cities, in which premium is attached to the branding and imaging the city as a brand ("the cityscape as a brandscape," as he puts it), that it is clear that "the lessons of imageability have been learnt only too well." Stephen Cairns, "Cognitive Mapping and the Dispersed City," in *Urban Space and Cityscapes: Perspectives from Modern and Contemporary Culture*, ed. Christoph Lindner, 201 (London: Routledge, 2006).

55. Bruno, *Atlas of Emotion*, 29.

56. "Couldn't an exciting film be made from the map of Paris? From the unfolding of its various aspects in temporal succession? From the compression of a centuries-long movement of streets, boulevards, arcades, and squares into the space of half an hour? And does the flâneur do anything different?" Walter Benjamin, *The Arcades Project* (Cambridge, Mass.: Harvard University Press, 1999), 83.

57. Richard Misek, "Mapping Rohmer: Cinematic Cartography in Post-war Paris," in *Mapping Cultures: Place, Practice, Performance* ed. Les Roberts (Basingstoke: Palgrave).

58. Teresa Castro, "Cinema's Mapping Impulse: Questioning Visual Culture" *The Cartographic Journal* 46(1) (2009): 9–15; Castro, "Mapping the City Through Film."

59. Castro, "Cinema's Mapping Impulse," 14.

60. *City in Film* http://www.liv.ac.uk/lsa/cityinfilm/catalogue.html.

61. Patrick Keiller, "Film as Spatial Critique," in *Critical Architecture,* ed. Jane Rendell, Jonathan Hill, Murray Fraser, and Mark Dorrian, 115–23 (London: Routledge, 2007).

62. See also Julia Hallam, "Mapping City Space: Independent Filmmakers as Urban Gazetteers," *Journal of British Cinema and Television* 4(2) (2007): 272–84; Julia Hallam, "'City of Change and Challenge': the Cine-Societies' Response to the Redevelopment of Liverpool in the 1960s," in Koeck and Roberts, *The City and the Moving Image;* Roberts, *Film, Mobility and Urban Space.*

63. Keiller, "Film as Spatial Critique," 117.

64. Keiller, "Film as Spatial Critique," 121.

65. Russell, *Experimental Ethnography,* xv.

66. Robert Kronenburg, "Informing Contemporary Architectural and Urban Design with Historic Filmic Evidence," in Koeck and Roberts, *The City and the Moving Image;* Roberts, *Film, Mobility and Urban Space,* 222–32, cited here at p. 232.

67. Benjamin *The Arcades Project,* N2a, 3.

68. Catherine Russell, "Dialectical Film Criticism: Walter Benjamin's Historiography, Cultural Critique and the Archive," *Transformations* November 15, 2007, www.transformationsjournal.org/journal/issue_15/article_08.shtml, accessed September 14, 2010.

69. Lefebvre, *The Production of Space.*

70. Doreen Massey, *For Space* (London: Sage, 2005).

71. David Crouch, *Flirting with Space: Journeys and Creativity* (Farnham: Ashgate, 2010), 12.

72. www.liv.ac.uk/lsa/cityinfilm/

73. Hallam, "City of 'Change and Challenge.'"

74. Les Roberts, "Making Connections: Crossing Boundaries of Place and Identity in Liverpool and Merseyside Amateur Transport Films," *Mobilities* 5(1) (2010): 83–109.

75. See Roberts, *Film, Mobility and Urban Space,* 122–24.

76. See, for example, BFI's Screenonline. Screenonline's Liverpool page was the first to document the film and television output of a specific city and was developed in partnership with the University of Liverpool, North West Film Archive, North West Vision and Media, Liverpool Libraries and Liverpool Record Office: www.screenonline.org.uk/liverpool.

TWO

Getting to
"Going to the Show"

ROBERT C. ALLEN

One of the first books I was assigned to read in graduate school more than thirty years ago was a collection of essays by Andre Bazin titled, in its English translation, *What Is Cinema?*[1] David Rodowick introduces *The Virtual Life of Film*[2] by arguing that nearly a half-century of scholarly books, journal articles, and conferences have still not produced a consensual answer to Bazin's foundational interrogative. For the most part, this "continual state of identity crisis," as Rodowick puts it, has concerned the aesthetic identity and character of cinema. But in the meantime, technological change has shifted the very material ground upon which cinema has rested for more than a century, pushing the cinema studies threat level from orange to red. As the reassuring physicality of celluloid is rapidly supplanted by immaterial digital simulations, what, Rodowick asks, is left of cinema? "Is this the end of film, and therefore the end of cinema studies? Does cinema studies have a future in the twenty-first century?"[3] Rodowick concludes (a few hundred pages later) that cinema and cinema studies can both withstand the metaphysical threat represented by technological change, even if that means adjusting the ontological boundaries a bit, so that a "film" shot, edited, distributed, and projected digitally in a movie theater is still "cinema," but watching YouTube videos on an iPhone is, well, something other than cinema.

In its most general outlines, my work is predicated upon a historicizing of Bazin's query: "What was cinema?" Or as I would rephrase it slightly, "What has cinema been understood to be and by whom?" More than ten years ago I argued that the assumptions that films studies scholars had made for a generation about Hollywood cinema as a cultural industry, the spaces in which it was encountered, and about the normative modes by which it was experienced were no longer valid.[4] There were a number of drivers of this transformation, but one of the most consequential was the extraordinarily rapid diffusion in the early 1980s of home video as an alternative exhibition outlet. By the early 1990s, Hollywood was making more money from selling movies on videocassette—for people to keep and watch wherever, whenever, and however they pleased—than it did from selling tickets to see a film one time in a place that had become a concession stand with small dark rooms attached to it. For the past twenty years, watching movies in a movie theater has been irreversibly declining as a normative mode of the experience of cinema in the United States and throughout much of the world, and in the meantime an entire generation has grown up with their earliest, most formative, and most common experiences of movies occurring in places that until recently Hollywood consigned to the category of "non-theatrical" exhibition sites: bedrooms, living rooms, kitchens, automobiles. In the process, a chasm has opened between what we might call the academic experience of cinema and the everyday experience of cinema. This experiential and, I would argue, ontological divide is generational as well.

Our daughter, Madeline, was born in 1994. Her earliest and formative experiences of cinema occurred not in a movie theater, but in front of a television set connected to a VCR. For her, cinema is a textually disintegrated phenomenon experienced through multiple and unpredictably proliferating sites and modalities. Her experience of cinema has always been decentered and fissiparous. Our students now studying some aspect of something identified by the academy as cinema at thousands of universities around the world are, figuratively speaking, Madeline's older demographic sisters and brothers. In the United States they are all members of the seventy-two-million-strong echo boom generation born between 1977 and 1995—the second largest generational bulge in American history next to the post–World War II baby boom. For them, theatrical moviegoing has never been more authentic than any other way of experiencing cinema.

My daughter's experience of cinema is historically located on this side of an epochal divide. On the far side of that divide lies "cinema" as it would have been understood and experienced by her grandmother and great-grandmother. Born in 1921 and 1887, respectively, they were part of the moviegoing epoch, the century-long period of theatrical and extra-theatrical moviegoing in America, which I would argue extends from the advent of projected motion pictures in the mid-1890s to the mass adoption of the videocassette player in the 1980s. What links their experience of cinema with other members of their epochal cohort—whether in the same town or on the other side of the world—is its sociality. It involved groups of people converging upon particular places to experience together something understood to be cinema. As an industry and as a cultural form, cinema depended upon the regular repetition of this social convergence under the sign of cinema, day after day, week after week, year after year, in hundreds of thousands of places by uncountable billions of people.

Despite the seemingly unending proliferation of cinema sites and modalities and the concomitant divergence between the academic and the everyday experience of cinema, film studies—as a scholarly and as a pedagogic practice—continues to privilege text over experience, the abstracted transhistorical screen over the historical spaces of cinematic performance, the reified, transhistorical spectator over the social practice of moviegoing. The historical experience of cinema at any particular moment in any particular place remains both undertheorized and—given its scope, diversity, and historical contingency—largely undocumented. The outcome of this neglect is that the full magnitude and implications of the sociality of the experience of cinema over the first century of film history have yet to be adequately considered.

At this stage in my own work, I am most interested in developing a scholarly and teaching practice that tries to understand cinema as a set of processes, practices, events, spaces, performances, connections, embodiments, relationships, exchanges, and memories—experiences, in other words, associated with but not reducible to films. Reimagining the history of cinema as *the history of the experience of cinema* is not a matter of supplying historical contexts for films, nor is it a playing out of the argument that contexts condition what a given film might have meant to some audiences. It is a matter of turning the assumed relationship of context to text, or of experience and the thing experienced, inside out. Context is not a frame, or backdrop, or setting for something else, but rather a necessary and irreducible element of experience. Surviving films from the past are the residue of a set of social and cultural practices. They are limited in what they can tell us about how they might have been experienced, and they say little about what cinema might have meant within the myriad of places within which it was constituted as "cinema," or how and for whom these meanings varied, were contested, or changed over time.

I'm certainly not the first to insist upon the historical situatedness of the experience of cinema—a sufficient body of scholarship has been building up on film exhibition, circulation, reception, audiences, publicity, regulation, and other empirical matters to earn it status as a tendency in film studies: the "historical turn," as it is called in a special issue of *Cinema Journal* devoted to it a few years ago. But, at least according to the editor's commentary, film scholars and teachers are not quite sure what they are supposed to do with this kind of work or how it might inflect their own research and teaching practice. Few are tempted to engage in empirical research themselves because, she says, they have not been trained to do so. The historical turn, she judges, has led to a dirt road.[5] The historical work that is most easily accommodated within cinema studies, not surprisingly, is work that winds up back at the intersection of film and interpretation, even if the analyst arrived back there carrying a good deal of historical/empirical/contextual baggage picked up along the way.

I am interested in developing a historiographic practice that points to, argues for, and, however problematically, represents some of what is representable about the historical experience of cinema. To borrow Nigel Thrift's description of his recently published account of non-representational theory, I am trying to develop a historical geography of what happened: "the beginning of an outline of the art of producing a permanent supplement to the ordinary."[6] One expression of my search for an appropriate historiographic and scholarly practice with respect to cinema is a digital library project with which I have been involved for the past four years and which was officially launched on July 1, 2009. Going to the Show (www.docsouth.unc.edu/gtts) uses data and content taken from city directories, photographs, postcards, newspaper ads and articles, architectural drawings, and business records to document and illuminate the experience of moviegoing in North Carolina between 1896 and 1930. Information about and content associated with more than 1,300 cinema venues in operation across two hundred communities in the state are displayed upon more than a thousand georeferenced urban ground plan maps (Sanborn Fire Insurance Maps).[7] Describing the contents of an interactive website in a journal article is a futile exercise: like cinema,

FIGURE 2.1. Sanborn map of Bijou Theater, Wilmington, North Carolina, 1910.

it is designed to be experienced. What follows is a reflection on some of the historiographic and practical issues the project raises for me and a consideration of some of the implications it has for my understanding of the history of the experience of cinema.

Going to the Show is a historiographic experiment on several levels. It asks, how has the experience of moviegoing been represented and what traces of those representations survive? How might those traces themselves be represented and manipulated in an interactive digital library? What aspects of the experience of moviegoing are highlighted in these representations and what aspects are obscured or remain unrepresentable regardless of how much or what kind of "data" my colleagues and I might be able to deploy? What is the historiographic and epistemological status of knowledge that might be generated from such data-rich projects?

My work on Going to the Show was based upon the premise that understanding the experience of cinema at any point in the past in any place also entails understanding the spatiality of the experience of cinema. Going to the Show is grounded, so to speak, in one form of spatial representation: the map, or to be more specific two hundred sets of morphological ground plans representing forty-five towns and cities in North Carolina between 1896 and 1922, some one thousand map pages in total.[8] Between 1867 and 1977 the Sanborn Map Company of Pelham, New York, produced large-scale (usually fifty feet to the inch) color maps of commercial and industrial districts of some twelve thousand towns and cities in North America to assist fire insurance companies in setting rates and terms. Each set of maps represented each built structure in those districts, its use, dimensions, height, building material, and other relevant features. The intervals between new map editions for a given town or city in the early decades of the twentieth century varied according to the pace and scale of urban growth—from a few years to more than five years. In all, Sanborn produced fifty thousand editions comprising some 700,000 individual map pages.[9]

Sanborn maps are widely recognized by urban historians and historical geographers as unique and invaluable resources, and they are the most requested historic maps at both public and academic libraries in the United States.[10] In accordance with U.S. copyright law, the Sanborn Company deposited two copies of each map it published with the Library of Congress. Between 1955 and 1978, the Library of Congress decided to give each state a copy of the maps produced to date for the towns and cities in it. Today, all fifty states possess a set of state maps—usually housed in the state library or in the library of a state university.

As soon as buildings begin to be used as regular cinema venues, they also begin to appear on Sanborn maps. Indeed, they were of special interest to insurance companies: the extremely flammable nature of film stock and its use only inches away from what was in effect an open flame made movie theaters potential fire traps for decades. The Sanborn maps show us how big each venue was, what it was made of, whether or not it had a balcony or stage, and, by comparing successive map sets of the same area, whether it was renovated or expanded and how long it stayed in business. But because several years or more elapse between Sanborn map iterations of a given town, they capture the spaces of cinematic exhibition in widely separated spatial snap shots.

Taken together, however, the two hundred map sets for forty-five communities covering the first twenty-five years of film exhibition in

North Carolina clearly show that moviegoing developed as a part of the experience of what urban historians call "Main Street"—the socially dense complex of commercial, civic, and cultural activity clustered around the town square or along the streets that made up the central business district. With the notable exception of African American theaters in black neighborhoods, the first generation of movie theaters in every town and city in North Carolina was located not only in the central business district, but as close to the commercial heart of downtown as it was possible for early entrepreneurs to get.

The Sanborn maps also show that moviegoing developed as a cultural and social practice at a time of enormous urban growth and change in North Carolina. New towns sprang up around cotton mills and furniture and tobacco factories; older towns grew and replaced wooden buildings along Main Street with more substantial and imposing buildings faced with stone or brick. But rapid urbanization in North Carolina did not produce big cities but rather hundreds of small towns, and more towns were chartered between 1880 and 1920 than at any other time in North Carolina's four-hundred-year history. Downtown commercial real estate development followed the same pattern from town to town: the erection of zero-lot-line (i.e., adjacent) buildings with twenty-five- to fifty-foot frontage, 100 to 150 feet deep, and two to four stories tall.[11]

The ground floor would be used for retail, and the upper floor or floors might be divided into commercial or professional offices or leased to fraternal organizations, of which there were dozens in nearly every town. Small businesses—hardware stores, drug stores, cigar stores, grocery stores, millenary shops—all vied to rent an affordable retail space in one of these buildings that was close to the center of downtown and passed by as many people as possible. Retail businesses might change locations when, at the annual lease renewal time (in Wilmington it was the end of October each year), a more central spot came open. No one would have thought it odd that one November a hardware store was transformed into a cigar store, or vice versa, and no one would have expected that someone starting a new retail business would have built a new structure to accommodate it. In the first place, few new retail businesses had the capital to do so, and it would have been much more advantageous to rent space in an existing building at the center of downtown than to build on available land elsewhere. A century ago, retail merchants were putting into practice

what urban economists now call agglomeration: the physical clustering of
enterprises in the same and complimentary business sectors.

In short, it is impossible to understand the early experience of cinema
in North Carolina except within its urban spatial context. This realization
drove a key representational strategy in Going to the Show. We would
manipulate and display the Sanborn maps in a way that they were never
intended to be: with individual map pages digitally stitched together to
form a composite overview of a town's central business district. This led to
a second key representational decision: to georeference the resulting map
mosaic—in other words, to align the map with the represented space's
longitude and latitude coordinates. With the Sanborn maps georeferenced, it made sense also to do the same for each venue and its associated
content, producing layers of data arrayed over the Sanborn map displays.
Pinning each venue to its spatial coordinates meant that we could view
over time the same place as represented in different map iterations.[12]

Another premise underlying Going to the Show—based upon research I and others had already done—was that race was the most important factor in the experience of moviegoing for all North Carolinians
between 1896 and the desegregation of white theaters in the early 1960s.
I wanted to make sure that we aggressively sought out data and content
that would help to document the racing of cinema spaces. This turned out
to be an especially challenging social and spatial phenomenon to research
and represent. White theaters seldom advertised their racial admission
policy in newspaper ads—whether that entailed complete exclusion of
African Americans, the creation of raced spaces within the theater, or the
admission of African Americans only for special screenings (frequently
called "midnight shows" because they tended to be held following the
final screening for white audiences on a Friday or Saturday evening).
There were, of course, African American theaters in operation in North
Carolina from the early 1910s through the 1950s. Both city directories and
Sanborn maps are themselves raced sources: black businesses, schools,
hospitals, and movie theaters are labeled as "Negro" or "colored" on the
Sanborn maps, and every African American resident, business, and social institution is noted as such in city directories. This made it possible
for us to include in our database all African American theaters that had
been documented in either source, and from city directory listings to
determine in most cases the race of the theater proprietor. However, few

African American theaters advertised in white newspapers, and although some larger cities in North Carolina had black newspapers, none of them were preserved and microfilmed in sufficient quantities and over long enough periods of time to be useful for our purposes. To supplement our local data about African American theaters, I scanned the annual listing of movie theaters for North Carolina compiled by *Film Daily Yearbook,* which began listing black theaters in the 1920s. The inventory of black movie theaters we have compiled covers the entire period of African American exhibition in North Carolina, making it—for now and so far as we know—the first and only such inventory assembled for any American state.

The imposition of Jim Crow laws, policing, and social practices across the South and bleeding into adjacent states spans the first sixty years of the history of moviegoing in America. Its authorizing Supreme Court decision, *Plessy v. Ferguson,* came down within weeks of the first commercial exhibition of projected motion pictures in New York City in the summer of 1896. The establishment of the first generation of movie theaters in the South around 1906–1908 occurs as towns and cities across the region were regulating the behavior and movement of African Americans through downtown streets and buildings and ruthlessly racing every urban space in which whites and blacks might come into contact. When the first movie theaters opened in North Carolina in the fall of 1906, some 90 percent of all African Americans still lived in the South and 70 percent of them lived in the rural South. In some key respects the social and cultural geography of North Carolina at the turn of the century would have been more familiar to most white and black Americans than that of Chicago or New York. Two-thirds of all Americans lived outside even the smallest town; for most Americans "urban" meant a town of fewer than five thousand people; downtown was a few blocks along Main Street or around the town square; a skyscraper was any building taller than four stories; the chances were good that if you spent more than a few minutes downtown you'd run into someone you knew or who knew you or your family.[13]

Going to the Show strives to be as comprehensive as possible in its coverage of cinema venues across an entire American state in the early decades of moviegoing, but this coverage is necessarily superficial. As a representational counterpoint, I chose Wilmington, North Carolina, as the site for a more fine-grain historical geography. I did not choose it because I thought it was representative of the urban environment of mov-iegoing for North Carolina as a whole. Indeed, in many ways Wilmington was atypical: the state's largest city (25,000) in 1900, its most important port, and an important regional rail hub, Wilmington was also the closest thing to a cosmopolitan urban area in the state at the turn of the century. Socially, it was the state's most ethnically diverse city. Racially, Wilming-ton was more than 40 percent black and was the scene of a devastating white supremacist political insurrection in 1898, an event that helped to shape politics and race relations throughout the South and one that cer-tainly conditioned the experience of everyday life for all Wilmingtonians for decades to come. Wilmington recommended itself for historiographic as well as historical reasons. The local public library has one of the oldest and largest local history collections in the state, including a collection of several million subject-catalogued newspaper clippings spanning the 1860s through the 1950s, but particularly strong between 1895 and 1930.

The project was shaped by other discoveries and offers of collabora-tion as the project unfolded between 2006 and 2009. An architect turned librarian in the mountain town of Hendersonville alerted me to the col-lection of more than four thousand architectural drawings housed in the public library there by Erle Stillwell, a local architect who practiced between 1915 to 1953 and designed hundreds of houses, churches, schools, hospitals, commercial buildings, and more than sixty movie theaters, more than twenty of them in North Carolina between 1922 and 1952. In addition to the light they shed on architectural styles, exhibition tech-nology, and construction practices, Stillwell's drawings also strikingly revealed the centrality of race as a design challenge in every theater he worked on. It has become commonplace to note that under Jim Crow policies in the South, black movie audiences were often forced to sit in the balcony if they wanted to be admitted to white theaters. This makes it sounds as if the balcony was a pre-existing feature of theaters and seg-regation a post-hoc seating policy decision. But Stillwell's drawings re-veal that the segregation of white theaters in the South was not merely a matter of assigning African Americans to one set of seats and in doing so denying them seating in another part of the theater. The construction of racially segregated balconies was but one element of a carefully and in some cases elaborately designed system of spaces, barriers, duplicate facilities, diversions, entrances, and passageways, whose purpose was to render the African American experience of cinema in white theaters invisible to white patrons and demeaning to African American patrons.[14]

My work on Going to the Show continues to unfold—in both predictable and unexpected ways. It has led to an opportunity to adapt, simplify, democratize, and distribute its underlying software applications so that local cultural organizations throughout the state of North Carolina can create, manage, and georeference content about the history of their downtowns (including the history of downtown moviegoing) and display this content on their own websites using the same georeferenced and stitched Sanborn maps we have produced for Going to the Show.[15] I have developed new undergraduate and graduate courses on the history of Main Street and on the use of digital technologies to document and represent that history. These courses also explore the ways university researchers, archivists, teachers, and students can partner with local cultural organizations and agencies in using archival resources and digital technologies for a wide array of purposes and audiences. I have just begun to work my way through some of the material now captured in Going to the Show and to provisionally piece together some of the patterns in the ways people experienced cinema in North Carolina at the beginning of the past century. One of the things that intellectually spans these activities is the relationship between the experience of cinema and the experience of urbanity, and the concomitant need to reconceptualize both terms of this relationship.

NOTES

1. A. Bazin, *What Is Cinema?* (Berkeley: University of California Press, 1971).

2. D. N. Rodowick, *The Virtual Life of Film* (Cambridge, Mass.: Harvard University Press, 2007).

3. Rodowick, *The Virtual Life of Film*, 11.

4. R. C. Allen, "Home Alone Together: Hollywood and the 'Family Film,'" in *Identifying Hollywood's Audiences: Cultural Identity and the Movies,* ed. M. Stokes and R. Maltby (London: British Film Institute, 1999).

5. S. Higashi, "In Focus: Film History or a Baedeker Guide to the Historical Turn," *Cinema Journal* 44(1) (2004): 94–100.

6. N. Thrift, *Non-representational Theory: Space/Politics/Affect* (London: Routledge, 2008), 2.

7. Going to the Show grew out of my use of local archival materials over the past thirty years in teaching and writing about the history of film exhibition and moviegoing. The scope and scale of this project are possible because my office is about two hundred

feet away from the largest archival collection of printed and published material about an American state in the world, and only because I found at our university library's Carolina Digital Library and Archives extraordinarily able collaborators with extensive experience in the creation of digital collections, databases, content management, GIS, display applications, and getting grants to digitize library collections. Their pioneering digital library work is showcased in Documenting the American South (www.docsouth. unc.edu). My project was also inspired by the example of a number of my colleagues in the United States, Europe, and Australia—Karel Dibbets and his team in Amsterdam chief among them—who have pioneered the use of digital technologies in a variety of innovative ways to collect, organize, and display data and materials that illuminate the historical experience of cinema. See Cinema Context (http://www.cinemacontext.nl/).

8. We are limited by U.S. copyright policies in the maps we can display online to those published prior to 1923.

9. See *Fire Insurance Maps in the Library of Congress: Plan of North American Cities and Towns Produced by the Sanborn Map Company* (Washington: Library of Congress, 1981). Most of the Sanborn maps published between 1867 and 1950 in the Library of Congress's collection were microfilmed and marketed by a commercial publisher in the 1980s. The large scale of the map pages required an 18X reduction when microfilmed, and cost considerations drove a decision to reproduce the maps in black and white rather than color. Despite this cost consciousness, the retail price of statewide map sets ranged from $110 (Alaska) to more than $15,000 (New York), with the complete collection priced at $195,000. More recently Sanborn maps have been made available electronically to institutions on a state-by-state basis, but the displayed map pages are taken from the black-and-white microfilms rather than from color originals. See Stuart Blumin, "Review of The Sanborn Fire Insurance Maps 1867–1950," *Journal of American History* 73(4) (March 1987): 1089–90. The fire insurance map publication industry emerges in the second half of the nineteenth century as a tool for managing risks associated with commercial and industrial real estate development. This need—common across cities around the world—led to the establishment of a number of companies and trade associations that undertook systematic urban mapping. In the United Kingdom, the Charles E. Goad Company produced fire insurance maps for more than one hundred cities, as well as cities in Canada, Denmark, Egypt, France, Mexico, South Africa, Turkey, and Venezuela. See Margaret Irene Fead, "Notes on the Development of the Cartographic Representation of Cities," *Geographical Review* 23(3) (1933): 441–56.

10. C. Moulder, "Fire Insurance Plans as a Data Source in Urban Research: An Annotated Bibliography of Examples," *Art Reference Services Quarterly* 1(3) (1994): 49–62.

11. R. E. Fogelson, *Downtown: Its Rise and Fall, 1880–1950* (New Haven, Conn.: Yale University Press, 2003); C. Bishir, *Architects and Builders in North Carolina: A History of Building Practice* (Chapel Hill: University of North Carolina Press, 1990).

12. There are several different GIS applications we could have used to display the maps and associated content, but we decided to use Google Maps. It does not require downloading of a map viewer, it is much easier to use than some other, more sophisticated GIS programs, and it allows the user to activate another layer of spatial data: the contemporary satellite image or street map of a given downtown, which enables the user to compare any urban location's contemporary use and appearance with its representation on Sanborn maps of a century ago. It also meant that we could take advantage of new Google imaging and mapping applications as they were developed, even if they

were not a part of our original plans for the project. The Google street view maps are a good example.

13. Population figures are extrapolated from various tables in United States Bureau of the Census, *Thirteenth Census of the United States (1910), Abstract of the Census—Population* (Washington, D.C.: Government Printing Office, 1913); and United States Bureau of the Census, *Fourteenth Census of the United States Population 1920* (Washington, D.C.: Government Printing Office, 1921).

14. http://docsouth.unc.edu/gtts/learn/commentary/Stillwell_Intro.html.

15. Main Street, Carolina is being developed with the support of the C. Felix Harvey Award for the Advancement of Institutional Priorities at the University of North Carolina at Chapel Hill and a Digital Start-Up Grant from the National Endowment for the Humanities.

THREE

Space, Place, and the Female Film Exhibitor: The Transformation of Cinema in Small-Town New Hampshire during the 1910s

JEFFREY KLENOTIC

A lot of people smiled, three years ago, when they heard that
Mrs. Richardson was going to manage the moving pictures....
When she started some influential citizens regarded her enterprise
with disfavor.... Now, it is safe to say, most of them realize that if
Milford is to hold its own and grow as ... a place where the "home
folks" will be contented and which outsiders will like to visit, it
is important to have an amusement place like the Star Theatre, a
place where clean, wholesome fun can be had at small cost.

By the mid-1910s, the town of Milford, New Hampshire, had established
a pattern of film exhibition in which only one proprietor was permitted
a license to present moving pictures.[1] To the surprise of many, a woman
vied to fill this role. Although women in the United States had not yet
gained full voting rights, they were becoming increasingly visible at work,
expanding to roughly 20 percent of the workforce as the number of female wage earners and retail merchants grew 43 percent and 82 percent,
respectively, between 1900 and 1910. The growth in women's work was
particularly strong in fields of trade, transportation, and communication.[2] Keeping with these trends, the moving picture trade (which relied
on transportation and communication to get prints to exhibitors) as it
developed in Milford created sufficient space to allow a female resident
the opportunity to become the lone cinema operator in her community.
Against considerable odds, she succeeded not only in occupying this posi-

tion but also in transforming it. By facilitating the movement of women into business, motion pictures produced a new kind of space in Milford, a "modern" space that was initially disruptive, creating disfavor among some prominent citizens. The nature of this disruption, however, had less to do with films than with who was showing films and the perceived seriousness of her enterprise. In the end, local disturbances created by the arrival of regular moving picture shows were negotiated in ways that enabled cinema to settle into place in a form that was fully embedded in the town's spatial and social identity.

This chapter emanates from my ongoing work using historical GIS methods to visualize contexts for early moviegoing in New Hampshire.[3] Among other variables, this work has mapped uneven patterns of population distribution by sex, raising questions about the impact this gendered landscape may have had on film exhibition across the state. Here I pursue these questions further by exploring the social, cultural, economic, and physical terrain that simultaneously enabled and constrained Mrs. Richardson's mobility as she navigated her journey as a woman and pioneer of early cinema. My objective is to sketch out some of the contours, pathways, and networks that gave definition to the experience of small-town life during the 1910s to suggest ways in which place and space mattered, not only as features of community identity but as forces shaping the uneven development of film exhibition amidst a time of pronounced urbanization, an expanding women's movement, and the emergence of a mass market for movies. Drawing upon wide social demographic patterns as well as narrow examples of local practices from Milford, this chapter considers cinema's spatially mediated, and spatially mediating, place in early twentieth-century modern life while also contributing to research on women's early film history[4] and the history of moviegoing, exhibition, and reception in rural and small-town America.[5] In doing so, a new layer is added to the project Jennifer Bean describes as "mapping a history of women's engagements with early film" by unearthing "the range of sites in which women produced, consumed, and performed in the growing industry."[6] In the case of Milford, I seek to recover part of the lost topography of women's enterprise at the site of exhibition, where Mrs. Richardson performed key roles as entrepreneur, civic leader, and producer of space and place.

Milford provides an excellent setting to explore the influence of sex, gender, and geography on the experience of cinema and the development of film exhibition in the 1910s. The town resides in lower Hillsborough County in southern New Hampshire, which is part of the Boston (Massachusetts) Metropolitan Area as well as the Manchester and Nashua (New Hampshire) Metropolitan Area. Well-served with transportation access, this portion of the state has historically been its population center, providing suburban living for Boston commuters and attracting immigrants and transplants to work in an industrialized and technology-based economy radiating from the state's two largest cities. At the turn of the twentieth century, many who relocated to the area were women, drawn by employment in the region's textile mills. Consequently, some parts of southern New Hampshire, including Hillsborough County, showed a slight majority of female residents, even though the state as a whole had more men than women (figure 3.1).[7] In this respect, Hillsborough County was closer in its demography to Massachusetts, which in 1910 had roughly ninety-seven males for every one hundred females, than to its upcountry neighbors in northern New Hampshire, Vermont, and Maine, all of which had significantly more men than women.[8] Research has shown that an emerging market of women workers with disposable incomes coincided with the success of early commercial amusements in some parts of the country, particularly the industrialized Northeast.[9] For this reason, sex and gender have been seen, along with class, race, and ethnicity, as key contexts shaping cinema's development as a social practice and regulated form of leisure. What makes Milford such an intriguing site for research is that it permits consideration of film exhibition not only as an aspect of women's leisure but also as a form of women's work and economic mobility, and, when placed in the context of the suffrage movement, as a dimension of women's transformative politics. At the same time, Milford offers a view of the changing dynamic of small-town life itself, which faced an uncertain future with dual forces of rural depopulation and metropolitan imperialism swirling around it. Milford's precarious place as a small town trying to hold its own in the twentieth-century landscape required active remediation, in part through the production of a new form of cinematic space that was simultaneously modern and traditional, urban and rural, global and local,

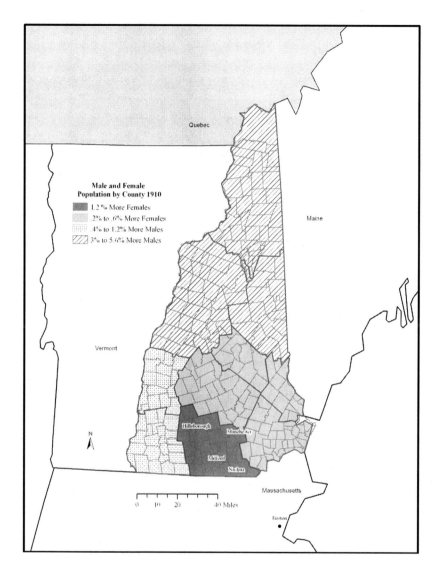

FIGURE 3.1. The gendered landscape of early twentieth-century New Hampshire.

a space connected to Hollywood and mass culture but grounded, quite literally, on the foundation of an old livery stable and blacksmith shop that was transformed through the hard work and enterprise of Mrs. May B. Richardson into the Star Theatre.

LOST IN TRANSLATION: SMALL
TOWNS IN THE 1910S

The 1910s were a watershed in the perception of American social geography. The decade began with the United States Census Bureau officially defining "urban" as "all incorporated places (including New England towns) having a population of 2,500 inhabitants or more."[10] This was a continuing decrease in the minimum threshold for urban from 8,000 inhabitants in 1880 to 4,000 inhabitants in 1890.[11] By the new measure, 45.8 percent of the U.S. population was classified as urban in 1910, which proved to be the last census to record a majority living in rural areas. Ten years later, the 1920 census reported 51.4 percent of Americans as urban dwellers.[12] Setting aside the legitimate question of whether 2,500 people adequately captured the dividing line between a rural lived experience and an urban one, the rebirth of the United States as an urban nation was under way, at least according to official maps produced by the Census Bureau.

When the new definition of urban was applied to past census data, it produced interesting results for New Hampshire. It now appeared the state's urban transformation had actually begun in 1890, when a slight majority of residents were recorded inhabiting places over 2,500 in population.[13] Twenty years later, 59 percent of the state's 430,572 residents were urban, a figure that rose to 63 percent in 1920.[14] It is important to note, however, that New Hampshire's urban population in the 1910s was distributed over a relatively small percentage of the state's 258 minor civil divisions (cities, towns, townships, grants, locations, and purchases).[15] In 1910, only twenty-six places in New Hampshire (10 percent) had populations exceeding 2,500. By 1920, two towns classified as urban had reverted to rural while three rural towns had become urban. This left twenty-seven places with populations over 2,500 (figure 3.2).[16]

The uneven distribution of urban population meant that, geographically speaking, New Hampshire presented a stubbornly rural landscape. The state had an average population per place of 1,669 in 1910 and 1,717 in 1920. Population density was also relatively low. In 1910, Coos County in northern New Hampshire ranked at the bottom with 17 inhabitants per square mile, while Hillsborough County with 141 was at the top. As a whole, the state averaged 48 persons to the square mile in 1910 and 49

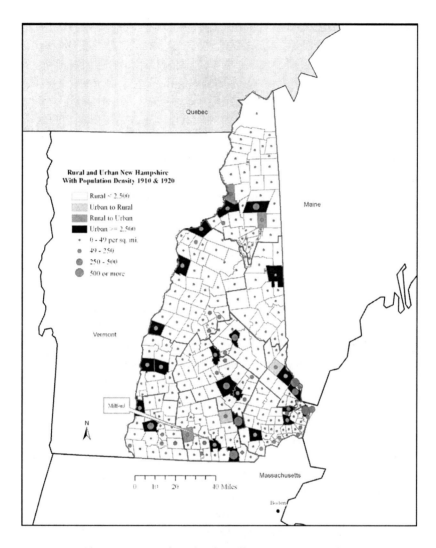

FIGURE 3.2. The persistence of rural and small-town New Hampshire; only 10 percent of the state's 258 minor civil divisions had populations above 2,500 in 1910 and 1920.

in 1920. Most places in the state fell below these averages. In 1920, for example, 204 of the state's 258 places (about 80 percent) had population densities less than 49 persons per square mile (figure 3.2). Compared with the rest of New England, New Hampshire's population density in 1920 was higher than Maine (26 per square mile) and Vermont (39), but far lower than Connecticut (286), Massachusetts (479), and Rhode Island (566).[17]

Over the course of the 1910s, New Hampshire arrived at an "in between" location in its spatial and social geography. It was an urban state, but not nearly as densely populated as its "modern" southern New England neighbors. At the same time, though large expanses of the state continued to have a strongly rural character, this measure of "traditional" New England paled in comparison to Vermont and Maine, both of which had urban populations well below 40 percent in 1920.[18] The mixing of rural and urban elements in New Hampshire produced an uneven layering of spatial and social experience, creating competing desires to pull closer to Boston metropolitanism while also maintaining older connections to northern New England and its rural traditions.

Similar dynamics also appertained, on a smaller scale, to the hybrid experience of America's small towns. The hybrid nature of small-town life had become evident to scholars and social observers of the time. Social and religious geographer Harlan Paul Douglass, for example, held particularly well-developed views on the subject. In *The Little Town,* published in 1919, Douglass observed that "somewhere between the country and the city lies that which is neither, but which partakes on a petty scale of the nature of both—the little town. After the isolation of one leaves off, but before the congestion of the other begins" sits the small town.[19] Because the census's bifurcation of America into either urban or rural populations "ignores the little town and obscures its significance,"[20] Douglass ventured his own definition of the "little town" as an "incorporated place of less than 5,000 people."[21] The act of a place's incorporation was the lower limit of this classification, indicating that "somebody must have felt that their group-interests constituted them a body of people different from their neighbors of the open country" such that they "separated themselves into a town."[22] The upper limit was 5,000 because at this size "people will still keep within walking distance of a single common centre which constitutes the business and institutional focus of their lives. Beyond that number, population tends to seek outlying sub-centers and to want a streetcar service. These are the beginnings at least of urban tendencies."[23] In New Hampshire, if unincorporated villages, townships, unorganized territories, land grants, and purchases are subtracted from the state's total of 258 places in 1920, this leaves 234 incorporated places. Of these, only fourteen had populations of 5,000 or more.[24] By Douglass's formula, New Hampshire had 220 small towns, amounting to 85 percent of all places and 94 percent of all incorporated places. Among these was the town of Milford, population 3,783.[25]

Douglass noted that the quality of life in small towns occupied a dubious place in America's spatial imagination. Such towns were thought of as "something between the worst and the best" and were held by many urbanites and small-town residents alike with a degree of ambivalence and conflicting attitudes as expressed in the folk saying, "God made the country, man the city, but the devil the little town."[26] Despite these misgivings, there were an estimated "twelve thousand such places in the United States, their life characterized by simple complexity, their people a distinct and mediating human type. More than twelve million Americans live in them and they supply the fundamental institutions of civilization for uncounted millions more."[27] To capture the hybrid character of small-town culture, Douglass adopted the term "rurbanism," by which he also intended to make the point that small towns were defined not simply by their distinctiveness as mediated places but by their mediating relationships to other places. This did not mean towns were merely provincial outposts of imperialistic cities and metropolises, but rather that they were key nodes in their own networks of relationships with proximate rural populations. As Douglass puts it, "a 'rurban' community consists of the village or town-centre with its surrounding farm population which uses the centre as its economic and ideal focus,"[28] adding that "the little town has its imperialism as well as its modesty."[29]

THE TRANSFORMATION OF CINEMA

The decade that saw the United States redefined as an ostensibly urban nation also witnessed the transformation of American film, which arrived at what André Gaudreault and Philippe Marion have called the "second birth" of cinema. If the film medium was first conceived as a technology dependent on ancillary industries and extant, frequently itinerant cultural practices, it was eventually reconceived as an autonomous and centrally located institution in its own right. The 1910s were the culminating stage in this transformation "from the *appearance* of a technological process, the apparatus, to the *emergence* of an initial culture, that of 'animated pictures', and finally to the *constitution* of an established media in-stitution."[30] The shift from the hodgepodge of "animated pictures" to the singularity of "cinema" was not, however, an immediate breakthrough. Rather, it was a gradual maturation, an uneven and not always orderly transition. In fits and starts, and amid much competition and resistance, new economic, aesthetic, social, and cultural practices (studio produc-tion, block booking, mass distribution, picture palaces, integrative narra-tives, feature-length films, stars, press kits, advertising trailers, fan maga-zines, etc.) were assembled and eventually constituted into a rationalized and nationalized cinema institution that placed a handful of companies at the center of a redrawn map of American film production, distribution and exhibition, a map that would ultimately produce Hollywood as its imagined capital city and cultural hub.[31]

But how did the medium's transformation develop, and under whose guidance and direction was the institution of cinema constituted, for those on the edges of this map? Gaudreault and Marion point out "a me-dium's second birth cannot be categorized as a discrete and momentary event which can be assigned a date and identified as occurring at a pre-cise instant."[32] This point is underscored by Ben Singer, who observes that the temporal complexities of transition present a major challenge for historians

> to figure out how to reconcile two essentially incompatible, but in this case equally legitimate, historiographical impulses: on the one hand, the need to accentuate radical transformation ... and on the other hand, the need to rec-ognize that transitions are never succinct or definitive shifts from one state of affairs to another. Transition is, almost by definition, a complex dynamic process in which disparate forces—competing paradigms and practices— overlap and interact.[33]

The process becomes even more complex when we acknowledge that transition is not only a matter of time, an amalgam of future and past pos-sibilities overlapping and interacting in an unfolding present, but of space, a heterogeneity of overlapping and interacting relationships between here and there, inside and outside, core and periphery, that shape the experi-ence of particular places. As Ian Gregory puts it,

> if geography is thought of as the study of places and the relationships be-tween them, then space must be important, as it enables and limits the

interaction between people and places. Almost everything that interests a historian—goods and services, capital and labor, ideas and innovations, fashions and epidemics—moves from one place to another; thus space enables and constrains their spread.[34]

By facilitating and constraining movement, space and its contingencies interlock with the contingencies of time. Doreen Massey describes space as the "dimension of multiple trajectories, a simultaneity of stories-so-far," and "the dimension of a multiplicity of durations."[35] Space is not flat, static, or closed, but uneven and dynamic, always in the process of being both unified and sedimented by competing forces and open to future possibilities. Stories of "here and there" will relate to stories of "now and then" in multiple ways. What appears as the present in one place may look like the past in another place and elsewhere be imagined as the future. Reconciling the impulse to accentuate the transition to a new state of affairs with the recognition that such transitions are rarely definitive therefore entails not only carefully identifying *when* practices were emerging, lingering, and expiring, but it equally involves locating *where* practices were emerging, lingering, or expiring.

One way to navigate through the complexities of cinema's transformation is to take bearings by what is on the screen. In this case, the best orientation point leading toward cinema and away from animated pictures is the regular presence of feature-length films as opposed to a variety program of shorter films. As Ben Brewster points out, during the 1910s "one phase of the cinema, that of the one-reel film, coexisted with another, that of the feature, at the same time that it was giving way to it."[36] Patterns in film programming thus offer a window through which to observe the horizon of each system expanding or receding. Ben Singer, for example, has charted film production in the United States, measured by the reel length of films made between 1908 and 1920, to identify trends in the circulation of shorts (three reels or less) and features (four reels or more). The data reveal the "short's free fall lasted for three years, 1916 through 1918. The production of shorts fell off 37 percent in 1916, then 50 percent in 1917, and another 57 percent in 1918."[37] Estimating that the typical feature program in the late 1910s was made up of 69 percent feature film reels and 31 percent short film reels, Singer asks, "At what point did manufacturers produce about 69 percent feature reels and 31 percent shorts?"[38] Production data indicate this ratio was reached in 1918, which Singer concludes was the year variety programs, with a few exceptions, disappeared. As for the rate of disappearance, the decline in excess production of short reels required to feed variety programs suggests that "in 1915 almost two out of three movie theaters employed the variety program format; in 1916 more than one third did so; and about one theater in six maintained that policy through 1917."[39]

Production trends reveal much, on a macro level, about the temporality of the film medium's second birth as cinema. To explore the spatiality of these findings, however, requires grounding them in particular locations, places where the topography of the transition to features can be unearthed as it took shape on the micro level of social and spatial experience. Moreover, by locating the transition in a local setting, it becomes possible to measure cinema's development as a modern, national institution not only by what was on screen, but also by the building in which the screen was stationed, as well as by the people who owned and operated the screen. As Giuliana Bruno observes, film "needs more than an apparatus in order to exist as cinema. It needs a space, a public site—a movie 'house.'"[40]

Sense of touch

A history of cinema as the transformation of space begins, following Bruno, with a "theoretical shift from the optic to the haptic—and from sight to site," a shift that relocates cinema in senses of touch (contact) and movement (kinesthesis) and positions the haptic as "an agent in the formation of space—both geographic and cultural."[41] Bruno's account of the haptic in cinema emphasizes architectural design, which shapes human contact and movement within the theater, and the capacity of motion pictures to produce a modern form of spectatorship characterized by immobile travel. But, not unlike a hotel, the production of space in the movie house also required managers, staff, and travel agents. Although the development of cinema occluded the routes itinerants once used to tote animated pictures intermittently from place to place, the contact and movement of exhibitors, distributors, and operators along new routes remained essential for the production of cinema as a fixed-site experience for audiences. The dynamic spatiality of the movie house was set in motion by people who procured, programmed, and projected films transported by trains, trucks, and cars to create places linked to other places, nodes in social and spatial networks. Cinema's imbrication in modernity owed as much to film cans as to films, and those cans were haptic agents

Overlapping or an overlapping pattern

in the contact and mobility they launched for persons managing their travel. Bruno's call for a map not "merely of spaces but of movements: a set of journeys within cultural movements . . . and historical trajectories"[42] leads to a psychogeography of spectatorship, but it might also direct us to reconstruct the geography of social and physical movements underpinning film exhibition itself.

In Milford, Mrs. Richardson's enterprise was to construct a geography from contact and movement that could produce the place and space of cinema for small-town audiences. Her performance in this work reveals much about the uncertain location of small towns in modernity and about the ways cinema's transformation in Milford hinged on the transformation of her own social and spatial footprint. The movement of films exerted a push to expand cinema's reach and a pull to attract audiences, forming a haptic space that held agency both for Milford's "rurban" growth and for women's mobility within southern New Hampshire's increasingly regional and metropolitan frames of reference.

WOMEN'S PROGRESS IS CINEMA'S PROGRESS IN MILFORD

The motion picture theatres are doing a fine work for the public, especially in the smaller communities where they are as competently managed as in Milford and Wilton. They furnish good amusement at a low price, and this, next to food, fuel, clothing and houses, is high in the list of necessities of modern life.

This praise for movie theaters and the people running them comes from the *Milford Cabinet and Wilton Journal's* columnist and town beacon, "The Observer," who though never identified by name or byline, was almost certainly a man.[43] The source of his enthusiasm? Narrowly defined, it was a Tuesday night screening of *Quo Vadis?* in late March 1914 at Milford's Star Theatre. The film capped a string of notable shows "given this winter" that in the eyes of the Observer helped "add much to the value of the 'movies.'" Such shows and the theaters presenting them contributed significantly to the stock of community welfare; they were a basic necessity, a compound source of energy, sustenance, and shelter that could feed the spirit and generate warmth on a cold New Hampshire night. The Observer's enthusiasm, however, was driven by more than just movies.

FIGURE 3.3. May B. Richardson made many border crossings into Massachusetts to secure films for the Star Theatre. Her trips to Boston elevated Milford's place in the regional landscape.

The people who "competently managed" the movies for "smaller communities" inspired his tribute as well. In this, the gender of the Observer did matter, for at least one of the managers called out for praise was a woman, Mrs. May Burnham Richardson, who owned and operated Milford's Star Theatre (figure 3.3).

In the particular case of *Quo Vadis?*, an eight-reel feature produced by the Italian company Cines, the newspaper had earlier reported that "Mrs. Richardson spent a day in Boston where she arranged for the *Quo Vadis?* films . . . and it is the first time they have ever been in this state."[44] That the theater manager herself made the fifty-five-mile journey to Boston to secure an early (for New Hampshire) contract[45] on an unusually good feature gave evidence of the energy she brought to her work, energy the Observer believed illuminated not only her small theater's screen but also the small town itself. Moreover, in forging personal and professional connections to film exchanges in Boston, where *Quo Vadis?* debuted in June 1913 at the Tremont Temple,[46] she was adding a new layer to local space, helping put Milford on the map by enlarging its stature not only within the state but in the region as well. This spatial recalibration of Milford's place in the landscape caught the attention of exchange men themselves, who in turn used it as part of a marketing rhetoric to further sell the little town on the benefits of movies. When Pathé-Frères sales agent J. E. Craig of Boston visited town, he offered that the Star Theatre was "quite up to the standard of the better Boston theatres. The pictures shown in Milford are as a whole superior to any in Nashua or Manchester houses, and it is surprising to find such a theatre in a town the size of Milford."[47]

If moving pictures were becoming powerful cartographic instruments in 1910s America, they were tools only Mrs. Richardson had yet been able to wield successfully in Milford. This was made evident in September 1914, when the paper ran a story titled "Theatre Needed a Woman to Run It," which noted that movies in Milford had "failed consistently until Mrs. Richardson became manager."[48] The story acknowledged that Mrs. Richardson's success created resentment among some businessmen, but it pointed out that she had simply beaten them at their own game, her acumen owing less to nineteenth-century notions of virtuous womanhood than to sheer nerve, grit, and ability:

> If any of the keen and shrewd business men of Milford wish they were owners of the business they can remember that they had a fine chance just a few years ago, when the movie business looked about as lucrative as selling straw hats in January. Mrs. Richardson was the only one with the nerve to take a chance, with grit and ability to see it through. Anybody is "small" indeed who begrudges her whatever measure of success she may attain.[49]

Who, then, was May Burnham Richardson? Census records show she was born in Milford in 1868 to Almus (b. New Boston, N.H.) and Helen (b. Thomaston, Me.) Burnham. Her birth name was Mary Helen Burnham. In 1900, she lived with her parents on Nashua Street in Milford with husband Fred Austin (married in 1899), born in the neighboring town of New Boston, and her two brothers, Frank and Atwood. Her name was Mary H. Austin. She had no children and no occupation. Fred also had no occupation. In 1902, Fred died and Almus soon followed. In 1905, Mary married Fred Richardson, five years her junior. Her name was Mary H. Richardson. Fred was born in Lawrence, Massachusetts, to a Scottish father and English mother. He was a woodworker at a furniture company. Mary was employed on her "own account" as a music teacher. Mary and Fred had no children. They resided at Helen Burnham's home, now on Monson Place, with Mary's brothers Frank and Atwood, and the latter's wife Florence. In 1920, Mary H. Richardson was replaced in the census by May B. Richardson, now head of household of the residence on Monson Place, a residence she owned and on which she held a mortgage.

Fred no longer resided with her, though her mother did, as did Atwood and Florence, and two boarders, one from Ireland. Her occupation was "theatre prop." May's mother died in 1922 and May and Fred were divorced. May remarried in 1925 to Augustin Tracey, a granite cutter born in Newfoundland. They lived on Nashua Street with three roomers and no children. May was once again a music teacher. She died in Milford in 1933 at sixty-five years of age.[50]

Census records are bloodless; on their own they usually fail to evoke the vitality of lived experience. But in this case they display a richness that suggests the trajectory of a fascinating life, one stationed in place, Milford, but connected and mediated through personal relationships with wider locations in New England and the world. While it remains difficult to know why, at age forty-four, May Richardson decided to enter the highly visible yet still dubious business of film exhibition (had she been an avid moviegoer?), it is not hard to imagine the courage this act required, in 1912, for a twice-married woman with no children in small-town New Hampshire. Although we may never know the full complexity of her motivations as an individual, we might still gain insight into her development as a modern woman, entrepreneur, and respected community member by considering it as an integral part of cinema's own development as a national institution that moved from the margins to the mainstream of society. If she could bring cinema successfully to Milford, despite whatever "disfavor" and "grudges" lay in the way, May would advance personally and professionally, and her mobility would help make the town itself more modern, not simply because she would have created a conduit for the arrival of Hollywood stars and feature films, but because she herself, as a successful businesswoman, would give proof that Milford was a progressive town. At the same time, because she remained anchored in Milford, she could see this transition through to its full fruition, mediating the experience of the new medium with the town's traditions, gender politics, and sense of place.

THE LOCAL TOPOGRAPHY OF
CINEMA IN TRANSITION

Before May Richardson entered the field, movies trickled into Milford at two venues, Eagle Hall, located in an old Congregational Church, and

Town Hall, a civic building run by Milford's board of selectmen. In November 1908, selectmen ended Town Hall shows "on account of the new rules by the insurance companies which demand that moving picture machines be incased [*sic*] in a steel cage and that special electric wiring be maintained."[51] Movies continued at Eagle Hall, sponsored by local groups such as Daughters of Pocahontas, who in January 1909 put on a show where it was "estimated there were four hundred present. There were many Italians there. The Italians like moving pictures."[52] Traveling exhibitors Cook and Harris from Cooperstown, N.Y., visited Eagle Hall in June to present their "World's Famous Exhibition of Moving Pictures."[53] In October 1910, the trickle of movies became a small stream as block advertisements appeared in the newspaper each week for "Motion Pictures. Eagle Hall. Entire Change of Program Tuesday, Thursday and Saturday. Admission 10 Cents to All." One month later, "Theatre Comique" was added along with "Pictures that will not hurt the most refined taste." By February 1911, "Under New Management" was inserted. The new manager was Mr. F. J. Reynolds, who exited town one year later, apparently "leaving his creditors wondering how they ever happened to give him credit."[54] It was then that Mrs. May Burnham Richardson was granted a license to "operate a moving picture theatre"[55] amidst "rumors of a theatre to be opened on Middle Street in the Shanahan building which was formerly used as a stable."[56] On February 29, 1912, she made it official, announcing "to Milford and surrounding towns that I propose to open a first class Motion Picture Theatre."[57]

Renovation of the former blacksmith shop and livery stable into the Star Theatre commenced immediately, with shows running at Eagle Hall in the interim. Though the building's construction continued throughout the year, the theater opened to the public on March 11. Mrs. Richardson was manager, employing four male staff members: J. A. McDonald, musician and assistant manager, Thomas O'Neil, ticket taker,[58] Atwood Burnham, machine operator, and Harold Goss, musician.[59] To ensure she could maintain order in her new theater, and to grant her authority to remove unruly patrons, the town appointed May B. Richardson Milford's first female police officer in 1912.[60] The rest of that year saw a pronounced absence of advertising and news relating to moving picture programs at the Star Theatre. The anomaly was a presentation of *Ben Hur* that was touring with Theodore Holman of Boston, who on April 8 provided lecture accompaniment to the film.[61] Despite limited advertising, the newspaper reported, "the Star Theatre is doing a big business."[62]

In 1913, news about the theater and its programs picked up. It was noted that Mrs. Richardson's husband Fred had painted a large star on the exterior façade, illuminating this with a single electric light bulb.[63] By end of January, the theater's remodel finally ended with completion of a stage in the front of the theater, an exit door on the side, and an enlargement of the auditorium to "nearly double the seating capacity" to accommodate three hundred patrons.[64] A new fireproof curtain was installed as a screen.[65] In April 1914 a metal front was added to the building.[66] Regular prices were ten cents, with shows on Monday, Wednesday, Friday, and Saturday. Throughout 1913 and into July 1914, the theater presented mostly variety programs from General Film Company, the national distribution arm of the Motion Picture Patents Company (MPPC). Titles of MPPC shorts were rarely advertised, with the notable exception of Vitagraph's two-reeler *The Strength of Men,* which Mrs. Richardson perhaps shrewdly opted to identify by name.[67] In a few cases, the theater showed longer "specials" such as Kalem's five-reel *From the Manger to the Cross,* which ran in March 1913 in observance of Easter Lenten season;[68] this religious passion play no doubt had great redolence for its audiences who were viewing it in an old stable. Serial films first appeared during this time, with Edison's *Who Will Marry Mary?* receiving headline status as it began its six-month run in October 1913.[69] By end of the year, it was possible to squeeze in a picture or two from outside General Film Company, such as *Pelleas and Melisande,*[70] a short distributed through Universal, or the Puritan Special Features Company two-reeler *Quincy Adams Sawyer,* which arrived in February 1914 with Theodore Holman from Boston again in tow for lecture accompaniment.[71] Throughout this period of General Film variety programs, manager Richardson supplemented her moving picture shows with vaudeville, occasionally from Boston, interspersed between films.[72]

The screening of *Quo Vadis?* in March 1914, which was "witnessed by most of the people in Milford," was a key marker in the transformation of cinema on the local level.[73] It was also a sign of May B. Richardson's growing stature in town and of the town's growing stature in the state and region. It was not, however, the culmination of the transition to feature films or the final constitution of an institutionalized "mass" cinema experience in Milford. Instead, the topography of film programming remained uneven, as the transition to features grew slowly but steadily over the next twenty months but did so without completely erasing variety pictures. *Quo Vadis?* was followed by other "big time" films distributed through George Kleine, including Ambrosio's *Last Days of Pompeii* and Cines' eight-reel *Antony and Cleopatra* in late April.[74] Prices for these specials were twenty-five cents, and they occasioned a limited number of reserved seats to be secured in advance by telephone with "ten cents extra charged."[75] In early summer, two MPPC features appeared, Lubin's five-reeler *The Third Degree* in June and Biograph's four-reeler *Judith of Bethulia* in early July.[76] Shortly thereafter, the theater announced the debut of "Universal Night" on July 14, a program priced at ten cents that included an educational short, *From the Mine to the Mint*, a two-reel drama, *The Step Mother*, a comedy short, *Serg Hoffmeyer*, and a five-reel feature, *Universal Ike Gets the Goat*. It was noted that "the Universal films are supposed to be the best there are, and this is the first time that a full Universal show has been put on in Milford."[77] Universal's Grace Cunard and Francis Ford serial, *Lucille Love, Girl of Mystery*, then began its twenty-two-week run Monday, July 27, and during the remainder of 1914 only two features received any mention in the newspaper: Universal's five-reeler *Neptune's Daughter*, which starred Annette Kellerman and played October 2 and 3, attracting eight hundred people over two days, and Famous Player's five-reeler *Tess of the Storm Country*, which ran October 31 and starred Mary Pickford. Though the latter received zero advertising in the newspaper, it broke the theater's attendance record by drawing nine hundred people across three shows in a single day.[78]

As demand for features grew, so did the risk that contracted "big" films would not arrive in Milford as scheduled, or that completed films would be delayed in their return to rental exchanges, incurring the wrath of exchange men and the potential cessation of services. In this, Milford's location in southern New Hampshire was advantageous, as access to an emerging network of paved trunk roads connecting the town to Boston via Nashua and Lowell provided a viable option, other than the train, that more remote towns did not enjoy. Accordingly, to mitigate the risk of distribution breakdowns, Richardson "inaugurated a messenger service from Milford to Boston. Every day somebody goes down, takes back the films used the night before, gets the new ones and brings them back. The cost in time and carfare is partly offset by the saving in express, insurance and delay on the rolls."[79]

Despite their momentum, features continued to share the theater with a healthy dose of three-reelers, which held a regular slot in the weekly program before trickling away over the last three months of 1915. For the first half of the year, serials (Universal's *Trey O' Hearts* and Thanhouser's *Million Dollar Mystery*) and three-reelers dominated the programming. Thereafter a notable shift took place in which only one of the four programs presented each week, often the Thursday show, was devoted to three-reelers as the lead attraction. Mrs. Richardson had contracted with Mitchell Granby, sales agent for Fox Film Corporation, to show Fox features, and these were frequently run on Friday nights.[80] Independent features distributed via World Film Corporation figured prominently on Mondays, while Saturday programs were indeterminate and could be either three-reelers or features. This system began to change again in October when films (and stars) from Famous Players–Lasky and Paramount began appearing much more frequently (*Such a Little Queen, Marta of the Lowlands, Brewster's Millions, The Typhoon*), exerting pressure on three-reelers and pushing them off the screen completely by end of 1915. The last three-reelers to play were *In the Clutches of the Ku Klux Klan,* an illegally distributed short version of D. W. Griffith's *Birth of a Nation,* and Selig's *War of Dreams,* released through General Film.[81] These were screened November 12 and November 27, respectively. Meanwhile, on the other end of the horizon, the highlight of late 1915 was a Thanksgiving Day showing of *Cabiria,* the Italian feature distributed through George Kleine and described as "the world's greatest motion picture, 12 parts, hand colored, 3 hour show. This is the greatest picture yet shown in Milford."[82] By February 1916, Paramount features often topped three of four programs a week, with the fourth reserved for features from World Film Corporation. The residual era of "animated pictures" had finally disappeared from view, at least in terms of onscreen space.

Once features were locked in on every program, Richardson put her energy into localizing the cinema experience for patrons. She did this by working with community constituencies, negotiating their relationships to movies, mass culture, and the Star Theatre. For the Milford Women's Club, there was a March screening of two Paramount features starring old stage favorites May Irwin (*Mrs. Black Has Come Back*) and Elsie Janis (*It*

Was Ever Thus). But instead of promoting a serious-minded progressive agenda, as might be expected, the screenings were designed to generate "ninety good laughs," and the women "voted it a unique innovation from studying social problems and reformation measures and a relief from making sponges and supplies for the fighting men in Europe."[83] Two months later, members of the East Milford Improvement Society, a social club for Italian immigrants who worked in Milford's granite quarries, were invited to enjoy an illustrated lecture with views of Italy and Switzerland, along with specially arranged documentaries, *Ancient Rome* and *Stone Quarrying in Italy*.[84]

For the national elections of November 1916, Mrs. Richardson transformed the theater into a modern heterosocial mingling of commercial, political, and gendered public spheres by arranging "a special wire to the Star Theatre for Tuesday night over which she will receive the election returns from all states and districts as fast as they are compiled. As received they will be flashed on the screen. A continuous series of pictures will be run during the night, with the bulletins 'cut in' as fast as they come."[85] Though May Richardson herself was denied the right to vote, this event undoubtedly served her own interest in politics and suffrage, and other women were also likely in attendance. But she deftly promoted the event to highlight the way women's interest in politics and in voting could benefit Milford's men, who at the very least might appreciate that the competence, ingenuity, and acumen employed to bring the national returns to Milford in "real time" created a unique opportunity for them to whet their own political appetites: "Mrs. Richardson's enterprise will be appreciated by many men who will enjoy a warm comfortable place to spend the evening and be entertained while watching the results of one of the most interesting and vital elections in the country's history." It was also noted that "after ten o'clock smoking will be permitted, and the theatre will be kept open as long as the bulletins are coming."[86]

In addition to localizing cinema, Mrs. Richardson tried "rurbanizing" it, promoting Milford as a cultural center by taking movies to town halls in the nearby hamlets of Brookline and New Boston.[87] As Gregory Waller has observed, by 1915 "the use of automobiles and trucks to transport film likely opened up greater opportunities for small scale distributors as well as itinerant exhibitors."[88] In this case, Richardson's itinerancy may have been driven by both a desire to expand her footprint into adjacent markets and by a judgment that once established, such connections could produce reverse traffic if residents saw fit to venture to Milford more frequently to enjoy cinema in an actual theater setting. Evidence of these itinerant activities is sparse, but her attempts to establish shows in both towns were apparently unsuccessful, and it is worth considering the ways in which space may have constrained the ability to facilitate such new movements and connections in cinema culture.

The success of "rurban" connections depended on transportation. Although Milford had access to streamlined rail service and improved roads leading southeast to Nashua and Boston, the conditions were more complex and often less tenable for shorter routes to towns located due south and north such as Brookline and New Boston. The crux of the problem originated twenty years earlier in maneuverings between the Boston and Maine Railroad and the Fitchburg Railroad to control traffic around Manchester, which today remains New Hampshire's largest city. Prior to that time, Fitchburg's northerly rail line from Ayer, Massachusetts, terminated in Brookline. In 1895, however, this line was extended to Milford. At the time there was no line connecting Milford north to Manchester. To block Fitchburg from profiting from such a line, Boston and Maine built a poorly designed branch between Manchester and Milford. Railroad historian Robert Lindsell explains that "the B&M built the Manchester & Milford Branch, with junctions at each end deliberately laid in the 'wrong' direction, in order to discourage Fitchburg RR traffic. By the time the line was completed in 1900, it was an anachronism, for that year the B&M took over the Fitchburg. The B&M now had a virtually useless line, owing to inappropriate junction layouts and almost no local traffic."[89] The Observer, writing in the *Milford Cabinet and Wilton Journal*, recognized immediately how spatial politics had doomed the new line: "it was intentionally circuitous, slow and undependable" and started "out of town on the Boston and Maine tracks, took off by itself beyond the Lorden Lumber Company, wandered toward Amherst (but didn't come too close to the center of town), meandered through Bedford and Grasmere, coming in sight of Manchester but then curving north before actually entering the city."[90] (See figure 3.4.)

In Milford's relation to Brookline, the fact that the new branch was "broken" meant that Milford remained cut off from Manchester, which also meant that Brookline remained cut off from Manchester. From

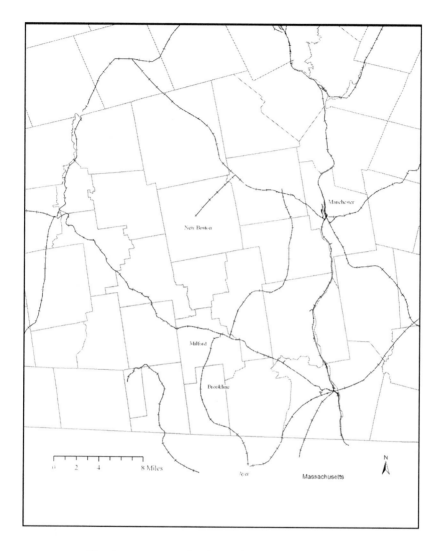

FIGURE 3.4. The circuitous spatial politics of dysfunctional rail lines made for difficult interconnections between Brookline, Milford, Manchester, and New Boston.

Brookline's perspective, Milford retained its status as the end of the Fitchburg line rather than an emerging node in a new network emanating from Manchester. This positioned Brookline to look south for its "rurban" center and to be pulled into the social, cultural, and economic

influence of Massachusetts rather than pushed into the orbit of Milford
to the north. May Richardson therefore faced considerable spatial odds
when she announced in 1916 "a moving picture show in the town house at
Brookline" with "a new booth" and a "new lantern,"[91] and indeed reports
soon followed that these shows "have not been very successful."[92] But
where May was unable to connect with an audience in Brookline, others
from the south had more success: "H. E. Woods of Ayer, who gave weekly
picture shows here for almost a year, until about two months ago, gave a
splendid show at the town hall."[93] One cannot help but wonder, of course,
whether Mr. Woods would have returned to the scene quite so quickly
had his substitute been a man, and it is possible that spatial politics and
gender politics combined to create an impossible barrier to entry for Mrs.
Richardson.[94]

Poor rail connection between Milford and Manchester also impacted
Milford's relation to New Boston, since traffic between the towns was
routed through Manchester. By rail, Milford was twenty-seven miles
from New Boston, by auto road twelve miles. The contours of space thus
favored cars as the cheaper and faster mode of transportation, but the
fact that nine of the twelve miles were dirt roads made this, too, a potentially costly choice (figure 3.5).[95] The Observer, ever attuned to the area's
transportation situation, noted, "in New Boston . . . the highways are a
menace" and they "make a sustained speed of ten miles an hour unsafe."[96]
In relational space, the unimproved road system could make the city of
Boston, fifty-five miles away, feel closer to Milford than the village of New
Boston. These conditions greatly raised the stakes of itinerant exhibition,
and May's shows in New Boston seem to have ground to a halt somewhere
on the muddied roads of "rurban" New Hampshire:

> Mrs. May B. Richardson, Atwood Burnham and J. A. McDonald had an
> unpleasant automobile experience last Thursday evening while returning to
> Milford from New Boston where they had been to give a moving picture ex-
> hibition. On the way home the machine got stuck in the mud and the party
> did not get home until after five in the morning.[97]

Cinema may have arrived on the screen in Milford, but it would be hard
pressed to take this show on the road; audiences in Milford's "rurban"
area would increasingly be invited to go to the movies rather than having movies brought to them. But what kind of theater would they find

FIGURE 3.5. Detail from 1928 map showing the road network connecting Milford to New Boston. Rope-like features indicate unpaved roads that made travel difficult and created roadblocks to successful itinerant film exhibition.

when they journeyed to Milford, and would the trip be worth the time and money?

CINEMA AND SUFFRAGE ARRIVE IN MILFORD

The Star Theatre that welcomed patrons in the late 1910s was largely the same venue as had been in service since the theater's remodel was completed in January 1913, which is to say that even though one could vicariously meet Mary Pickford, Douglas Fairbanks, Charlie Chaplin, or any other big-name stars there, the structure itself was not much more than an old blacksmith shop and stable retrofitted for movies. As early as 1914, May Richardson had plans to increase the size of the theater to six hundred seats and to enhance its comforts, but these plans went unrealized, in part because they hinged on acquiring an adjacent parcel of land owned by the American Thread Company.[98] American Thread would sell the parcel, but a lack of capital stymied May's ability to execute the purchase. For small exhibitors, the movie business had become a difficult proposition; Hollywood's grade "A" feature films were in great demand, but they were expensive to obtain and required higher ticket prices to offset costs. In a theater with only three hundred seats, there was a limit to how much revenue could be produced. Moreover, as Hollywood consolidated and rationalized its business practices, unprofitable small theaters were increasingly relegated to the "end of the line" of film distribution, unable to get the best films early in their release, which further suppressed attendance and revenues. This demotion was evident, according to Deb Verhoeven, in every scratch and poorly executed splice in a well-traveled print, which revealed "the layers of a film's meaning for those in the cinema. They are a film's defining marks, serving to both position and address its audiences, alerting them to their status at the end of the line."[99]

With profits squeezed, there was reduced potential for capital investment in the building and its appointments, or in projection equipment so vital to the quality of the image and narrative experience. For example, the *Milford Town Clerk's Record: 1900–1920* indicates that after leasing her first projector, a Power's No. 6 Cameragraph, in March 1912 at a cost of $264,[100] May Richardson made only one further mechanical upgrade over the next seven years, advancing in November 1913 to the Power's No. 6A, leased at $265.[101] Records for these machines make no references to motor drives, which were often leased separately, and though it is hard to prove conclusively, it is possible that film projectors at the Star Theatre were manually operated long after the transition to features had been completed. Indeed, when the theater finally received a new projector in June 1919, it made front-page news because the motor was stolen. The report noted that on "Monday a new picture machine came, a dandy, with a glass case and fine lens and a motor drive," only to have somebody walk away with the motor, "which was in a box, weighed about 40 pounds, made a bulky package, and cost $35. The picture machine is being cranked by hand until the motor can be recovered or a new one secured."[102] Though cinema had come three years earlier to the Star's screen, the building and its operators were still actively exerting their presence, producing a hybrid experience, a kind of hand-cranked Hollywood.

However long it took to replace the stolen motor, the truth remained that even with a motorized projector, feature films at the Star were presented on a single machine. Every reel change produced a break in the narrative as the next reel was mounted. The completely integrative and absorptive narrative experience that defined the second birth of cinema required at least a dual system of film projection to sustain it, and such a system would not be installed in Milford until June 1920. When the second machine at last arrived, this too was front-page news: "A new picture machine has been received at the Strand Theatre, and a new operator's booth will soon be installed for it. With the new equipment and two machines there will be no delay between reels. Heretofore there has been a short delay after a reel was shown before the next one could be loaded. The enterprising proprietors will do away with even this slight annoyance."[103]

It will be noted that the increased number of projectors came amidst an increased number of proprietors and a theater name change. Indeed, the Star was being transformed into the Strand, and upon completion of this metamorphosis, "cinema" would finally, and fully, have arrived in Milford, both on and off the screen. It was a process May Burnham Richardson had initiated and cultivated but could not complete entirely on her own, so she reached out, not to a local businessman or bank, but to another businesswoman in her own field. If the social and economic limitations of small-town film exhibition had proven too intractable for one exceptionally enterprising female proprietor, they would be no match for two.

Mrs. May B. Richardson and Mrs. Lottie M. Pierce announced their partnership on May 1, 1919 ("May Day"). Unlike Richardson, who was native-born to native parentage, Pierce was a foreign-born Scottish Canadian immigrant from Quebec who came to the United States in 1899. Pierce was thirty-six years old when the partnership was formed, which made the collaboration an intergenerational one given that her partner was fifty-one years of age. Similar to Mrs. Richardson, Mrs. Pierce had been in the exhibition business many years, having owned and operated one of the first purpose-built movie theaters in Manchester, The Lyric, since 1909, and subsequently opening a second theater there.

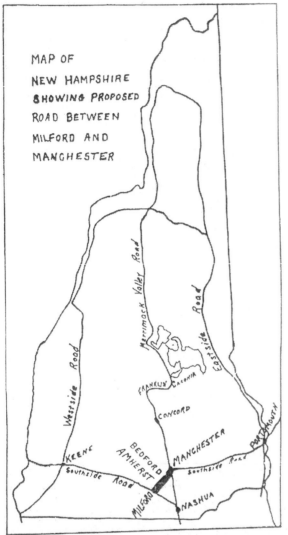

The heavy black line between Manchester and Milford is the route of the proposed new highway. But seven miles of this road is uncompleted.

FIGURE 3.6. Hand-drawn map from a 1917 issue of the *Milford Cabinet* showing the new road that would shrink relational space and improve flows of capital and resources between Milford and Manchester.

The partnership between Richardson and Pierce was no doubt predicated on many factors, including their shared bond as female entrepreneurs in a male-dominated field, but it was also aided by passage of a state highway bill that would greatly reduce the physical and relative space between Milford and Manchester, two places long separated by poor roads and dysfunctional rail. The bill set aside state funds to build an improved state highway directly connecting Milford to Manchester. Voicing support for the bill, the Observer noted that the new road would make "Milford and Manchester only 15 miles apart instead of, in effect, 28 miles," adding:

> At Milford the traveler from the west has his choice of following the state road 11 miles to Nashua and thence 17 miles to Manchester, or "cutting across" through Amherst and Bedford to Manchester and saving 13 miles. ... If travelers choose the long way round, as many do, it is because of the 7 or 8 miles between Bedford village and Baboosic Lake. This part of the road is in Bedford and is one of the roughest, muddiest, rockiest, narrowest bits of highway in any populated part of the state. Yet it is the road connecting the largest city with one of the largest towns only 15 miles away![104] [figure 3.6]

With a boost from the prospects of improved transportation, Mrs. Pierce's success in Manchester now enabled her "to bring new capital into the business here, and by teaming the Milford theatre with the two Manchester houses will secure better service from the film producers who rent the pictures." The infusion of capital also meant that a new lease on the "present theatre has been secured until 1932, together with a lease and option on land to the north, 35 feet deep. The plan is to enlarge the building, put in a sloping floor and cushioned seats, a new heating plant and electric ventilating system, new commodious lobby at the back, new curtains and picture machine, and in every way make the theatre attractive."[105] Work on these renovations progressed steadily over the next year, culminating in June 1920 with the addition of the second film projector, a Simplex model with motor drive leased at a charge of $495.[106] In the near term, effects of the partnership included a switch from four programs per week to daily changes (excluding Sunday), and a theater name change to the Strand, which went into use on May 29, 1919. That same day trademarks for Paramount and Artcraft Pictures (Paramount's specialty division devoted to Mary Pickford films) appeared at the top of the Strand's advertising and would continue to do so until December 9, 1920.

The years 1919 and 1920 were also culminating moments in the long struggle for women's suffrage. By mid-June 1919, both the U.S. House of Representatives and U.S. Senate had passed the Nineteenth Amendment, giving women the right to vote, and the proposal was sent to individual states, with the approval of thirty-six states required for ratification. On September 10, 1919, New Hampshire became the sixteenth state to approve the amendment, and on August 18, 1920, Tennessee became the thirty-sixth state. The Nineteenth Amendment was enacted on August 26, 1920. Given that the development of cinema in Milford overlapped a key era in the suffrage movement in the United States, was there any connection between the two? More bluntly, was Mrs. May B. Richardson a suffragist?

An exhaustive reading of the *Milford Cabinet and Wilton Journal* from 1909 through the end of 1920 suggests that Richardson was indeed a suffragist. But this fact did not emerge until one week after the Nineteenth Amendment was enacted. Before this, there was not a single reference in the newspaper to the political views of Mrs. Richardson or her stance on suffrage. Evidence of her participation in the movement became visible only in an "Open Letter to the Women Voters of New Hampshire" dated September 2, 1920, on which she was one of fifteen female signatories to a missive that begins, "As full fledged enfranchised voters of this great republic, we greet you. At last the great power of the ballot has been rightly placed in the hands of womanhood. Let us all make the best possible use of it." The letter recounts the hard-fought effort for suffrage in New Hampshire, deemed of great importance for its "bearing on the subsequent action of other states," which made New Hampshire "a pivotal state in the enfranchisement of women." The purpose of the letter was to solicit votes for New Hampshire councilor Windsor Goodnow, a candidate for the state's Republican gubernatorial nomination, whose "longstanding interest in the enfranchisement of women" and "success in bringing about the special legislation is well known and appreciated by the leaders of woman suffrage in the state."[107]

If May Richardson was a suffragist, what did this mean for her business? Here again the local press, though noting the "theatre needed a woman to run it," never explicitly connected the dots to women's suffrage. There were no signs of suffrage films, lectures, or rallies. Perhaps such events occurred but were not reported, but it is equally plausible that May's work at the theater supported suffrage primarily as a pragmatic demonstration that women could be strong, independent, and successful in spheres dominated by men. She performed, in an embodied way, the equality of the sexes. The visibility of this performance was magnified by

Star Theatre

May B. Richardson, Prop. and Mgr.

MIDDLE STREET

MILFORD - - N. H.

Telephone 101-5

FIGURE 3.7. In transforming cinema, May B. Richardson was herself transformed, emerging in the public sphere as a successful businesswoman and civic leader.

her frequent, almost constant, engagements with the local newspaper. In small-town New Hampshire, this may have been the most effective of all political strategies; her emergence in the public sphere meant those opposed to suffrage for *all* women had to contend with the fact that there were *particular* women, such as May Richardson, who were disenfranchised as a result. Perhaps those inclined to do so found it easier to deny voting rights to the person in figure 3.3, represented in cameo as an ideally generalized woman, than to the person in figure 3.7, transformed two years later by specificity and naturalism, indexing a powerful and influential local businesswoman.

May B. Richardson demonstrated courage, energy, and ingenuity running a successful small business that was built from scratch and transformed from dubious origins into a local symbol of Milford's status in the region and a sign of the small town's connection to modern life and larger national institutions. She shaped the landscape of a new media technology and expanded women's footprint on early cinema and social history. With each passing year her reputation and audience grew. Movies were a stepping-stone into the public sphere, and on December 30, 1920, with women's place in society transformed by the right to vote, May handed day-to-day operations of her now fully established movie business to new managers, remaining co-owner with Lottie, but moving on, perhaps, to more explicitly political forms of social and civic engagement.[108]

CONCLUSION

Cinema historians have begun to rethink cinema's relation to modernity in ways that move beyond the confines of the film text. Paul Moore, for instance, makes use of the spatial category of the "region" as a scale of analysis that mediates between grounded, local, embodied experiences of cinema and general, global processes of modernity. In his study of cinema's role in the formation of regional mass markets and publics, Moore contends that cinema culture in the 1910s was a metropolitan, rather than a cosmopolitan, phenomenon because it connected life in the hinterlands to a regional metropolis by way of the shared social practice of moviegoing. Like the act of reading a newspaper, the act of moviegoing—widely publicized and spatially indexed through print channels such as event reporting, town news and note columns, paid advertising, and local society news—grew in visibility to the point where it was perceived as available to everyone, from a region's center to its periphery:

> The modernity of cinema was not simply the electric apparatus, nor just the commercial form of its pastime, nor the edited sensations of its depictions. It was also, and perhaps primarily, a mass practice that connected all places in a region, not to each other so much as to the mass market. Whatever was on the screen, cinema provided a way to practice modernity as it constructed a modern mass public.[109]

Going to the movies became a way for rural and small-town people to stay in step with the times and in touch with other places. Their growing awareness of moviegoing as a social movement and shared form of regional then national leisure practice served to embed them haptically in a culture of "metropolitan modernity" constructed through a capitalist mass market: "Cinema gave local publics a strong relation to the metropolis and to modernity at large, and yet always grounded in a specific place, through a particular showman-entrepreneur, and focused on a precisely timed, promoted, and priced show."[110]

In Milford, May B. Richardson was one such mediating figure, a female "showman," bringing films from around the country and the world to her small theater and developing personal, political, and professional connections in the region that raised the visibility of women, movies, and the town itself, helping to relocate the place of each within trajectories of larger social and spatial movements. These connections enabled her to forge a public venue out of an old blacksmith shop and transform the experience of cinema for local and "rurban" audiences by producing a new layer of modern space that was simultaneously local and global. Because the production of this space was not an abstraction but a concrete achievement, GIS methods can map these connections and locate them within micro- and macro-historical geographic contexts. Such methods can bring into sharp relief the topographies of space that enabled and constrained mobility and shaped relations between people, and between people and places. As Doreen Massey puts it: "The global is just as concrete as is the local place. If space is really to be thought relationally then it is no more than the sum of our relations and interconnections, and the lack of them; it too is utterly 'concrete.'"[111] Or, in the parlance of the times, "To the Public: Did you know that nobody nowhere is getting from anybody anywhere, better pictures than we are showing everybody here? Come and see for yourself!"[112]

NOTES

Epigraph: "Theatre Needed a Woman to Run It," *Milford Cabinet and Wilton Journal,* September 24, 1914, 1.

Throughout this chapter, the spelling "theatre" is preserved as it originally appeared in documents and names from the period.

The author wishes to acknowledge the contributions of undergraduate researchers Robyn Black, Cara Mahony, and Judy McGurk to this study.

1. "Milford Items," *Milford Cabinet and Wilton Journal* (hereafter *Cabinet*), February 15, 1912, 5.

2. C. E. Persons, "Women's Work and Wages in the United States," *The Quarterly Journal of Economics* 29(2) (1915): 201–34.

3. J. Klenotic, "Putting Cinema History on the Map: Using GIS to Explore the Spatiality of Cinema," in *Explorations in New Cinema History: Approaches and Case Studies,* ed. R. Maltby, D. Biltereyst, and P. Meers, 58–84 (Oxford, UK: Wiley-Blackwell, 2011).

4. V. Toulmin, "Women Bioscope Proprietors—Before the First World War," in *Celebrating 1895: The Centenary of Cinema,* ed. J. Fullerton, 55–65 (Sydney: John Libbey, 1998); S. Stamp, *Movie-Struck Girls: Women and Motion Picture Culture After the Nickelodeon* (Princeton, N.J.: Princeton University Press, 2000); J. Bean, "Toward a Feminist Historiography of Early Cinema," in *A Feminist Reader in Early Cinema,* ed. J. Bean and D. Negra, 1–26 (Durham, N.C.: Duke University Press, 2002); K. W. Mahar, *Women Filmmakers in Early Hollywood* (Baltimore: Johns Hopkins, 2006); M. G. Cooper, *Universal Women: Filmmaking and Institutional Change in Early Hollywood* (Urbana: University of Illinois Press, 2010); K. H. Fuller-Seeley and K. W. Mahar, "Exhibiting Women: Gender, Showmanship, & the Professionalization of Film Exhibition in the United States," in

Women Film Pioneers Project, ed. J. Gaines, R. Vatsal, and M. Dall'Asta (Center for Digital Research and Scholarship, New York: Columbia University Libraries, forthcoming).

5. G. Waller, *Main Street Amusements: Movies and Commercial Entertainment in a Southern City, 1896–1930* (Washington: Smithsonian Institution Press, 1995); K. H. Fuller, *At the Picture Show: Small Town Audiences and the Creation of Movie Fan Culture* (Washington: Smithsonian Institution Press, 1996); R. C. Allen, "Relocating American Film History," *Cultural Studies* 20(1) (2006): 48–88; R. Maltby, M. Stokes, and R. C. Allen, eds., *Going to the Movies: Hollywood and the Social Experience of Cinema* (Exeter, UK: University of Exeter Press, 2007); K. H. Fuller-Seeley, ed., *Hollywood in the Neighborhood: Historical Case Studies of Local Moviegoing* (Berkeley: University of California Press, 2008).

6. Bean, "Toward a Feminist Historiography," 3.

7. United States Census Bureau, *Thirteenth Census of the United States Taken in the Year 1910—Abstract of the Census With Supplement for New Hampshire* (Washington: Government Printing Office, 1913), 583.

8. United States Census Bureau, *Fourteenth Census of the United States—1920—Volume 2—General Report and Analytical Tables* (Washington: Government Printing Office, 1921), 108.

9. K. Peiss, *Cheap Amusements: Working Women and Leisure in Turn-of-the-Century New York* (Philadelphia: Temple University Press, 1986).

10. United States Census Bureau, *Thirteenth,* 14.

11. United States Census Bureau, *Geographic Areas Reference Manual* [Portable Document Format File]. [1994] http://www.census.gov/geo/www/garm.html [July 14, 2011]. Chapter 12–2.

12. W. S. Rossiter, *Increase of Population in the United States 1910–1920* (Washington: Government Printing Office, 1922), 74–75.

13. United States Census Bureau, *Fourteenth,* 49.

14. United States Census Bureau, *Fourteenth,* 46.

15. United States Census Bureau, *Thirteenth,* 569–70.

16. United States Census Bureau, *Fourteenth,* 520–22.

17. United States Census Bureau, *Fourteenth,* 29.

18. United States Census Bureau, *Fourteenth,* 45.

19. H. P. Douglass, *The Little Town, Especially in Its Rural Relationships* (New York: The MacMillan Company, 1919), 3.

20. Douglass, *Little Town,* 4.

21. Douglass, *Little Town,* 11.

22. Douglass, *Little Town,* 10.

23. Douglass, *Little Town,* 11.

24. New Hampshire Office of Energy and Planning, *1830–1920 Decennial US Census,* http://www.nh.gov/oep/programs/DataCenter/Population/1830–920.htm, accessed July 24, 2011.

25. United States Census Bureau, *Fourteenth,* 521.

26. Douglass, *Little Town,* 4.

27. Douglass, *Little Town,* 3.

28. Douglass, *Little Town,* 51.

29. Douglass, *Little Town,* 53.

30. A. Gaudreault and P. Marion, "The Cinema as a Model for the Genealogy of Media," *Convergence,* 8(4) (2002): 12–18, italics in original. Cited here at 14.

31. E. Bowser, *The Transformation of Cinema* (Berkeley: University of California Press, 1994); C. Keil, *Early American Cinema in Transition: Story, Style, and Filmmaking, 1907–1913* (Madison: University of Wisconsin Press, 2001); C. Keil and S. Stamp, eds., *American Cinema's Transitional Era: Audiences, Institutions, Practices* (Berkeley: University of California Press, 2004); C. Keil and B. Singer, eds., *American Cinema of the 1910s: Themes and Variations* (New Brunswick, N.J.: Rutgers University Press, 2009).

32. Gaudreault and Marion, "The Cinema," 14.

33. B. Singer, "Feature Films, Variety Programs, and the Crisis of the Small Exhibitor," in Keil and Stamp, *American Cinema's Transitional Era*, 76–100, cited here at 76.

34. I. Gregory, "'A Map Is Just a Bad Graph': Why Spatial Statistics Are Important in Historical GIS," in *Placing History: How Maps, Spatial Data and GIS Are Changing Historical Scholarship*, ed. A. K. Knowles, 123–49, cited here at 126–27 (Redlands, Calif.: ESRI Press, 2008).

35. D. Massey, *For Space* (London: Sage, 2005), 24.

36. B. Brewster, "Periodization of Early Cinema," in Keil and Stamp, *American Cinema's Transitional Era*, 66–75, cited here at 74.

37. Singer, "Feature Films," 86.

38. Singer, "Feature Films," 95.

39. Singer, "Feature Films," 95.

40. G. Bruno, *Atlas of Emotion: Journeys in Art, Architecture, and Film* (New York: Verso, 2002), 44.

41. Bruno, *Atlas*, 6.

42. Bruno, *Atlas*, 6.

43. The Observer self-identifies using the male pronoun, as in *Cabinet*, January 26, 1911, 4. The epigraph above is from "The Observer," *Cabinet*, April 2, 1914, 2.

44. "Special Features Arranged," *Cabinet*, February 26, 1914, 1.

45. On early film distribution practices, see R. Abel, "The 'Backbone' of the Business: Scanning Signs of US Film Distribution in the Newspapers, 1911–1914," in F. Kessler and N. Verhoeff, *Networks of Entertainment: Early Film Distribution 1895–1915* (Eastleigh, UK: John Libbey Publishing, 2007), 85–93.

46. On the distribution of *Quo Vadis?* see R. Abel, *Americanizing the Movies and 'Movie-Mad' Audiences* (Berkeley: University of California Press, 2006), 35–36.

47. "Says Star Is O.K.," *Cabinet*, January 28, 1915, 1.

48. "Theatre Needed a Woman to Run It," *Milford Cabinet and Wilton Journal*, September 24, 1914, 1.

49. "Theatre Needed a Woman to Run It," 1.

50. Census information from original enumeration reports filed in 1900, 1910, 1920, and 1930, http://www.ancestry.com, accessed July 7, 2011. See also Genealogy Index Card, Almus Burnham, Lull History Room, Wadleigh Library, Milford, New Hampshire.

51. "No More Moving Pictures at the Town Hall," *Cabinet*, November 12, 1908, 1.

52. "Milford Items," *Cabinet*, January 14, 1909, 2. On Milford's immigration history, see W. Wright, *The Granite Town* (Canaan, N.H.: Phoenix Publishing, 1979); and C. A. Reese, "The Immigrants' Influence on Milford," *Cabinet*, March 23, 1916, 1, 7.

53. "Social News," *Milford Daily Pointer*, June 2, 1909, 1.

54. "Theatre Needed a Woman to Run It," 1.

55. "Milford Items," *Cabinet*, February 15, 1912, 5.

56. "Milford Items," *Cabinet*, February 15, 1912, 3.

57. "Announcement," *Cabinet*, February 29, 1912, 1.

58. The film industry's gendered division of labor made male ticket takers a rarity; see Mahar, *Women Filmmakers*, 33–35.

59. "Theatre Needed a Woman to Run It," 1.

60. Wright, *The Granite Town*, 129. On the rise of policewomen in relation to the suffrage movement, see J. Olsson, *Los Angeles Before Hollywood: Journalism and American Film Culture, 1905 to 1915* (Stockholm: National Library of Sweden, 2008), 251–65.

61. *Cabinet*, April 4, 1912, 5; April 11, 1912, 2.

62. "The Observer," *Cabinet*, October 31, 1912, 2.

63. "Milford Items," *Cabinet*, September 26, 1912, 2; October 17, 1912, 2.

64. "Milford Items," *Cabinet*, January 2, 1912, 2. Seating capacity is confirmed in "Milford Women's Club," *Cabinet*, March 16, 1916, 1.

65. "Milford Items," *Cabinet*, January 23, 1913, 6.

66. "Milford," *Cabinet*, April 30, 1914, 2.

67. "This Week at Star Theatre," *Cabinet*, August 7, 1913, 1.

68. *Cabinet*, February 27, 1913, 2.

69. *Cabinet*, October 9, 1913, 1, 2.

70. "The Observer," *Cabinet*, November 27, 1913, 2.

71. "Milford," *Cabinet*, February 19, 1914, 5; "Special Features Arranged," 1.

72. "At the Star Theatre," *Cabinet*, July 31, 1913, 2; "This Week at Star Theatre," *Cabinet*, August 7, 1913, 1; "Milford Items," *Cabinet*, June 25, 1914, 3.

73. "The Observer," *Cabinet*, April 16, 1914, 2.

74. "Special Features Arranged," 1; "Reserved Seats at the Movies," *Cabinet*, April 26, 1914, 1.

75. "Reserved Seats at the Movies," 1.

76. "*Third Degree* June 9th," *Cabinet*, June 4, 1914, 1; "Theatre Improvements," *Cabinet*, July 2, 1914, 2.

77. "At the Star Theatre," *Cabinet*, July 9, 1914, 1. Cooper, *Universal Women*, details the key roles played by women directors, writers, and performers at Universal in the 1910s.

78. "New Movie Feature," *Cabinet*, July 23, 1914, 1; "*Neptune's Daughter*," *Cabinet*, September 24, 1914, 5; October 1, 1914, 1; "Will Enlarge Theater," *Cabinet*, October 8, 1914, 1; "Milford Items," *Cabinet*, November 5, 1914, 2.

79. "Theatre Needed a Woman to Run It," 1. On the complexities of transporting film prints, see M. Alvarez, "The Origins of the Film Exchange," *Film History* 17 (2005): 431–65.

80. "New England News Notes," *Moving Picture World*, July 24, 1915, 693.

81. "At the Star Theatre," *Cabinet*, November 11, 1915, 1; "Star Theatre," *Cabinet*, November 25, 1915, 1.

82. "Star Theatre," *Cabinet*, November 25, 1915, 1.

83. "Women's Club Attends the Movies," *Cabinet*, March 23, 1916, 1.

84. "Sunday Afternoon at Star Theatre," *Cabinet*, May 4, 1916, 1.

85. "Elections Returns Tuesday Night," *Cabinet*, November 2, 1916, 1.

86. "Elections Returns," 1.

87. In 1910, Brookline had a population of 501, New Boston 982.

88. G. Waller, "Mapping the *Moving Picture World:* Distribution in the United States circa 1915," in F. Kessler and N. Verhoeff, *Networks of Entertainment: Early Film Distribution 1895–1915* (Eastleigh, UK: John Libbey Publishing, 2007), 94–102, cited here at 99.

89. R. M. Lindsell, *The Rail Lines of Northern New England* (Pepperell, Mass.: Branch Line Press, 2000), 125.

90. As quoted in Wright, *The Granite Town,* 296.

91. "Milford," *Cabinet,* December 7, 1916, 2.

92. "Brookline," *Cabinet,* December 14, 1916, 7.

93. "Brookline," *Cabinet,* January 4, 1917, 7.

94. Mrs. or Miss invariably preceded female names in the newspaper. No such designation preceded H. E. Woods, making it highly probably this person was a male.

95. The status and mileage of early auto roads in New Hampshire found in *Rand McNally Commercial Atlas* (Chicago: Rand McNally & Co., 1928), 252.

96. "The Observer," *Cabinet,* July 17, 1919, 2.

97. "Milford," *Cabinet,* April 27, 1916, 2.

98. "Will Enlarge Theatre," *Cabinet,* October 8, 1914, 1.

99. D. Verhoeven, "Film Distribution in the Diaspora: Temporality, Community and National Cinema," in *Explorations in New Cinema History: Approaches and Case Studies,* ed. R. Maltby, D. Biltereyst, and P. Meers, 243–60, cited here at 245 (Oxford, UK: Wiley-Blackwell, 2011).

100. *Milford Town Clerk's Record: 1900–1920,* Lull History Room, Wadleigh Library, Milford, New Hampshire, 216.

101. *Milford Town Clerk's Record: 1900–1920,* Lull History Room, Wadleigh Library, Milford, New Hampshire, 259.

102. "Stole Motor at Theatre," *Cabinet,* June 5, 1919, 1.

103. "Improvements at Strand Theatre," *Cabinet,* June 17, 1920, 1.

104. "The Observer," *Cabinet,* February 1, 1917, 2.

105. "Will Improve Star Theatre," *Cabinet,* May 1, 1919, 1.

106. *Milford Town Clerk's Record: 1900–1920,* Lull History Room, Wadleigh Library, Milford, New Hampshire, 541.

107. "To the Women Voters of New Hampshire," *Cabinet,* September 2, 1920, 8.

108. "Announcement," *Cabinet,* December 30, 1920, 1.

109. P. S. Moore, "The Social Biograph: Newspapers as Archives of the Regional Mass Market for Movies," in *Explorations in New Cinema History: Approaches and Case Studies,* ed. R. Maltby, D. Biltereyst, and P. Meers, 263–79, cited here at 264 (Oxford, UK: Wiley-Blackwell, 2011).

110. Moore, "The Social Biograph," 276.

111. Massey, *For Space,* 184.

112. "To The Public," *Cabinet,* September 11, 1919, 1.

changes in a linguistic system
between successive points in time

FOUR

Mapping Film Exhibition in Flanders (1920–1990): A Diachronic Analysis of Cinema Culture Combined with Demographic and Geographic Data

DANIEL BILTEREYST AND PHILIPPE MEERS

INTRODUCTION

Ever since the start of the film industry, Belgium was widely considered an open and lucrative film market.[1] Being one of the most industrialized and prosperous countries in Europe before the First World War,[2] the small kingdom had a vivid film exhibition scene with a high attendance rate as well as a wide range of cinemas. Before the war, Brussels, which was a transportation center, grew into an important film distribution center for international exports to the Netherlands,[3] while in the capital and other major cities cinemas prospered. After the Great War, which had a more devastating impact on social, economic, and cultural life in Belgium than in any other country, Belgium largely maintained its liberal film policy. Because Belgium was one of the few countries without any adult film censorship and no significant film production of its own, movies from all major film production centers flew into the country, although with a large dominance of American and French titles. In practice, film distributors or exhibitors were not obliged to show their movies to a state or any other film censorship board and could distribute their film products freely—leading to a wide choice for audiences.[4]

Historical comparative data on cinema attendance and the international film exhibition scene are scarce and often unreliable, but the few existing insights mostly support this analysis of the small but lively

Belgian film exhibition market. This dynamic Belgian film exhibition culture, however, is widely underresearched.[5]

This chapter reports on a collaborative research project on the history of the film exhibition scene in Flanders and Brussels.[6] A core enterprise in this project was to build a longitudinal database with references to cinemas and—in a larger sense—other movie exhibition spaces, mainly from the First World War onwards. The file—which contains more than forty thousand references or entries to film exhibition spaces, including data on architectural, economic, and personnel issues—is based on a wide variety of sources and traces, mainly industry yearbooks, but also on film programs in newspapers and trade journals and research in public and private archives. The construction of this database, which also serves as the basis for further research and case studies on the history of Flemish/Belgian film (exhibition) culture,[7] throws up many questions—not least heuristic and broader methodological ones. The findings from the database are analyzed in relation to sociogeographic data on population density and the differences between rural and urban settings. When writing on mapping film exhibition in Flanders, we apply the concept of mapping not in a metaphorical, but in a literal way: to see how the geographic spread of cinemas (and thus cinema culture) relates to demographic data (population density) and geographic data (spread of venues over provinces). We link classical (existing) geographic and demographic data with new original data on cinema venues. The spatial specificities of cinema are analyzed: rural, urban, and metropolitan areas are compared. This mapping is then translated in quantitative data; some of these data will be illustrated with maps, visualizing the diachronical analysis. The analysis presented here thereby positions itself at the core of what Richard Maltby has coined "new cinema history,"[8] a movement that pleads for multidisciplinary empirical research in cinema cultures.

This chapter concentrates on the main results coming out of this large database. Keeping the methodological issue in mind, the main part of the chapter is organized around some key tendencies and tensions within the Flemish/Belgian film exhibition history. Besides overall longitudinal tendencies in terms of cinema exploitation and film attendance, we concentrate upon tensions between rural and urban forms of film exhibition. These findings are put in international perspective in the final discussion.

CONSTRUCTING A DATABASE
ON CINEMA EXHIBITION

Before looking at the Belgian film exhibition scene, it might be useful to briefly sketch the institutional and sociocultural context of our case, Flanders as a part of Belgium. Belgium is a constitutional monarchy that since the 1960s has developed into a federal state, with a highly complex federal system of (geographical) regions (Flanders/Wallonia/Brussels) and (cultural-linguistic) communities (Flemish, French, and German). Flanders is the Dutch-speaking region in the northern part of Belgium. It has an area of 13,522 square kilometers, a population of 6.3 million (around 60 percent of the Belgian population) and a population density of 462 inhabitants per square kilometer. Flanders is divided into five provinces and currently counts 308 municipalities. Two of them are metropolitan cities (Antwerp and Ghent). Brussels (equally included in the research) is the bilingual capital city of Belgium (and of Flanders), composed of nineteen municipalities and counting more than a million inhabitants.

Our research consisted of the construction of an extended inventory of existing and historical cinemas in Flanders, paying attention to the geographical distribution in rural and urban areas, based on archival research.[9] We use the term "movie theater" for any place where films were shown on a more or less regular basis. Research was therefore not limited to permanent movie theaters, as alternative exhibition places with occasional movie screenings were included. The data gathering on which a large part of this chapter is based was done mainly through analyses of industry yearbooks that provide us with a detailed list of cinemas in Flanders by location, compiled by various interest groups related to the Belgian exhibition landscape.[10] Other data covering the entire region of Flanders was provided by the National Institute for Statistics (from 1973). To these centralized, systematic data, we added local data gathered through program schedules, company files, building licenses, local history studies, interviews with local key players, photographs, etc. These alternative data were not just purely an enrichment of the database, but were also seen as a necessary tool to correct certain, though non-systematic, omissions and errors between the various non-continuous industry yearbooks.[11]

Different sources reveal different numbers and data. Once one goes deeper into comparing the different datasets, it becomes clear that each source has its particular flaws. These differences necessarily call for a discussion about the value of the various yearbooks. The data presented in the following parts consequently must be read with a strong caveat. We know for instance from elaborate case studies on particular cities or towns that the yearbook data are not always correct. Notwithstanding these shortcomings, they are the most comprehensive historical data on cinema exhibition in Flanders and Brussels. As we did not uncover any systematic biases, one can presume that for the analysis of main tendencies, the several shortcomings in different directions flatten out the possible bias. Once one goes into detailed town-by-town or year-by-year analysis, however, another story altogether is revealed.

We therefore stress that our analysis is based on what is (as far as we know) the first systematic collection of cinema exhibition data in Flanders and Brussels, and that it presents a general overview of the field of film exhibition in that area, to be complemented by in-depth case studies. In order to make a diachronic analysis about the movie theater landscape in Flanders, all these data were organized chronologically by year, resulting in a database that contains more than forty thousand records, with information about a specific cinema situated in a precise year.

The analysis of the database was organized around two major themes. First, we did a diachronic analysis on the number of theaters per year in Flanders and Brussels, illustrating long-term tendencies in the rise of cinemas, the boom of cinemagoing, the decay of cinemas, and the rise of multiplexes. Special attention was paid to the discrepancy between the decline of cinemas and the rise in the number of screens in the cities after the 1970s. In a second part, we take a closer look at the geographical division of movie theaters, as we put these general tendencies in an urban versus rural perspective and question the classic view connecting film experience and cinema exhibition with a city environment and urbanity.

FILM EXHIBITION IN BELGIUM AND FLANDERS: GENERAL TENDENCIES

One of the key results from this broad structural investigation underlined the high density of cinemas and the vibrancy of the Belgian film exhibition scene. The database reconfirmed the rapid emergence of cinemas from the start of permanent film exhibition, especially in major Belgian cities like Antwerp and Brussels. International comparative data are scarce for this period, but if we can believe a correspondent of the German trade journal *Der Kinematograph,* who visited Brussels in February 1907, the Belgian capital must have been a "paradise for cinema." He was amazed by how the city at night was immersed in light coming out of the many fixed film houses.[12] Three years later, another *Kinematograph* correspondent compared Brussels with Berlin, claiming that "[w]hen you come from Berlin, you are struck by the abundance of cinemas in the Belgian capital, and not less by the dignified splendor and elegance of their interior design."[13] Three more years later, as the Brussels and Belgian film exhibition sector continued to boom, a Dutch film trade journal, *De Kinematograaf,* estimated that Belgium with a population of about 7.5 million counted some 625 cinemas, of which 115 were located in Brussels. These were extreme figures by Dutch standards, but it was high even compared to Germany (2,000) and Berlin (200), or England (2,000) and London (400).[14] By this time, when the first substantial taxes on film exhibition were introduced all over the kingdom,[15] the Belgian film scene prospered, attracting investors from different horizons.

Cinema, which was first introduced in November 1895,[16] had first been mainly exploited for commercial reasons by people working in the broader field of fairground attraction and variety shows.[17] By the start of the twentieth century, film screenings were common in nearly all major towns and cities. Similar to what happened in the United States and countries like France and Germany, film theaters appeared in cities in the period between 1905 and 1907. The first fixed Belgian film theater started in December 1904 in Brussels (Théâtre du Cinématographe) and very much resembled American nickelodeons or German *Ladenkinos.*[18] Due to a lack of tough regulation, cinemas mushroomed in the period till 1908, leading many people and investors to step into this highly lucrative market. A widely popular form of film exhibition, not only in Brussels, Antwerp, and other major cities but also in minor towns in rural areas, was the *café-ciné.* Many pub and bar owners opened cinemas as a sideline. The high penetration of cinemas in such a strongly urbanized country as Belgium must thus be linked to the intensive Belgian *café* culture. A wider factor, explaining the rapid expansion of the local cinema and leisure industry in this period, is linked to socioeconomic developments such as better salaries for workers and the growth of leisure time.

After the First World War the practice of filmgoing grew into the most popular leisure form, not only in urbanized but also in rural areas, where even in small towns one or more cinemas appeared. One of the first statistical sources is an overview of the number of movie theaters in the different provinces of Flanders in 1920.[19] Of the 776 movie theaters in Belgium, 55 percent (426) were located in Flanders. According to the different available sources, during this golden age of cinema in the 1920s the number of cinemas reached its height around 1925, followed by a strong decline toward the end of the decade.[20] According to one source, Belgium counted some 1,129 cinemas in 1925, but lost one-third of them by the end of the decade (772 in 1929).[21] The first industry yearbooks containing a detailed list of movie theaters in the different towns of Flanders and Brussels were published in the years 1924 through 1930.[22] In 1924, there were 498 movie theaters active in Flanders, which indicates a rise of 15 percent from 1920. Within the next years there were serious fluctuations, ending with a steep decline by 1928. This decline was due, in addition to the economic crisis at the end of the 1920s, to increasing taxation on cinemas, leading to a storm of protest from exhibitors and the organized local film industries.[23]

Although taxes were still considered to be heavy in 1930 according to international standards,[24] a new fiscal regulation softened the pressure on Belgian cinemas. The introduction of sound came as an additional financial burden and took quite some time to enter cinemas, especially in theaters in more rural areas. The number of theaters in Flanders and Brussels had already stabilized by 1930, when nearly the same number (499) were registered as in 1924 (498). During the next decade the number of film theaters grew steadily; in eight years there were 118 more movie theaters. The fastest increase happened between 1932 and 1934, when 95 movie theaters opened in Flanders and twelve in the city of Brussels. And it continued to stay comparatively high—also by international standards. In an international overview on the introduction of sound systems in 1931, Howard T. Lewis counted some 740 film houses in Belgium, a much higher figure than those for countries with comparable numbers of inhabitants, such as the Netherlands (266) or Switzerland (330).[25] In a later article on the international film exploitation sector published in an academic economic journal in 1938, Belgium's high profile in terms of film attendance was reaffirmed. With its huge cinema landscape (1,103 theaters, 57 percent of them in Flanders and Brussels), the small kingdom came up with a figure of 138 screens for every one million habitants. This was again high compared to England (5,000 cinemas, with a density of 109 screens for every one million people), France (4,100 theaters and a density of 100), Germany (5,000 theaters and a density of 77) or Holland (300 theaters and a density of 38).[26]

In this period, many cinemas started, reopened, or were heavily modernized. The introduction of sound had a major impact on technological equipment as well as on the architectural design of cinema in Belgium. The cinema landscape became more diversified, with a system of different runs, the arrival of theaters specializing in newsreels and news films (mainly part of the international Cinéac circuit), as well as the clear presence of *studios* or *cinemas d'art et essai* (film clubs specializing in art or avant-garde pictures).[27] The city of Brussels, for example, gained twenty-seven venues between 1930 and 1938; 19 percent of these theaters were newly built movie palaces, including Métropole (1932) and Eldorado (1933), each holding three thousand seats, making them the largest one-screen movie theaters Belgium would ever know.[28] Brussels witnessed the rise of the *art et essai* cinemas like Studio Arenberg (1936) and gained five urban newsreel cinemas, Cinéac-Nord (1932), Cinéum (1935), Actual (1936), Cinémonde (1937), and Cinéac-Centre (1938). These urban cinema tendencies were followed in Ghent and Antwerp: both cities gained two film palaces (Rex and Capitole in Antwerp; Rex and Capitole in Ghent) and one newsreel cinema (Cineac in Antwerp and Actual in Ghent).

An important drive behind the growth of the Belgian cinema landscape, which would still count more than 1,100 cinemas when the Second World War broke out, was the flowering of cheaper theaters in suburbs and small towns.[29] Another special feature, which may be typical for the Belgian market and which throws up additional methodological questions for all these figures and tendencies, is that film attracted increasing attention from ideologically and/or politically inspired groups.[30] Key players in this seemingly marginal part of the film market were what is commonly called in sociopolitical terms the different "pillars" of Belgian society.[31] From the mid-nineteenth century onwards, Belgian society was strongly segregated along politico-ideological lines, referred to as pillarization. In a pillarized society Catholic, socialist, liberal, and Flemish-nationalist organizations tried to organize the lives of citizens within the same pillar of institutions. Film exhibition soon became a key feature in the strategy to use motion pictures as a modern means to influence citizens. One might speculate about the impact of these initiatives, but it is clear that this politico-ideological exploitation of cinema strongly stimulated the film exhibition. This situation continued after the Second World War, only to decline at the end of the 1950s and afterwards.[32]

The impact of the Second World War was sharply felt by the film exhibition industry, but in 1942, 76 percent of the cinemas of 1938 (625) were still standing; Brussels saw only twelve cinemas disappear. When the first statistics of the Federation of Cinema Owners emerged in 1945, an amazing 967 movie theaters were counted in Belgium, 560 of them located in Flanders and Brussels. That same year, cinema attendance broke loose with a staggering 147.6 million visitors for Belgium.[33] These record numbers for cinema attendance were never exceeded in Belgium, but the overall expansion of the cinema landscape in Europe lasted well into the 1950s. For Flanders and Brussels there was an amazing 37 percent increase in movie theaters—327 cinemas opened between 1946 and 1953—while in 1950 the cinema attendance rate for Belgium had already dropped 22 percent since the roaring postwar years. The number went down to 115 million by the mid-1950s. Clearly, this did not match investors' hopes for a final recovery of cinema.[34] Starting in the 1940s, board members of the Federation of Cinema Owners constantly stressed in their monthly meetings the need to limit the number of theaters because of the failing attendance rates, but their calls were ignored by entrepreneurs wanting to participate in the profitable film business.[35] Between 1954 and 1957 another 247 movie theaters opened in Flanders and Brussels. That year Belgium had a record 1,585 movie theaters for eight million people, with only bigger countries like Germany, Italy, France, and Spain with more.[36] In comparison, the Netherlands had about three hundred movie theaters for ten million people.[37] But by then the nearly doubling of the number of cinemas (from 560 in 1946 to 984 in 1957[38] in Flanders and Brussels) and the halving of cinema attendance (from 147 million in 1945 to 79.56 million in 1960 in Belgium) had led to a crisis.

All in all, in the post–Second World War period until the pivotal years of 1957 and 1958, cinema seemed to be able to maintain its role as the most popular form of entertainment, with many new huge cinemas built, often in a modernist architectural style. Television, which was introduced in Belgium by the end of 1953, would only play a significant role from 1958 onwards at the occasion of the prestigious World Exposition, which strongly promoted the television medium by increasing the amount of (live) television broadcasts. More research needs to be undertaken to determine the various reasons for the postwar drop in cinema attendance, but a combination of several reasons seems plausible. Besides television, the availability of new forms of entertainment (e.g., the success of popular music and dance halls), leisure activities (e.g., boom in tourism), and transportation (e.g., the growth in the number of cars, better public transportation), it is important to refer to sociodemographic trends in the 1950s (a baby boom leading to record number of births in 1961). The turning point 1957–1958 marked the beginning of a continuous decline in the number of movie theaters. In ten years, Flanders lost 541 cinemas; by 1970 only 46 percent of the Belgian movie theaters from 1960 were left. Yet what is now the Brussels Capital Region held on to a surprising 75 percent of its venues, losing only thirty-three cinemas over ten years, even though cinema attendance lost a massive 57 percent in the Brussels region, from 19.19 million in 1960 to a mere 8.39 million in 1969. National cinema attendance rates kept declining, falling in 1970 to a mere 38 percent of what it had been in 1960. Flanders and Brussels lost more than thirty-four million visitors in the 1960s, leaving them in 1970 with only 37 percent of the attendance rate of 1960. As in other countries, television became more successful in the 1960s and 1970s, and there were also changes in the urban structure and the role of the city. More people were living outside the big urban centers, there was an exodus from urban areas, and city centers often became commercial ghettos at night. In Belgium, however, it is also important to refer to the gradual implosion of the pillarization system after the 1960s[39]—which is important for film exhibition. In many rural areas, cinemas or theaters that regularly showed films were often linked to the showing of Catholic films; these declined in the 1960s.

During the 1960s there were two distinct events that affected movie theaters in Flanders and Brussels. In 1962 the agreement between the Belgian cinema owners and the public television broadcaster that restricted the showing of films to one per week was annulled;[40] the next year there were 98 fewer movie theaters in Flanders and a drop of 15 percent in admis-

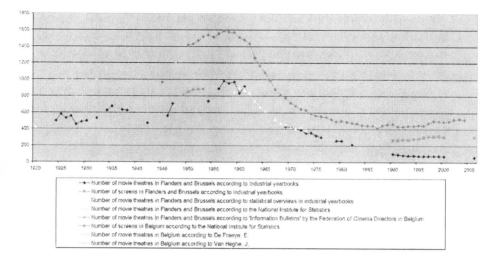

FIGURE 4.1. Number of movie theaters and screens for Flanders, Brussels, and Belgium (1920–2005). The data in this figure are based on forty-eight industrial yearbooks, the *Inlichtingsbulletijns* of the *Vereniging van Kinemabestuurders* from the year 1946 until 1953, and statistics received from the National Institute of Statistics.

sions. In April 1967 stricter tax regulations were imposed, which caused many small cinemas to close their doors[41]: there were 104 fewer cinemas in Flanders than in 1965. Big cinemas were transformed by new technologies in sound, image, and experience, which were common in most film markets, and they also were transformed into multiscreen theaters that offered a variety of films. The first reference to a multiscreen cinema in Flanders is found in 1969, when the Colisée in Brussels reopened with three screens after renovations. This trend continued throughout the 1970s in an attempt to reverse declining cinema attendance by offering more choice in films. Figure 4.1 shows that at the beginning of the 1970s, Flanders and Brussels lost 39 percent of their movie theaters but only 20 percent of the total number of screens. This, however, did not stop the rapidly declining cinema attendance rate: between 1970 and 1979 cinema attendance dropped 35 percent in Belgium and 32 percent in Flanders and Brussels.

In the 1970s and 1980s, sociological studies indicate that deep transformations in public trust, community life and leisure also affected the traditional social role of public spaces such as bars and community centers as well as suburban cinemas. The role played by family-owned cinema was over, while the surviving theaters were part of bigger networks that could only survive through a strategy of concentration, synergy, and market control. The former film palaces in city centers such as those in Brussels and Antwerp were transformed into multiscreen cinemas directed at adolescents. This resulted in the 1980s in a continuing decline in the number of movie theaters in Flanders and Brussels, which lost 159 theaters (61 percent) between 1980 and 1990. Only 74 screens (22 percent) were lost. The region of Brussels lost 27 screens and 27 theaters. In the ten years after 1980, the Brussels cinemas lost a little more than 700,000 visitors, in comparison with the loss of 2.65 million visitors in the 1970s. In Flanders, the downward trend of the 1980s was less rapid, with a 21 percent loss (from 9.53 million in 1980 to 7.62 million in 1990).

At the end of the 1990s, the decline and the crisis were curbed: Flanders and Brussels lost only thirty movie theaters in this decade, and by 2006 another fourteen movie theaters disappeared. But for the first time the number of screens started to rise. The pivotal year is 1992: by 2000 Flanders and Brussels gained thirty-nine screens, and by 2006 Belgium gained 11 percent of screen capacity compared to 1990. These shifts were mirrored in the cinema attendance rate, which increased for the first time since the Second World War, with a 21 percent increase in the 1990s. A major player in this process was a smaller local exhibitor, Albert Bert, who was inspired by U.S. and British tendencies to build multiplexes. In 1981, Bert had already built a twelve-screen multiplex in Ghent (Decascoop), followed in 1989 by what was then considered a gamble of building a twenty-five-screen complex in Brussels (Kinepolis). Bert's concept was new for the continent, and it consisted of offering a wide choice of movies (mostly American movies, one must add) aimed at teenagers or young adolescents, at the outskirts of a major city. These shopping-mall-inspired multiplexes also had the advantage of wide transportation and car parking facilities. The gradual introduction of similar multiplexes in other Belgian cities (as well as in neighboring countries and other foreign markets) made Bert and his Kinepolis Group into an important player—in the Belgian context even into a dominant, near-monopolistic player. The Belgian cinema landscape in 2005 counted 121 cinemas (118,085 seats), offering 527 screens, controlled by a small number of exhibitors (mainly the Kinepolis Group and the French UGC), selling 21.9 million tickets annually (in 2005).[42] Theaters in Flanders and Brussels represent 47 percent of all

Belgian movie theaters; 21 percent are monoscreen cinemas, 49 percent are multiscreen cinemas (two to eight screens, renovated or newly built) and 30 percent of those venues are multiplexes. Flanders and Brussels in 2005 had 307 screens; 195 of them, or 63 percent, are within multiplexes.

We see the same general evolution when looking at the evolution in the number of cinemas per township for the province of Antwerp. There is a clear trend toward the spread of cinemas to smaller towns and villages from the 1920s on, together with a steady, high number of cinemas in the main city (Antwerp). There is almost total coverage at the end of the 1950s, during which only ten entities go without cinema. There is a gradual downward movement from the 1960 until the 1980s, where we see an almost complete disappearance of village and small-town cinemas, with the multiplexes dominating in the city of Antwerp.

The new positive balance in screen numbers and cinema attendance since the early 1990s contradicts the traditional view of the "death of the cinema." Cinematic exhibition is blossoming again. As the geographical analysis will show, the evolution is strongly linked to the differences between urban and rural cinema culture. The new cinema culture reflects a thorough change in movie exhibition culture, where geographical distribution and variety have made way for concentration—economic and geographic—which slowly added up to an increase in cinema attendance.

THE TENSION BETWEEN METROPOLITAN, URBAN, AND RURAL FILM EXPLOITATION

It is a classic view in film history to link film exhibition and the experience of moviegoing with urbanity. Robert C. Allen recently stated:

> One of the most enduring and striking features of American film historiography is its assumption of a particular and in some accounts determinative connection between the experience of metropolitan urbanity and the experience of cinema.[43]

Over the last decade, however, this general assumption has been thoroughly revised by scholars focusing on cinema culture in more rural and small-town areas in various countries.[44] In this part of the chapter, we empirically test the connection between urbanity and cinema culture for the Flemish situation using the database. We argue that an in-depth social-geographic analysis of the distribution of movie theaters throughout Flanders can add crucial additional information to the general overview presented. This analysis, linked with demographic data, allows for much more nuanced and fine-grained conclusions on the spread of cinemas in Flanders and on the relation of cinema with metropolitan, urban, small-town, and rural contexts. We thus stress that we use a continuum between metropolitan and rural, whereas urban has a far broader meaning than solely metropolitan. Similar studies on the spread of cinemas have been done in other countries, but the systematic analysis in combination with demographic data as applied here is original.

To investigate the connection between urbanity and cinema in Flanders, one must take into account the specific social-geographic situation of the Flanders region. From the foundation of the kingdom of Belgium in 1830, urbanization was a key factor in the geographic reality. For many municipalities in Flanders, urbanization is a heritage from before the Industrial Revolution in the nineteenth century. Vandermotten and Vandewattyne[45] estimate that in 1831, almost 30 percent of the population of Flanders already lived in cities, as opposed to only 21 percent of the population in Wallonia, the southern part of the country. Since 1831, urban population has increased from 51 percent of the total Belgian population in 1910 to 61 percent in 1976. Between 1841 and 1976, the total population of Belgium grew 2.6 times, but the urban population increased its total 5.7 times, while population outside the cities only grew 41 percent. An important part of the urbanization, however, took place outside the cities. The construction of railways (since 1835) and local branch lines (since 1885) made sure that at the end of the nineteenth century, most municipalities in Belgium were connected to the railway network. Together with the establishment of local industry settlements, surrounding residential areas, and the historical tradition of dispersed habitation and ribbon development in the Flanders region, the improved mobility resulted in what is described as a general urbanization in Flanders.[46] Where in the southern part of the country, the expansion of the cities was accompanied by a decrease of the non-urban population, in Flanders the growth of the urban population went hand in hand with the growth, although smaller, of the non-urban population.[47]

This short historical overview illustrates that Flanders was already a densely built-on region at the start of permanent movie theaters in 1906, with large parts more or less urbanized and half the population living inside cities. The historic Flanders is hardly comparable to the rural south of the United States Robert Allen is talking about. Although a large part of the population did not live in cities, many "rural" villages in Flanders lay close to each other, had achieved some form of urbanization, and were connected through local railways.

In the second part of the nineteenth century and the beginning of the twentieth century urban population expansion was far more important than that of non-urban areas. (In the last thirty years of the nineteenth century, urban population doubled.) As cities became more and more important and the center of attraction, it is not surprising that at least for the first decade of permanent film exhibition, movie theaters were an urban phenomenon. The emergence of permanent cinemas in Flanders took place in geographically determined waves. Between 1905 and 1910 movie theaters boomed in an urban context. This boom was first located in the three metropolitan cities, then in the provincial cities. Only ten years after the first theaters opened in the big cities, the earliest permanent cinemas in little towns in more rural areas emerged.[48] By that time, movie exhibition had already taken a firm grip on the leisure culture in the cities.

From the first industry yearbooks in the 1920s, we are able to pinpoint all existing movie theaters in Flanders to an exact location. This enables us to investigate in detail to what extent the geographic spread of movie theaters was determined by urbanization and to what extent people who did not live in cities had the opportunity to go to the movies.

A large-scale analysis of this geographic spread again poses several problems. There are no official and workable standards in historical perspective to distinguish cities from urbanized and agrarian or rural villages. Furthermore, the region of Flanders initially was divided into more than 1,200 different municipalities of unequal size. In 1977, this administrative structure was completely altered as Flanders was reorganized as a region with 335 municipalities.[49] After that year, all official statistics only take into account the 335 new municipalities. Moreover, later scientific typologies for Flanders predominantly focus on the 1970s onwards, in other words, a period when most movie theaters were already gone.

Although we realize that urbanization can take different forms and consist of different components (morphological, demographic, functional, etc.), we choose to make a geographic analysis purely based upon

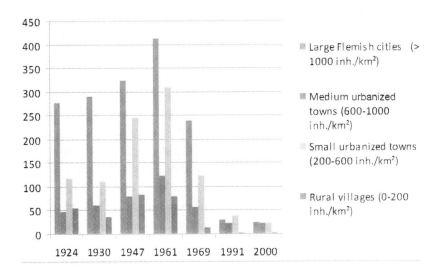

FIGURE 4.2. Absolute numbers of cinemas according to population density in Flanders (1924–2000).

morphologic elements (i.e., size and population). This information was gathered in a census every ten years and is therefore historically accurate for each period. We work with population density instead of absolute population numbers.[50] Such a classification is a workable parameter for comparing different municipalities with different sizes and histories. This classification, for the period before 1977 consisting of all 1,250 existing villages,[51] counts four categories according to population density: rural villages, small urbanized towns, medium urbanized towns, and large urban cities.[52]

There are several ways of representing and analyzing the relation between cinemas and population density. A general overview of the evolution of absolute numbers of cinemas in relation to population density (see figure 4.2) more or less mirrors the general overview we gave in figure 4.1. But it distinguishes between four levels of urbanization, making the picture more detailed and complex.

For analytical clarity, we look at the division over the four categories in an alternative manner, focusing on the relative importance of the categories in percentages. Figure 4.3 then gives an overview of the distribution of movie theaters in Flanders and Brussels throughout the past

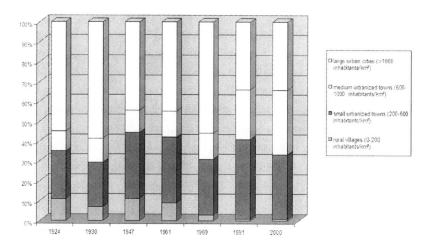

FIGURE 4.3. Geographic spread of movie theaters in Flanders and Brussels (in terms of percentage) according to population density (1924–2000).

century according to these four categories. A first look at the graph clearly shows a steady—but far from exclusive—connection between urbanity and cinema throughout the entire past century. In 1924, 55 percent of all movie theaters were located in large urban cities.

The 276 movie theaters in these thirty-eight municipalities account for an average of 7.3 cinemas per city. This could appear as astonishing, taking into account that these cities represent only 4 percent of the total number of municipalities in Flanders. But in the year 1924 Flanders is of course only at the beginning of a widespread diffusion of cinema culture toward less urban and more rural areas in the decades to follow. Still, until the Second World War, more than half of the movie theaters were still located in this small number of cities with the highest population densities. The even slighter amount of medium urbanized towns, only 3 percent of the total number of municipalities in Flanders, adds up to slightly more than 10 percent of the number of movie theaters until the Second World War.

In 1924, small urbanized towns represented only 7 percent of the total number of municipalities, but the theaters in those towns represented 25 percent of all movie theaters. Rural villages were by far the largest portion with 58 percent of all municipalities.[53] Although these predominantly rural villages embody the lion's share of municipalities, their movie theater share is relatively marginal. In 1924, the cinemas in these villages represented 11 percent of all cinemas; only 44 villages of the 727 villages in this lowest category owned a movie theater. After the crisis in 1927/1928, only 25 villages in this category still had a movie theater. We can conclude for this period that although more than 30 percent of all movie theaters were not located in the most densely populated municipalities, these movie theaters were in general not to be found in the predominantly rural or agrarian villages. Movie theaters outside the cities were to be found in the small and medium urbanized towns with higher than average populations.

After the Second World War, we see a rapid growth in the installment of permanent movie theaters all over Flanders. As has been illustrated, the period between 1945 and 1960 can be considered the heyday of movie theaters in general. The growth of cinema in Flanders was, however, largely by virtue of new cinemas opening in smaller villages and towns. The postwar period was the time when non-urban cinema flourished as more than 40 percent of all movie theaters were located outside the large cities or the densely populated towns. The major share, however, was still situated in those non-urban towns that had a larger-than-average population density.[54] Nonetheless, our analysis clearly proves that in these decades, cinema was no longer an urban phenomenon, but fully permeated everyday life in all areas of Flanders, be it metropolitan, urban, or rural.

Just as with the establishment of the movie theater industry in Flanders, there is a clear geographic thread in the disappearance of movie theaters. The rapid decline of cinemas in the 1960s took place simultaneously in metropolitan cities, towns, and villages. However, the decline of movie theaters in areas with a low population density was more overwhelming and occurred at a much faster pace. In 1969, only thirteen of the seventy-nine original movie theaters remained in rural villages, an 83 percent drop in ten years. The 60 percent drop of neighborhood cinemas in small urbanized towns and the 54 percent drop in medium urbanized towns are equally upsetting. Movie theaters in the most densely populated larger cities survived a bit better, as "only" 42 percent of these cinemas had to close their doors.

The same situation can be found at the beginning of the 1990s.[55] Only one village with a population density below two hundred inhabitants per

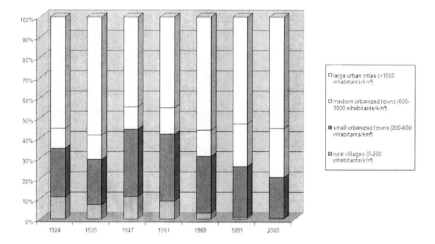

FIGURE 4.4. Geographic spread of screens in Flanders (in terms of percentage) according to population density (1924–2000).

square kilometer could hold on to its movie theater.[56] Small urbanized towns lost another 70 percent of their cinemas, while medium urbanized towns lost 60 percent of their theaters. By this time, however, movie theater owners in the most densely populated cities who survived the 1960s could no longer postpone the inevitable. Between 1969 and 1991, 87 percent of all movie theaters in the most densely populated cities had to close their doors. At the beginning of the twenty-first century, cinema is an urban phenomenon more than it ever was, as only 1 percent of movie theaters are located in the predominantly rural villages.[57] These last numbers, however, have to be revised in light of the recent tendency to split up movie theaters and the building of multiplexes and megaplexes, which brings us to the next level of analysis: the rural-urban divide in cinema screens.

In the 1980s the total movie offer slowly stabilized; large movie theaters were broken up into smaller ones, and multiplexes with newer and better infrastructure were established. But these structural adjustments proved to be too expensive for many rural movie exhibitors. Their market was just not densely populated enough to create enough demand to make these adjustments economically profitable. Figure 4.4 clearly shows that when we look at the available screens in the second half of the twentieth century, the disappearance of rural cinema in the movie theater landscape is even more complete, as by the year 2000 the total number of screens in rural villages represents no more than 20 percent of all available screens. Of all screens, 55 percent are located in large cities and 25 percent in medium urbanized towns. The 307 screens in 2000 are spread over just 71 movie theaters in 47 towns. In other words, for those cities that still have movie theaters, the evolution of screens is not that different from half a century ago. The forty-five screens available in Antwerp in 2000 are close to the fifty screens half a century earlier, and the twenty screens available in Ghent are not that far from the thirty screens in the 1950s. Moreover, in provincial cities like Diest or Leuven where multiplexes are located, screen capacity has never been as high as at the turn of the century. Again the thorough change in movie exhibition culture is illustrated as geographic distribution and variety make way for concentration of screens and cinemas.

It is now safe to conclude that population density has proven to be a good indicator to explain the presence of movie theaters in a town, city, or village. It is not a surprising outcome, but taking into account the overall high population of Flanders and the general urbanization of a region that is overall densely built-on, it is remarkable how cinemas were in general located precisely within those areas where population density was the highest.

When we take demographic elements like population density as an indicator to measure the morphologic urbanization level of villages and towns, it becomes clear that the higher the level of urbanization is, the higher the chance that a specific town or village will have at least one movie theater and the higher the average number of movie theaters per town or village is. Moreover, the urbanization level of the location of cinemas also shows a clear link with the exhibition routine in these locations. The higher the urbanization, the bigger the movie theaters get and the more movies are shown per week. Movie theaters in villages in the lowest categories often showed movies only two or three days a week and almost never more than two or three movies a day. Movie theaters in the highest populated areas, on the other hand, mostly showed movies seven days out of seven and often in a continuing loop, where visitors could just walk in at any time and stay in the theater until they had seen the whole show.

Demographic elements are nevertheless just one component to pinpoint the urbanization level of a specific area. Other elements, such as functionality, prosperity, centralizing function, etc., also come into play. More research needs to be undertaken to analyze the geographic spread of movie theaters according to various classifications, but the overall conclusion seems to be very much the same: there is indeed a clear link between urbanization on the one hand and the location of movie theaters on the other hand. This link, however, is not exclusive and has proven to vary throughout the past century. The theory of central places by Walter Christaller (1933/1969) can also help to shed light on this variation. Christaller says that services (such as movie theaters) are not offered just everywhere, but only in places that have a certain central function in regard to surrounding places. Those surrounding places are restricted by the range of a service (i.e., the maximum distance one is willing to undertake in order to obtain that service). The minimal demand necessary to make the service economically possible is the threshold of that good. Based upon these hypotheses, Christaller makes up a hexagonal network of cities and principal villages.[58] The result given above—that cinemas are mainly localized in the large cities or in urbanized villages while the less-developed villages are dependent upon those villages to be able to go to the movies—seems to correspond with this theory of centrality. The level of regional function is however not static. (One of the major critiques against the Christaller theory is its static nature.) A descent of regional function can be explained by a growing demand, through which the regional function undergoes a stronger spread. This is what happens after the Second World War in the movie theater landscape when more and more villages open a movie theater. After 1960, the service of movie theaters clearly rises in regional function, because it needs a continually larger economic basis to be profitable. Therefore, most cinemas in villages and towns need to close doors in order for the service of movie theaters to be able to rise to a higher level (provincial and regional cities).

CONCLUSION

Putting the Flemish cinema landscape in historical perspective has proven to be a challenging case. This chapter has drawn on data and insights from a major research project on the history of film exhibition and cinemagoing in the Dutch-language part of Belgium (Flanders), the Enlightened City project. Here, the focus was on the first phase of the project, the analysis of an extended inventory of existing and historical cinemas in Flanders, paying attention to the geographical distribution. This kind of analysis is fruitful, but there are certain pitfalls: it is always hard to get reliable data, and once the data are localized, building and filling the database takes an immense amount of work, which allows for large-scale evolutions. We highlighted some of the major tendencies and changes in film exhibition in the twentieth century identified through analysis of empirical data in the database, such as the rise of cinemas in rural and urban environments, the boom in cinemagoing, the decay and closure of many provincial and neighborhood cinemas, and the rise of multiplexes.

We have shown how there is indeed a link between urbanization on the one hand and the exploitation of movie theaters on the other hand. But this link is far from exclusive and has proven to vary throughout the past century. Especially in the 1950s, rural cinema culture was thriving. Further comparative research projects can help us put these findings in perspective. Is Flanders fully in line with international developments, or is this a specific situation? We can already agree that there is a parallel with the international trends, such as the fall in number of cinemas from the late 1950s on, but we equally showed how regional characteristics interact with broader social geographic and demographic developments. The widespread presence of cinemas in less-than-urban areas illustrates how cinema culture permeated every region in Flanders.

The close quantitative analysis of data in large databases such as the Enlightened City database makes a strong case for the value in (new) cinema history of large-scale findings on the relationship between cinema exhibition venues and population density as a marker for the degree of rurality vs. urbanization. With these kinds of analyses, we can slowly draw a more detailed map of cinema culture in Flanders, and we can hope to inspire similar research in other countries.

NOTES

1. J. Trumpbour, *Selling Hollywood to the World: U.S. and European Struggles for Mastery of the Global Film Industry, 1920–1950* (Cambridge: Cambridge University Press, 2002), 213.

2. In 1903, Belgium was considered to be the fifth industrial nation in the world with an open, export-driven, and expansive economy. Its high position in international

trade was also due to the exploitation of rubber and all kinds of minerals in its colony of Congo. See G. Deneckere, "Nieuwe geschiedenis van België," in *Nieuwe Geschiedenis van België I: 1830–1905*, ed. E. Witte et al., 460, cited here at 460 (Tielt: Lannoo, 2005).

3. In 1908, the Belgian railway system was much more elaborate than those of neighboring countries and used lower tariffs for transportation. See Deneckere, "Nieuwste geschiedenis van België," 461. For transport and distribution of motion picture reels to the north, see I. Blom, *Jean Desmet and the Early Dutch Film Trade* (Amsterdam: Amsterdam University Press, 2003), 147.

4. L. Depauw and D. Biltereyst, "De kruistocht tegen de slechte cinema: over de aanloop en de start van de Belgische filmkeuring (1911–1929)," *Tijdschrift voor Mediageschiedenis* 8 (2005): 3–26.

5. See Daniel Biltereyst and Philippe Meers, eds., *De Verlichte Stad* (Leuven: LannooCampus, 2007).

6. The research project "The Enlightened City": Screen Culture between Ideology, Economics and Experience. A Study on the Social Role of Film Exhibition and Film Consumption in Flanders (1895–2004) in Interaction with Modernity and Urbanization, funded by the FWO/SRC-Flanders, 2005–2008, promoters: Philippe Meers/UA, Daniel Biltereyst/UGhent, and Marnix Beyen/UA, was based at the universities of Antwerp (UA) and Ghent (UGhent). The project concentrated upon the Dutch-speaking part of Belgium (Flanders) and the bilingual capital of Brussels. The overall research project contains (i) a longitudinal database on the film exhibition structures (1919–2005), (ii) case studies on particular cities and towns (e.g., Antwerp, Ghent, Mechelen), and (iii) an oral history project on cinema experiences.

7. See e.g., D. Biltereyst, Ph. Meers and L. Van de Vijver, "Social Class, Experiences of Distinction and Cinema in Postwar Ghent," in *Explorations in New Cinema History: Approaches and Case Studies,* ed. R. Maltby, D. Biltereyst, and Ph. Meers, 101–24 (Malden: Wiley-Blackwell, 2011); D. Biltereyst, Ph. Meers, K. Lotze, and L. Van de Vijver, "Negotiating Cinema's Modernity: Strategies of Control and Audience Experiences of Cinema in Belgium," in *Cinema, Audiences and Modernity. New Perspectives on European Cinema History,* ed. D. Biltereyst, R. Maltby and Ph. Meers, 186–201 (London: Routledge, 2012).

8. R. Maltby, D. Biltereyst, and Ph. Meers, eds., *Explorations in New Cinema History: Approaches and Case Studies* (Malden: Wiley-Blackwell, 2011).

9. The authors wish to express their gratitude to Gert Willems and Lies Van de Vijver, the researchers on the Enlightened City project in Antwerp and Ghent respectively, who under the supervision of the authors built the database and made the first analyses on geographic and demographic data.

10. Interest groups that have published industry yearbooks include the Chamber for Film Distributors (Syndicale Kamer der Filmverhuurders), the Federation of Cinema Directors in Belgium (VKBB), the Belgian Chamber for Cinema Publicity (Chambre Syndicale belge de la publicité cinématographique a.s.b.1.), the Ministry of Economic Affairs and the Royal Belgian Film Archive.

11. All collected data have been imported in a database for further analysis and research. Four types of information were included in the database. First, information about the movie theaters mentioned in the industry yearbooks and other sources (location, name of cinema, address, opening and closing date, ideological identification, number of screens, number of seats, infrastructure, architecture, ticket prices). Second, information

about the cinema employees (names and functions) was added. Third, information about the companies behind the cinemas (name, judicial organization, and board members) was included. Finally, general information about exhibition (frequency and programming) was added.

12. G. Convents, *Van kinetoscoop tot café-ciné: De eerste jaren van de film in België 1894–1908* (Leuven: Universitaire Pers Leuven, 2000), 300, cited here at 302–3.

13. (Authors' translation.) "(W)enn man von Berlin kommt, dann staunt man über die Fülle der Cinémas in den belgischen Hauptstadt, nicht minder aber auch über die gediegene Pracht und Eleganz ihrer Inneneinrichtung." Convents, *Van kinetoscoop tot café-ciné* 302.

14. Blom, *Jean Desmet and the Early Dutch Film Trade*, 93. Similar data can be found in an article published in the Flemish newspaper *De Kleine Burger* (Zottegem, June 12, 1913). This article claims that Brussels had some 115 cinemas, while Paris (with its 3.5 million inhabitants) had 200 film theaters; London counted 400 cinemas, New York 470 cinemas, Berlin 280.

15. See Stad Gent, *Taks op de Openbare vermakelijkheden* (Ghent: Electra, 1912). By March 1913, cities like Brussels or Antwerp did not yet have a specific regulation for taxes on film exhibition. Later that year, taxes on cinemas were installed by a special law (September 3, 1913); see G. Convents, "Le cinema et la guerre mondiale en Belgique," *Revue Belge du Cinéma* 38–39 (1995): 29.

16. In fact, Belgium was the first country outside France where the Lumières showed their *cinématographe* projections. In March 1896, the first commercial screenings were organized (Convents, *Van kinetoscoop tot café-ciné*, 15).

17. Convents, *Van kinetoscoop tot café-ciné*, 348.

18. Convents, *Van kinetoscoop tot café-ciné*, 303.

19. J. Van Heghe, "Film als bron voor geschiedschrijving (in België tussen 1920–1940)" (Master's thesis, Ghent University, 1977), 48.

20. V. Peeters, *Bioscoop en televisie, op zoek naar een evenwicht*, vol. II (Brussels: Filmdienst van de Belgische Radio en Televisie, 1965); S. Van Aerschot-Van Haeverbeeck, "Film ... film theaters," *Monumenten en Landschappen* 7 (1988): 12–39; Van Heghe, "Film als bron voor geschiedschrijving"; see also the data for the period between 1924 and 1929 in the Belgian trade journal for the spectacle and leisure industry, *Annuaire du Spectacle de la Musique et du Cinéma* (Brussels: Editorial Office, 1924, 1925, 1926, 1927, 1928, 1929).

21. Van Heghe, "Film als bron voor geschiedschrijving," 48.

22. *Annuaire du Spectacle de la Musique et du Cinéma 1924* (Brussels: Editorial Office, 1924, 1925, 1926, 1927, 1928, 1929, 1930).

23. In the journal *Revue Belge du Cinéma*, considered to be the main film industry journal in the kingdom, many articles appeared on these protests in 1928 and 1929. In an article ("Le monde du cinéma," *Revue Belge du cinéma*, January 27, 1929, 8) the journalist claims that Belgian cinemas have the heaviest tax rate in the world. In other articles, comparative tax rates are published to bolster this statement. Again, it is difficult to evaluate these comparative international data.

24. See an article in *Revue Belge du Cinéma* (June 1939, 5–40) on an international conference on the issue of film exhibition (Congrès de la Fédération Internationale des Directeurs Cinématographiques), which seemed to have taken place in Brussels in June 1930.

25. Based upon a figure from H. T. Lewis, *The Motion Picture Industry* (New York: Van Nostrand, 1933), reprinted in I. Jarvie, *Hollywood's Overseas Campaign: The North Atlantic Movie Trade, 1920–1950* (Cambridge: Cambridge University Press, 1992), 141.

26. S. François, "Les représentations cinématographiques en Belgique," *Revue des Sciences Economiques* (April 1938): 53.

27. See for instance J. Braeken, "Paleizen voor de hoofdstad," *Monumenten en Landschappen* 7 (1988): 59; Van Aerschot-Van Haeverbeeck, "Film . . . film theaters," 32.

28. M. Crunelle, *Inventaire des salles de cinéma de la région de Bruxelles* (Bruxelles: La Rétine de Plateau asbl, Service Monuments et Sites, 1994).

29. Van Heghe, "Film als bron voor geschiedschrijving," 48.

30. L. Schokkaert and R. Stallaerts, *Onder dak. Een eeuw volks- en gildehuizen* (Ghent: Bijdragen Museum van de Vlaams Sociale Strijd, Uitgave Provinciebestuur Oost-Vlaanderen, 1987). For a closer view of pillarization, see D. Biltereyst, "The Roman Catholic Church and Film Exhibition in Belgium, 1926–1940," *Historical Journal of Film Radio and Television* 27(2) (2007): 193–214. Biltereyst, Meers, Lotze, and Van de Vijver, "Negotiating Cinema's Modernity: Strategies of Control and Audience Experiences of Cinema in Belgium."

31. Some sociologists argue that this pillar system created strongly organized subcultures between the individual and the state. See J. Billiet, ed., *Tussen bescherming en verovering. Sociologen en historici over verzuiling* (Leuven: Universitaire Pers, 1988); Els Witte et al., *Nieuwe Geschiedenis van België I* (Tielt: Lannoo, 2005).

32. Besides the intriguing question on the role of cinema in society, this "marginal" fraction in film exhibition, however, throws up many methodological and heuristic questions for today's researchers of the vivid Belgian film scene. In many industry yearbooks these pillarized forms of cinema exhibition were often omitted. Most of these yearbooks were published by commercial exhibitors' networks, and they considered political and ideological film exhibition to be an illicit form of competition. See also Biltereyst, Meers, Lotze, and Van de Vijver, "Negotiating Cinema's Modernity: Strategies of Control and Audience Experiences of Cinema in Belgium."

33. D. Biltereyst and B. Vriamont, "De filmsector in Vlaanderen," in *Audiovisuele media in Vlaanderen*, ed. J.-C. Burgelman, D. Biltereyst, and C. Pauwels, 57–90, cited here at 60 (Brussels: VUB Press, 1994).

34. Biltereyst and Vriamont, "De filmsector in Vlaanderen," 57–90.

35. Federation of Cinema Directors in Belgium, *Inlichtingenbulletijns*, 1946–1953.

36. www.mediasalles.it.

37. J.-P. Everaerts, *Film in België, een permanente revolte. Inleiding tot een geschiedenis en actualiteit van de filmproductie; -distributie en -exploitatie in België* (Brussels: Mediadoc, 2000), 220.

38. It's important to mention that this source—s.n., *Annuaire Général du Spectacle en Belgique* (Brussels: Editions l'Epoque, 1957)—also takes forty-nine 16 mm movie theaters into consideration and movie theaters with the "permission under special conditions." These were local town halls or schools that regularly showed films.

39. For a wider analysis of this process, see L. Huyse, *De verzuiling voorbij* (Leuven: Kritak, 1987).

40. J. Peeters, *Van dorpscinema tot megabioscoop: bioscoopexploitatie in Vlaanderen* (Brussel: Rits—Erasmushogeschool, 1997), 50.

41. Peeters, *Van dorpscinema tot megabioscoop: bioscoopexploitatie in Vlaanderen*, 50.

42. Data from FCB (Federatie van Cinemabestuurders van België, Brussels, e-mail June 6, 2006). See also: MediaSalles, *European Cinema Yearbook—2005 Advance Edition*, www.mediasalles.it/yindex05advedition.htm; *Jaarboek van de Belgische Film* (Brussels: Koninklijk Belgisch Filmarchief, 2003–2004).

43. See R. C. Allen, "Relocating American Film History: the 'problem' of the empirical," *Cultural Studies* 20(1) (2006).

44. E.g., on the U.S. contributions by R. C. Allen and C. Fuller-Seely in R. Maltby, Biltereyst, and Meers, *Explorations in New Cinema History;* for the UK, B. Doyle, "The Geography of Cinemagoing in Great Britain, 1934–1994: A Comment," *Historical Journal of Film, Radio and Television* 23 (2003): 59–71, and contributions in Biltereyst, Maltby, and Meers *Cinema, Audiences and Modernity* on Sweden (A. Jernud), the Netherlands (T. Van Oort), Wales (S. Moitra), and Hungary (A. Manchin).

45. C. Vandermotten and P. Vandewatteyne, "Groei en vorming van het stadsstramien in België," *Driemaandelijks Tijdschrift van het Gemeentekrediet van België* 54 (1985): 41–62.

46. J. Sporck, H. Van der Haegen, and M. Pattyn, "De ruimtelijke organisatie van de steden," *Driemaandelijks Tijdschrift van het Gemeentekrediet van België* 54 (1985): 153–63.

47. Vandermotten and Vandewatteyne, "Groei en vorming van het stadsstramien in België."

48. This does not mean that rural villages did not come into contact with cinema before the opening of permanent theaters. Traveling entrepreneurs visited fairs and music halls in urban villages with mobile film projectors.

49. Because of this administrative reorganization, the number of predominantly agrarian entities dropped dramatically. The National Institute of Statistics defines an agrarian area as one where 20 percent of the male population works within the agrarian industry. Due to the clustering of many municipalities in 1977, almost none of the new entities lived up to this criteria. In 1977, there were only seven agrarian municipalities in Flanders, in 1991 only three. None of these municipalities had a movie theater.

50. To avoid unproductive generalizations such as to say that each town with a population of less than 2,500 inhabitants is an agrarian town. Many towns of equal population were in fact incomparable, because of different size and structure.

51. To save as much detail as possible about the exact location of the movie theaters, we chose to pinpoint the movie theaters to the smallest administrative entity possible and not to make a clustering of municipalities based upon urban district or range of influence.

52. The largest category by far was the category of villages and towns with a population density between 17 and 200 inhabitants per square kilometer, which we name rural villages. Until after the Second World War, more than half of all municipalities in Flanders were in this category. The majority of these towns have a predominantly agrarian profile. A second category of municipalities we distinguish are municipalities with a population density in between 200 and 600 inhabitants per square kilometer, or small urbanized towns. Most towns in this category are still not urban, but do have a more urbanized profile (due to industry settlements, mining industry, etc.). Throughout the twentieth century, this category gained importance as a general urbanization occurred in the Flanders region. As a third category we defined all municipalities between 600 and 1,000 inhabitants per square kilometer, or medium urbanized towns. Many towns in this category have a clearly different profile than towns in the two previous categories,

as most regional and provincial cities are in this category. A fourth and last category is made up of municipalities with a population density higher than 1,000 inhabitants per square kilometer, or large urban cities. This is the smallest group of municipalities, but it consists of all large metropolitan cities (Brussels, Antwerp, and Ghent) and most of the municipalities in their surroundings. When we compare this last category with the research Sporck, Van der Haegen, and Pattyn (see note 46) did on urban districts, we see that this last category encloses the average (large) city center, the core city, and most agglomeration areas. Municipalities in the "banlieu" of a city (forensic residential areas), however, are mostly in the category of small urbanized towns.

53. The average population density in Flanders at that time was well below 200 inhabitants per square kilometer.

54. In 1947 and 1961 respectively, 35 and 34 percent of all villages in this category owned at least one movie theater (in both years worth one-third of the total available cinema), whereas only respectively 12 and 11 percent of villages with a population density below 200 inhabitants per square kilometer owned at least one movie theater, still representing just over 10 percent of the total cinema offer in the after-war years.

55. In 1977, the administrative organization of municipalities in Flanders changed thoroughly as Flanders went from a region with more than 1,200 separate administrative entities to a region with 335 municipalities. The result of this clustering of municipalities was that the number of predominantly agrarian entities dropped dramatically.

56. This movie theater remained open until February 2006, when it was closed by its owner due to economic reasons and rebuilt into a fitness center.

57. The other remaining cinemas are split in three by the other three categories.

58. The situation of the Belgian cities corresponds to a large extent to this Christaller network. But there are some differences, such as the central function of Brussels Capital Region, which is clearly of a higher hierarchical position than the other metropolitan cities (Antwerp, Ghent, and Liège).

FIVE

Mapping the Ill-Disciplined?
Spatial Analyses and Historical
Change in the Postwar Film Industry

DEB VERHOEVEN AND COLIN ARROWSMITH

Making maps is hard, but mapping Guizhou province is especially
so.... Southern Guizhou has a multitude of mountain peaks. They
are jumbled together, without any plains or marshes to space them
out, or rivers or water courses to put limits to them. They are vexingly
numerous and ill-disciplined.... Their configurations are difficult to
discern clearly, ridges and summits seeming to be the same. Those
who give an account of the arterial pattern of the mountains are thus
obliged to speak at length. In some cases, to describe a few kilometers
of ramifications needs a pile of documentation, and dealing with
the main line of a day's march takes a sequence of chapters.

—*GUIYANG PREFECTURAL GAZETTEER* (1850)

INTRODUCTION

As part of a broad disciplinary shift from a focus on measuring the value
and meaning of cultural artifacts to understanding the import of cultural flows, humanities researchers are progressively turning to other
disciplines and disciplinary practices to inform their research. For film
scholars, rather than providing a reading of specific media texts and their
qualities, there is an increasing focus on the contextual events that shape
and formulate cinema practice. This chapter is an example of how cross-
disciplinary relationships, for example between cinema studies, geospatial science, statistics, and the creative arts can uncover new research
questions and test methodologies across uncharted disciplinary terrain.
It also offers an opportunity to reflect on some of the key assumptions

MAPPING THE ILL-DISCIPLINED? · 107

around collaborative research, through its reorganization of academic spaces and sites of knowledge.

In the following case studies we examine how films circulate in specific ways, revealing how their itineraries and destinations are equally as significant as the content of a given cultural object. Our focus in this chapter is to demonstrate how different spatial methodologies can reveal the circulatory matrices of film exhibition. Following Jeffrey D. Himpele we use circulation, "as a frame to overcome the misleading bifurcation between political and corporate structural conditions, seen as production, and the cultural meanings within them, seen as consumption."[1] One of the real values of our collaborative study of postwar cinema lies in our exploration of the relationships between the cinemas themselves. In developing our collaboration, however, a series of ancillary questions has also arisen: How tractable is the research landscape of the humanities? How easily can we delineate its disciplinary configurations and confusions? In appropriating and adapting approaches from science-based disciplines, how can we continue to acknowledge and speak of the jumbled, the vexingly numerous, and the ill-disciplined?

Cinema data is characteristically highly complex, heterogeneous, and interlinked. Its use for research requires collaboration not just between previously unrelated disciplines (cinema studies, geospatial science, statistics, information management, computer science, to name a few) but also between career academics and non-academics (such as amateur researchers, curators, collectors, enthusiasts, industry bodies, and policymakers) and between different registers of academic practice (professors and postgraduates for example). Simply recognizing that film industries generate data with a temporal and a spatial element enables the building of connections that can reveal previously obscure influences and relationships. For cinema studies, for example, there is the question of the most appropriate geographical visualization (geovisualization) approaches for portraying and measuring the spatial arrangement of film circulation and cinema location. For geospatial research, on the other hand, there is the question of how we manage time within what is essentially a static technology, namely geographic information systems (GIS). The geographic analysis of micro-historical data, then, has implications for research across both fields.

But at a more fundamental level, these case studies demonstrate how resourceful research configurations built around solving specific problems result in new, contingent sites of knowledge production. In galvanizing teams made up of differently specialized researchers that are *problem*-oriented, rather than discipline- or program-specific, we are proposing a model for collaboration that is itself mindful of the temporalities of contemporary academic practice. In the words of Mario Biagioli, this model foregrounds "a new and distinct pattern of postdisciplinarity."[2] For Biagioli, modular research practices such as the ones we will outline constitute "neither a family of disciplines, nor a new bud or branch of the tree of knowledge. It is a problem specific collaboration that takes place within a limited temporal window and in places that may have little to do with standard departments and institutes.... What matters the most is to maximize the quality of one's skills and to expand their range so as to be able to move from one fruitful collaboration to the next."[3]

Specifically, this chapter will discuss two preliminary studies that link film histories to geospatial science in order to examine spatial influences in cinema history. We are not proposing these cases as exemplars for a newfound disciplinary rapport between the familiar binary distinction "humanities and sciences." Nor are we suggesting that there is an identity crisis underlying every instance in which the contemporary humanities encounter new methodologies. Instead we would like to see these time-specific collaborations as demonstrations of how shared problems can be the catalyst for creative partnerships between different researchers, each possibly motivated for entirely different reasons. These "tactical" problem-based teams do not propose or require institutional recognition to succeed. In fact they most often thrive in the interstitial cracks of research funding regimes or outside the provenance of ordinary departmental and disciplinary administration. They present a formidable challenge to the academy's laborious attempts to administer and streamline research output using commensuration strategies such as discrete "field of research" codes.

Both our case studies are concerned with the distribution and exhibition of films in Melbourne in the postwar period. The first of these builds on previous research into the Greek film circuit in Australia.[4] The second study draws upon a more comprehensive cinema database (Cinema and Audience Research Project—CAARP) to ascertain the key factors that

influenced the nature of cinema venues for the period following the introduction of television broadcasting in the mid-1950s in Melbourne.[5] Both
studies utilize the analytical tools provided by geographical information
systems (GIS) technology to reveal spatial patterns that emerged during
the periods of time covered by the research. The studies differ in terms
of personnel. The first study, which uses a statistical process referred to
as Markov chains to extract patterns of film movement, employed a specialist statistician to model the data. These patterns were then visualized
by a creative artist to facilitate the analysis. The second case study draws
on research undertaken by a postgraduate candidate and relies on prior
research by information management and computer science specialists.
Both case studies are excellent examples of how historical cinema data
can be expanded through the analysis of spatial arrangement and geography. And both reveal the value of problem-based research for articulating
focused collaborative opportunities.

CASE STUDY 1: MARKOV CHAIN ANALYSIS
OF GREEK FILM DIFFUSION IN AUSTRALIA

This study investigates whether or not spatial patterns of film movement
from one venue to the next existed for the diffusion of Greek cinema in
Australia between 1956 and 1963. A Greek "cinema circuit," or sequence of
venues, emerged in Australia in the postwar period, coinciding with significant Greek immigration into Australian cities and changes in both the
Australian and Greek film industries.[6] It has been anecdotally noted that
the patterns of movement of films within the Greek cinema circuit during
this period were determined by the provenance of the films, in particular
the identity of the production company.[7] We were led to believe that films
produced by rival Greek studios were distributed around Australia differently, suggesting the existence of sophisticated practices of market segmentation within the Greek diaspora. We wanted to test whether or not
this was the case and, if so, which patterns were statistically significant.
These patterns could then be examined by film researchers as a mecha-
nism for extracting information about the latent relationships between
Greek film producers and Australian venue operators, patterns that have
been, to date, largely noted as hearsay. The rationale for our study was
to demonstrate the role of geographic and statistical analysis in under-

standing cinema circuit behavior. For example, why did particular films show in particular cinemas first before moving to another? Did different cinema circuits exist for different film production companies and/or for different film genres? Do these spatial patterns also reveal social delineations? Which geospatial and/or statistical techniques might be gainfully used in micro-historical studies? And, beyond micro-historical studies, can we more broadly ask, how are divergence and discontinuity a factor in cinema history?

For the purposes of pattern extraction in this study we adopted a statistical process referred to as Markov chain analysis. Markov chains provide a powerful technique for analyzing time series events where an initial condition results in a number of alternative outcomes that can be predicted through a probability distribution. For example Xia, Zeephongsekul, and Arrowsmith have adopted Markov chains to show patterns of movements of tourists visiting Phillip Island in Victoria, where different attraction options on the island result in a range of alternative visiting patterns.[8] The graphic representation of film distribution as a Markov chain demonstrates spatial discontinuities (individual venues), the production of temporal divergence (emphasizing the passage of time between screenings), and the multiplicity of simultaneous events (emphasizing synchronous releases). Using Markov chains, we can see graphically how film diffusion (and film history) moves both forwards and sideways at once from a singular point of origin.[9]

We restricted our research period to the years between 1956 and 1963, and two particularly well-known and popular Greek film production companies, Finos Films and Anzervos Films. Between 1956 and 1963 alone some twenty-seven venues made up a thriving Greek cinema circuit throughout several Australian cities at a time when hundreds of thousands of Greeks migrated to Australia. These years are defining ones for the evolution of the Greek film circuit in Australia, as mass migration ensured steady customers and proclivity of film production in Greece ensured steady supply.[10] Reliable data for capital city screenings is available for this period from a single source, the Greek-language newspaper *NeosKosmos*. It was also during these years that the acquisition of newly abandoned cinemas began and major commercial alliances between rival distributors were developed within Australia and with Greek companies such as Finos and Anzervos. Finos Films was the largest and most successful film production company in postwar Greece, specializing in lavish musicals. Anzervos Films, established in direct competition with Finos, developed a reputation for the production of melodramas.

The specific objective of our research was to establish whether or not there existed distinct cinema circuits for these popular Greek film production companies. This would enable us to evaluate anecdotal assertions that exclusive agreements between venue operators in Australia and Greek film production companies influenced the specific configuration of Greek film diffusion in Australia. The implications of this analysis also propose the significance of social segmentation or ranking *within* marginal film distribution businesses (who got to see which films first), revealing film circuit behavior as having both spatial and social dimensions.[11] Earlier studies by Verhoeven and Arrowsmith have shown significant spatial correlation of Greek cinema venues to demographic concentration.[12] By interrogating collected data on Greek film diffusion in Australia and extracting statistically valid patterns of movement from one venue to the next, this study offers significantly more granularity in its correlation of spatial and temporal patterns.

For this project a research assistant collected data including film title, production company, date of screenings, and venue name and address, including city of venue. Data was sourced from archival newspaper and oral history research as well as from government records, including censorship documents, and theater license and company records. The data was then stored in a project spreadsheet developed by the research assistant. For valid Finos films, a total of eighteen cinema venues and twenty-nine different films were extracted and transferred to the GIS database. Anzervos provided twenty-four films shown within sixteen different venues. Venues were located via street address or actual GPS recorded locations where street address was not given. For the cinema venues, a letter was assigned from A through W (table 5.1). For each of the films numbered from 1 to 29 for Finos and 1 to 24 for Anzervos, patterns of cinema venues were derived from the dates of screenings. These sequences were then drawn in the form of a tree graph. Sections of these tree graphs are shown in figure 5.1.

For each of the film movements a probability was calculated by an expert statistician. Initial probabilities were calculated for the number of films that commenced at each of the venues (table 5.1 shows frequencies for Finos Films).

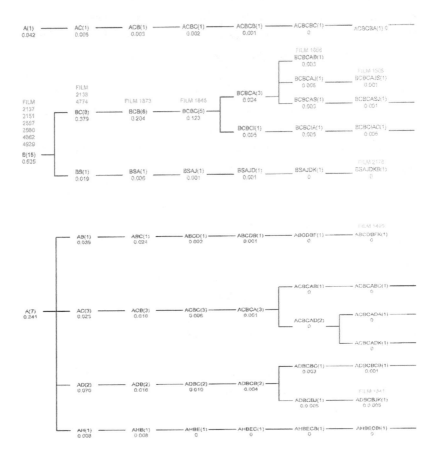

FIGURE 5.1.a and b

TABLE 5.1. Probabilities from Venue A to All Others for Finos Films

PATH	FREQUENCY	PROBABILITY
AB	5	0.161
AC	3	0.097
AD	9	0.290
AH	1	0.032
AI	2	0.064
AJ	7	0.226
AO	1	0.032
AW	1	0.032
AFinal	2	0.065
sum	31	1.000

TABLE 5.2. Primary and Secondary Key Markov Chains for Anzervos
and Finos Film Circuits for Venues in Melbourne and Sydney

NUMBER OF VENUES	ANZERVOS		FINOS	
	PRIMARY	SECONDARY	PRIMARY	SECONDARY
1	B	C	B	A
2	BC	CB	BC	AD
3	BCB	CBC	BCB	BCA
4	BCBC	CBCB	BCBC	BCBA

For subsequent movements of films between venues, conditional
probabilities were calculated from moving from one venue to the next
venue in the sequence. These probabilities were conditional based on an
initial venue being visited first. Patterns of probabilities were determined
for each successive movement and the probability of moving along an
entire chain (Markov chain) was then calculated. Key Markov chains
identified for each of the film producers are shown in table 5.2.

The key difference between pathway patterns for Anzervos and Finos films is in the number of cinemas that films were shown at, which is
generally greater for Finos (twenty-nine films screening at eighteen different venues) than for Anzervos (twenty-four films at sixteen venues).
The number of different venues at which films were permitted to launch
was also greater for Finos (eight) than for Anzervos (six). In addition,
there are many more bifurcations for the Finos trees, which indicates
that these films were more likely to screen at a greater number of cinemas
through the course of their release, while for Anzervos these movements
are generally more linear and do not persist throughout a circuit to the
same degree. Bifurcation also occurs much earlier in the circuit, indicating that more current films were shown more extensively throughout
the Greek cinema network and that the distributors of Finos Films had
working relationships with a greater number of film venues.

ANALYSIS

Approaching cinema history from a detailed problem-based approach
such as the one outlined above invariably reveals more complexity than
answers per se. We were motivated by our findings to ask more detailed
questions and to search beyond the data itself for further explanation.

And the emergent shortcomings of our application of Markov chain analysis to cinema data prompted us to adjust and reformulate our techniques as the research progressed. Nevertheless, working with data, and with specialist data researchers, is enormously valuable for cinema historians since it can sanction new readings, recommend new lines of inquiry, and present unfamiliar angles to our accustomed analytical maneuvers and perspectival complacencies.

Analysis of the Markov patterns shows that there was a strongly defined primary release circuit for both Finos and Anzervos films, made up of four venues (two in Melbourne and two in Sydney). This demonstrates that the Greek circuit conformed in principle with contemporary mainstream practices of film distribution in Australia at the time, in which venues were sequentially divided between "first-run" (venues A and B) and "move-over" or "second-run" (venues C and D) exhibition. The analysis clearly shows that only single prints of these films were released in Australia. By regularizing and maximizing first-run release in the separately operated Greek cinema chains of either Sydney (venues B and C) or Melbourne (venues A and D) before transferring between cities, the Australian distributors of these films were able to minimize their costs relative to box-office returns. The analysis also challenges aspects of the anecdotal record that propose an exclusive arrangement between Finos Films and Melbourne venue operators; eleven Finos films premiered in Melbourne (in four different venues) but sixteen opened in Sydney (at only two venues) and almost all titles were screened in both cities. The data suggests instead a higher level of commercial cooperation between Melbourne and Sydney venue operators than otherwise supposed. The Melbourne-based film importer Peter Yiannoudes of New World Entertainment has claimed that Finos Films granted his company exclusive rights to distribute their movies in Australia[13] but that from the end of 1958 he established a close working relationship with the Sydney-based exhibitor Chris Louis, whose advantage during this period is attributed to his use of permanent theaters (venues B and C, the Lawson and Doncaster cinemas) rather than "four-walled" occasional venues (such as the Melbourne venues A and D, the Melbourne Town Hall and Nicholas Hall).[14] Melbourne-based Greek film importers did not acquire a purpose-built cinema until early 1962 (Venue J, the National). The data also reveals a sharp distinction between diasporic community cinema circuits and foreign-language screenings at nearby art house cinemas (such as venue H, the Savoy). Celebrated Greek film auteur Mihalis Kakogiannis's *The Girl in Black* (*To Koritsi Me Ta Mavra*) screened at the Savoy some two and a half years before appearing on the Greek circuit and *Stella* moved over from the art house to popular circuits after almost a year. Only one film moved in the other direction: *To Telefteo Psema* (*A Matter of Dignity*) opened at the Melbourne Town Hall before moving quickly to the Savoy and then reappearing more than a month later in Sydney at the Lawson.

There are a number of limitations that have been noted with the research methodology so far. First, the small number of records used in the Markov chain determination has not enabled any model validation to take place. Ordinarily data would be randomly selected as "training data" to be used in determining the transition probabilities and "test data" to be used to validate the patterns using a simple statistical test, such as the chi-squared test, to compare the test data against the training data.[15] Second, the original advertisements used to source the database did not always specify exact screening times. This has affected the detail of our analysis because in the case of film titles screening at two venues on the same date, it is not possible to accurately determine which venue should be allocated the first position in the chain. Third, the assumption of "stationarity" was adopted whereby sequential movement probabilities were calculated under the assumption that the probability of moving from one venue to another was the same irrespective of where along the Markov chain it occurred. This is possibly not always the case; the likelihood of a particular one-step transition may diminish as we move further along the Markov chain such as would occur in the case of repertory screenings.

Finally, future research is required into the representation of temporal lag from one cinema to the next within an individual circuit. Despite absolute time being implicitly shown in figure 5.1, there is no consideration to the relative time differences ("windows") between these movements. For example, following the Markov chain sequence BCKC for film 16, we can infer that film 16 commenced its screening at venue B before moving onto C, K, and then back to C. But there is no indication in this figure of the time the film spent at venue B before moving to C, and whether or not there was any delay in that movement. The identification of "clearance periods" is particularly significant for determining the distinctiveness of different forms of a release (e.g., first or second run,

FIGURE 5.2

revival, or repertory) in the ordering of a film's movement between venues. It would also enable contextual analysis of film circuit behavior that accounts for the acquisition of new cinemas over time.

To address these concerns and the evident limitations of our previous attempts to represent film circuit movement, we undertook preliminary visualization of the temporal lag in Greek cinema Markov chain analysis using the visual metaphor of olive trees (in reference to the Greek nature of the data). Markov chains are sometimes referred to as "trees," which they resemble when tilted ninety degrees. In this visualization, the lengths of the tree's branches correspond to the length of interval between screenings at consecutive venues (see figures 5.2 and 5.3). The olives convey the city in which films finished (where light gray is a Sydney venue and dark gray a Melbourne venue). The leaf color indicates the location of screenings (pale gray is Queensland, light gray is New South Wales, darker gray is Victoria, dark gray is South Australia). The branch length is days between screenings and is drawn to scale. A bushy tree indicates a generative venue from which many films are launched into the circuit (see figure 5.3). A sparse tree with few branches and olives indicates a venue

FIGURE 5.3

lower in ranking that seldom launches films (see figure 5.2). In the case of Melbourne Town Hall (figures 5.2 and 5.3) we can immediately see that there was a privileged relationship between this venue and a particular type of film, namely high-budget films produced by Finos rather than the films of the rival studio Anzervos. In one glance, these images suggest that the Greek film circuit used deliberative strategies of segmentation, linking particular films to particular venues in order to create distinct market differentiation.

CASE STUDY 2: MAPPING THE MOVIES: SPATIAL ANALYSIS OF METROPOLITAN MELBOURNE CINEMA 1954–1970

Like the first case study, the second case study also demonstrates the value of spatial analysis, data mining, and visual representation in historical cinema studies research. This study investigates the changing nature of Melbourne cinema venues in a turbulent period for the industry. In particular, it examines the spatial arrangement of various changes to film venues, including seating capacity, screen numbers, management and ownership, and the primary purpose of venue as well as times and locations for the opening and closing of venues. And like the Greek cinema circuit exemplar, this case study combines spatial, historically temporal, and multivariable data to explore the geographic patterns of cinema operation and influence in the postwar period. This study developed research inquiries prepared by a PhD student, a cinema historian, and a geospatial scientist, and it relied on technical assistance from a GIS specialist.

The postwar years are usually characterized as a period of arbitrary or wholesale cinema decline. According to one influential Australian study, "What the trade found hardest to accept was that the closings were indiscriminate."[16] Using spatial analyses within GIS, we have been able to demonstrate through proximity analyses and clustering techniques how changes to the various facets of cinema venues have not been random, and we have been able to identify which variables might explain the survival of cinemas in particular locations.

Throughout the period of analysis there were more than 200 cinema venues in operation. There is a decrease in total cinema venue numbers from 181 in 1950 to 117 in 1970 (an overall decrease of around 35 percent in twenty years). This decrease, however, has not been uniform with respect to time. While only fourteen closures took place from 1950 to 1954, this increased to forty-eight closures from 1955 to 1959 and fifty-three in the period from 1960 to 1964. These figures challenge conventional historical accounts of cinema exhibition in this period, which claim that 33 percent of Melbourne venues had closed as early as 1959.[17] In addition, our geographic study has also shown that the occurrence of closures corresponds to a particular geographic pattern.

Figures 5.4a through 5.4h show a sequence of geographical distributions for cinema openings and closures for the twenty years between 1950 and 1970. For 1950 to 1954 openings can be seen extending outwards from the Melbourne central business district (CBD) in an easterly direction, extending in some cases up to and beyond fifty kilometers. These openings tend to follow urban growth during this period with new suburbs being developed up to twenty kilometers from the CBD along primary arterial roads.

During 1955–59 openings extend toward the newly developing western and northern suburbs. Linear patterns indicate location along key

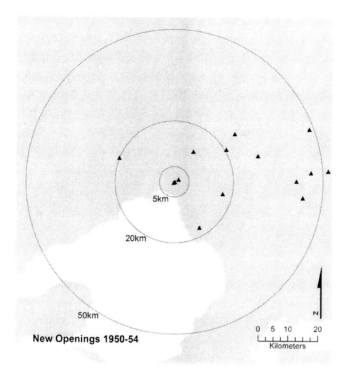

New Openings 1950-54

FIGURE 5.4 a

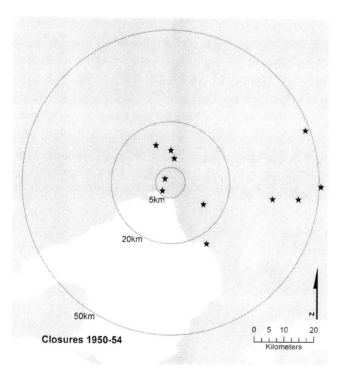

Closures 1950-54

FIGURE 5.4 b

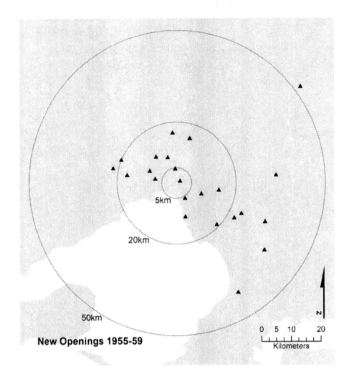

5km
20km
50km
New Openings 1955-59

0 5 10 20
Kilometers

N

FIGURE 5.4 C

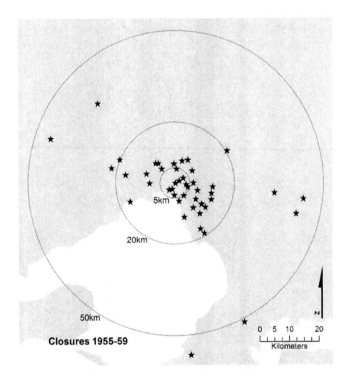

5km
20km
50km
Closures 1955-59

0 5 10 20
Kilometers

N

FIGURE 5.4 d

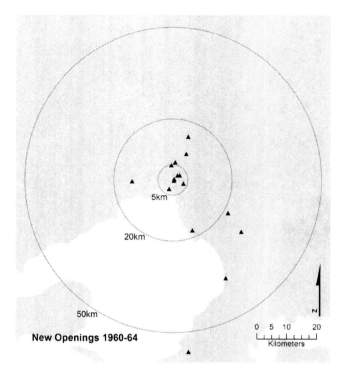

New Openings 1960-64

FIGURE 5.4 e

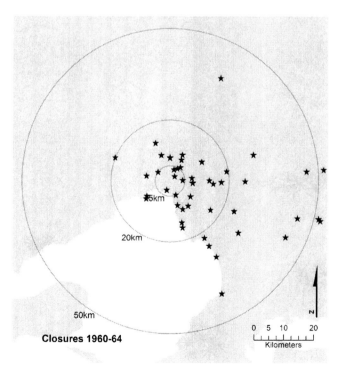

Closures 1960-64

FIGURE 5.4 f

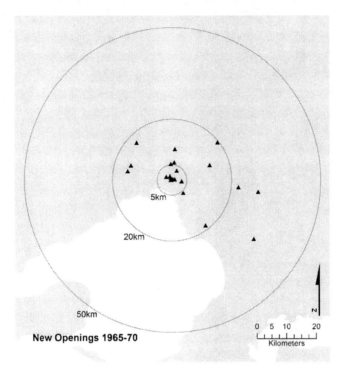

5km

20km

50km

New Openings 1965-70

0 5 10   20
Kilometers

N

FIGURE 5.4 g

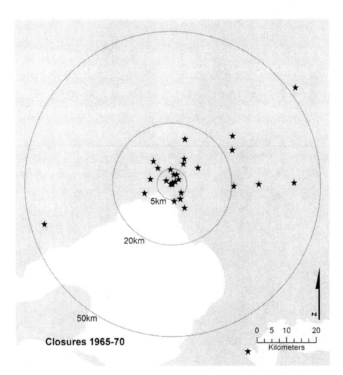

5km

20km

50km

Closures 1965-70

0 5 10   20
Kilometers

N

FIGURE 5.4 h

arterial roads. Closures are extensive but again are concentrated within twenty kilometers of the CBD toward the southeast. These patterns are replicated in 1960–64, with substantially fewer openings for this period but again concentrating along one arterial road passing through the northern suburbs of Melbourne. By 1965 to 1970 we see significantly fewer closures particularly in the southeast suburbs and comparatively greater numbers of openings throughout Melbourne.

ANALYSIS

Contextual analysis typically associates the increase in velocity of cinema closures with the introduction of television to Melbourne in November 1956. Commentators frequently and explicitly attribute the decline of cinema businesses to the arrival of television from the mid-1950s to the early 1960s.[18] Certainly, Melbournians were particularly enthusiastic early adopters of television. In 1956, 5 percent of households in Melbourne possessed a TV set compared to only 1 percent in Sydney.[19] According to cinema historian Diane Collins, by 1957 the number of set owners in Melbourne had risen to more than 25 percent, by 1959 to more than 50 percent, and in 1960 (only four years after the inaugural broadcast) to more than 70 percent.[20] For Collins, "in the end it was in the suburbs and in country towns that television had an almost fatal impact."[21] For cinema historian Trevor Walters, the connection between the introduction of TV and the closure of suburban cinemas is also obvious:

> Television took away the majority of suburban theatre pictures in only a few short years. Some fell instantly with the white flag waved immediately. Why bother fighting an unwinnable war was the cry from many a theatre owner out in the suburbs? Even then the cinema companies could not be jolted into any action that required spending money to modernise their theatres and make them a more attractive alternative to staying at home watching television. . . . Instead of planning for the future and redesigning their theatres, it was lock the front door and sell everything.[22]

For Walters, television is the catalyst for venue change, but some of the responsibility also lay with theater owners. And so there might be other explanations the data could also support. For example, specifically analyzing the evident survival of prestigious city-based venues *at the expense* of local, suburban theaters can provide further insight.

In the very early 1960s, as the pace of venue closures accelerated, the larger cinema chains initiated a policy of "splash" releasing (opening films in the city and at select suburban venues simultaneously), a practice that had a particularly deleterious effect on the independent suburban cinemas, which were restricted to screening films only at the conclusion of their city release. This practice ensured that unlike previous periods of significant cinema closure such as during the 1930s economic depression, city cinemas would be more durable than suburban and rural venues.

It is also possible that the various measures by which some businesses chose to bolster themselves *before* the arrival of TV had just as much impact as television itself. For Diane Collins, the sad passing of suburban cinemas was in part the result of competition between city and suburban venues and was already indicated by declining attendance at the cinema in the late 1940s and early 1950s:

> Television was in much more direct local competition with the local flicks than with those special occasions when people went to town to see a big first-release film. . . . On the way to this big night out families and dating couples passed the old neighbourhood cinema, its awning now advertising butcher shop specials. As there was nothing to take its place as a community facility—the venue of countless charity appeals and school speech days – passers-by momentarily regretted their defection. But as the doors of the Boomerangs, Odeons, Royals and Magnets closed, it seemed obvious that television had killed the cinema. The truth was that when television became monarch of the living room, the movies' reign had long since ended.[23]

In the early 1950s, cinemas experimented with new business practices that emphasized the prestige "event" of cinema attendance (such as showcase releasing) and that progressively drew audiences away from the suburbs into more luxurious city venues. Following the example of U.S. exhibitors, who were already grappling with the arrival of television, they also introduced new wide-screen exhibition formats designed to enlarge the cinema experience. This is especially apparent if we look at the data for seating capacity changes, which reveals that the balance of change was weighted in the *pre*-television years and was not a rejoinder to the introduction of television.

Years before the arrival of television, many cinema businesses began installing expensive wide-screen formats. Cinemascope arrived with fanfare in Melbourne in December 1953. Other formats came later.

Melbourne's first Cinerama screenings were post-television (December 1958), and within the year 70 mm had also arrived. These technologies usually required the removal of venue seating to accommodate the expanded screens and projection facilities necessitated by the new formats. For example, the Plaza cinema was reduced from 1,235 seats to 865 when it installed Cinerama. The Esquire went from 1,526 to 1,125 seats when it adopted 70 mm. But as Trevor Walters has noted, "By the time television started, Cinemascope films were old hat as far as audiences were concerned, and were no longer a novelty factor to entice patrons along."[24] Here Walters suggests that the pace of change in cinema technologies is more relevant to the introduction of television in the U.S. than locally and is mistimed in terms of its impact on the sustainability of local businesses.

In reading the seating capacity changes in relation to the venue closure data we can see that suburban venue operators frequently chose to close rather than undertake expensive renovation of their theaters. Taking into account the organization of cinemas into chains reveals that venues associated with the dominant Hoyts cinema chain are particularly unlikely to have survived from 1950 until 1970. Those Hoyts cinemas that continued were the ones that experienced some form of change to their operations, such as adding a screen and/or decreasing seat capacity. Greater Union cinemas, on the other hand, changed more readily and experienced, on average, a longer life span than Hoyts venues.[25]

What is also revealed in the data and underanalyzed in accounts of cinema operation in this period is the occurrence of cinema openings. Openings in some suburban areas can be attributed to the construction of drive-ins. As drive-ins required about 5.5 hectares, they are not located in cities and inner suburban areas. The first Australian drive-in opened in the east Melbourne suburb of Burwood in February 1954 (again, prior to the introduction of television in Melbourne). Construction of drive-ins also appears to have had a negative impact on other suburban cinema venues. For George Ivanoff, the widespread construction of drive-ins through the suburbs (in 1968 there were twenty within the Melbourne metropolitan region) was especially influential on hard-top cinema decline: "The introduction of the drive-in into Australia, two years prior to the coming of television in 1956, had an adverse effect on conventional cinema attendance."[26]

The proliferation of drive-ins and the changes they wrought on the film industry are also indicative of other events, such the rise of car ownership. As noted by Ivanoff, transportation was also a major issue in the location of cinemas during this period.[27] Between 1947 and 1954 Melbourne's motor registrations trebled. In its ready embrace of car culture, Melbourne also became an automotive manufacturing center. In 1948 Australia's first locally made car was produced at Fisherman's Bend (to the immediate south of the Melbourne central business district), with a succession of new factories opening in the suburbs of Dandenong (southeast of Melbourne) (1956), Lang Lang (toward Gippsland approximately seventy-five kilometers southeast of Melbourne) (1957), Broadmeadows (north of Melbourne) (1956), and Westall (to Melbourne's southeast) (1959). In 1950 the government abolished gasoline rationing. Increases in car ownership meant the proximity of a cinema to a major road was just as important as its proximity to demographic concentrations. Major thoroughfares such as Whitehorse Road (to Melbourne's east) and the Nepean Highway (to Melbourne's southeast) featured multiple cinema openings during this period.

In addition, the introduction of the forty-hour week in 1948 prompted widespread diversification and dispersal of the locations in which Melbournians spent their spare time including new suburban commercial centers, race courses, suburban swimming pools (inspired by the 1956 Melbourne Olympics), bowling alleys, and even bingo halls.[28] Also important was the development of road-based tourism destinations. Between 1957 and 1963, the number of regional motels in the Melbourne hinterland grew from 7 to 122.[29] All this additional contextual information strongly suggests that further detailed study of the impact of rival attractions in relation to the road network (particularly major arterial thoroughfares) and their impact on the location of cinema closures is warranted.

CONCLUSIONS

Recent years have seen the widespread application of spatial analyses to non-traditional fields of study. These "new geographies," sometimes described as the "spatial turn," have resulted in collaboration between researchers from disparate disciplines.[30] In this chapter we have presented two case studies derived from a cross-disciplinary research project based around the use of different techniques for understanding spatial patterns in the postwar Australian film industry. In the first study we applied Markov chain analysis to the Australian distribution of films produced by two different Greek film companies, Finos Films and Anzervos Films. In undertaking further research using this approach we intend to expand our data set and explore the effect of time lag on these movements. In the second study we used an existing information database (CAARP) and linked cinema-specific data to location in an effort to ascertain spatial patterns within the extensive industrial changes that occurred in the postwar period. The preliminary outcomes of this study suggest that by analyzing venue attributes in various combinations we can produce a more accurate picture of change in a notoriously volatile era for film industry businesses. While Case Study 1 concentrated on the analysis of film movement from one venue to another, it highlighted the temporal and sequential nature of this movement within a cinema circuit. Case Study 2 concentrated on the geographic distribution of cinema operations (including opening and closing and seat capacity) in Melbourne throughout the 1950–1970 period and highlighted an increasing spatial concentration of closures in the period.

Both studies reveal the geographical significance of historical events and demonstrate the manifold benefits of a cross-disciplinary approach, pointing to the collaborative opportunities afforded by focused attention on specific research problems. In practice, they revealed some immediate challenges for our research, particularly around the availability (and therefore attendant cost), quality, and scale of data required for these small, intensive research inquiries. They are also suggestive of future challenges for establishing cross-disciplinary inclination in research. This is particularly so for the ways we currently organize research training in the humanities both at undergraduate levels (which is invariably discipline-specific) and at postgraduate levels (where it is obdurately oriented to monolithic, singular outcomes rather than a multitude of short-term tactical achievements). Finally, the evident expansion of methodological possibility that results from the introduction of data analysis in humanities research also suggests broader questions. For example, to what extent is the humanities' inclination for finding further complexity rather than definitive answers an opportunity or an insurmountable challenge for other disciplines? Is the convention of serendipitous discovery in the humanities necessarily at odds with research practices that rely on procedures of logic, consistent application, and measured behavior? As the *Guiyang Gazetteer* quoted at the outset observes, to speak adequately to these questions will take nothing less than a sequence of chapters (and a pile of documentation).

ACKNOWLEDGMENTS

The authors would like to acknowledge the indispensible research efforts of Alwyn Davidson (including the visualizations of cinema openings and closings), Michelle Mantsio (especially for the Markov chain olive tree visualizations), Surag Kulkarni, Jenny Anderson, and Olympia Szilagyi. We would also like to thank Panlop Zeephongsekul for his generous help with statistical modeling and Ronan Buick for his technical assistance. Any errors remain our own.

NOTES

The epigraph is from *Guiyang Prefectural Gazetteer* (1850), cited in Mark Elvin, *The Retreat of the Elephants: An Environmental History of China* (New Haven, Conn.: Yale University Press, 2004), 236.

1. J. D. Himpele, Circuits of Culture: Media, Politics and Indigenous Identity in the Andes (Minneapolis: University of Minnesota Press, 2008), 13.

2. M. Biagioli, "Postdisciplinary Liaisons: Science Studies and the Humanities," *Critical Inquiry* 35(4) (2009): 821.

3. Ibid.

4. D. Verhoeven, "Twice Born: Dionysos Films and the Establishment of a Greek Film Circuit in Australia," *Studies in Australasian Cinema* 1(3) (2007): 275–98.

5. D. Verhoeven et al., Cinema and Audiences Research Project (CAARP) database, http://caarp.flinders.edu.au.

6. D. Verhoeven, "Twice Born."

7. D. Verhoeven, K. Bowles, and C. Arrowsmith, "Mapping the Movies: Reflections on the Use of Geospatial Technologies for Historical Cinema Audience Research," in *Digital Tools in Film Studies* (Bielefeld: Transcript Verlag, 2009), 1–13.

8. J. Xia, P. Zeephongsekul, and C. Arrowsmith, "Modeling Spatio-temporal Movement of Tourists Using Finite Markov Chains," *Mathematics and Computers in Simulation* 79(5) (2009): 1544–53.

9. F. Moretti, *Graphs, Maps, Trees: Abstract Models for Literary History* (London: Verso, 2007).

10. P. Yiannoudes, *Greek Cinema across Australia* (Melbourne: Peter Yiannoudes, 2010), 107.

11. D. Verhoeven, "Film Distribution in the Diaspora: Temporality, Community and National Cinema," in *Explorations in New Cinema History: Approaches and Case*

Studies, ed. R. Maltby, D. Biltereyst, and P. Meers, 243–60 (Malden: Wiley-Blackwell, 2011).

12. C. Arrowsmith, D. Verhoeven, S. Kulkarniand, A. Davidson, "A Geographical Analysis of Greek Cinema Circuits," unpublished conference paper presented at the 24th Biennial Conference of the Film and History Association of Australia and New Zealand "Remapping cinema, remaking history," University of Otago, Dunedin, November 27–30, 2008. See also Verhoeven, Bowles and Arrowsmith, "Mapping the Movies" 76–78.

13. Yiannoudes, *Greek Cinema across Australia,* 22, 30, 49.

14. Ibid., 44, 78.

15. Xia, Zeephongsekul, and Arrowsmith, "Modeling Spatio-temporal Movement of Tourists Using Finite Markov Chains."

16. D. Collins, *Hollywood Down Under: Australians at the Movies. 1896 to the Present Day* (Sydney: Angus & Robertson, 1987), 229.

17. Ibid.

18. D. Catrice, "Cinemas," in *The Encyclopedia of Melbourne,* ed. A. Brown-May and S. Swain, 135 (Port Melbourne: Cambridge University Press, 2005); Collins, *Hollywood Down Under.*

19. Heritage Victoria, *Survey of Post-war Built Heritage in Victoria: Stage One, vol. 1: Contextual Overview, Methodology, Lists and Appendices* (Melbourne: Heritage Victoria, 2008), 15, http://www.dpcd.vic.gov.au/__data/assets/pdf_file/0016/47203/Post_War_Study_volume_1.pdf.

20. Collins, *Hollywood Down Under,* 225.

21. Ibid., 231.

22. T. Walters, *The Picture Palaces of Melbourne* (Melbourne: Walters, 2009), 244.

23. Collins, *Hollywood Down Under,* 232.

24. Walters, *The Picture Palaces of Melbourne,* 129.

25. See also A. Davidson, C. Arrowsmith, and D. Verhoeven, "A Method for the Visual Representation of Historic Multivariate Point Data," *Advances in Cartography And Giscience. Volume 2, Lecture Notes in Geoinformation and Cartography* 6(2) (2011): 163–78.

26. G. Ivanoff, "Victoria's Suburban Cinemas," *Victorian Historical Journal* 6(2) (1995): 156.

27. Ibid., 150.

28. "Bingo Blamed for Cinema Closing," *The Australasian Cinema,* September 23, 1977.

29. Heritage Victoria, *Survey of Post-war Built Heritage in Victoria: Stage One,* 30.

30. B. Warf and S. Arias, *The Spatial Turn: Interdisciplinary Perspectives* (London: Routledge, 2009).

SIX

Mapping Film Audiences in Multicultural Canada: Examples from the Cybercartographic Atlas of Canadian Cinema

SÉBASTIEN CAQUARD, DANIEL NAUD, AND BENJAMIN WRIGHT

INTRODUCTION

Canadian cinema has historically been framed, much like Canadian society, by the tensions between French and English culture as well as by the large influence of its imposing neighbor to the south: the United States of America. This double influence is perfectly illustrated by the film *Bon Cop Bad Cop* (dir. Erik Canuel, 2006). This "buddy action comedy" set on the border of English-speaking Ontario and Francophone Quebec plays with Canadian bicultural stereotypes while simultaneously catering to the more populist Hollywood genre sensibilities of the mass-market Canadian audience. With a gross of $12.6 million from Canadian box offices, *Bon Cop* is the most financially successful Canadian film of all time.

Although Canadian cinema and society have often been shaped by cultural tensions between Francophones and Anglophones, new cinematographic voices have emerged from other communities, which is characteristic of a new postnational and multicultural Canadian society.[1] Film directors such as Zacharia Kunuk, Atom Egoyan, and Mina Shum express these voices and bring to the screen alternative perspectives on Canadian identity. In *Atanarjuat* (2001), Inuit film director Zacharia Kunuk offers unique insights into Inuit culture, history, and territory. With *Ararat* (2002), Armenian Canadian director Atom Egoyan tells the story of a young Canadian of Armenian descent who lives in Toronto and struggles to find his place in a cultural history deeply marked by the Armenian genocide of 1915. Finally, in her film *Long Life, Happiness*

& *Prosperity* (2002), Chinese Canadian director Mina Shum portrays the everyday life of a twelve-year-old girl and her single mother living in the Chinese community of Vancouver, British Columbia. With stories unfolding in different Canadian communities, these films characterize the emergence of new forms of expression that ultimately expand the cinematographic geography of Canadian cinema beyond the historical limits of Francophone and Anglophone duality.

Drawing from Benedict Anderson's imaginary community, Shohat and Stam include cinema as a national identity vector.[2] As with other forms of mass media, the collective dimension of moviegoing and contributes to the belonging in a community. This collective consciousness ultimately allows approval or disapproval of values or behaviors. Although the mere existence of these aforementioned films is an indication of the emergence of a postnational Canadian identity, it is not enough to really understand how these voices shape this new identity. We need to find out how this ethnic plurality actually breaks the strong relationship between territory and national identity. If we only associate a national cinema with its production system, then we neglect how those films are consumed and understood by local audiences.[3] If we agree with Higson that cinema contributes to the production of a national identity, then it has to be consumed by the citizens in order to fully contribute to its production.[4] However, as Northrop Frye once stated, the production of Canadian identity is "less perplexed by the question 'Who am I?' than by some such riddle as 'Where is here?'"[5] Consequently, in this Canadian context, it then seems essential to link identity production processes and geography. In this chapter we therefore propose to map the geography of the audiences of these contemporary Canadian films in order to better understand how cinematographic territories and audiences overlap and how films associated with places and communities can reach diverse audiences and contribute to the development of a collective multicultural identity.

This chapter begins with the presentation and contextualization of the four selected films within the framework of contemporary Canada. This contextualization is followed by the cartography of the audiences of each of these films. This cartography has been developed in the context of the Cybercartographic Atlas of Canadian Cinema as discussed in the second section. The third section introduces a methodology developed to assess the sociodemographic profiles of these audiences, as well as a geovisualization tool (and some statistical analysis) designed to compare these sociodemographic profiles with the revenues of each film. The results are finally discussed in the context of Canadian multicultural and postnational identity.

CONTEXTUALIZATION OF THE
FOUR SELECTED MOVIES

The opposition between French- and English-language films is one of the major historical components of Canadian cinema, reflecting a similar tension in Canadian society.[6] This opposition is at the center of the film *Bon Cop Bad Cop.* When a body is found hanging on the border sign of English-speaking Ontario and French-speaking Quebec, Ontario Provincial Police constable Michael Ward (Colm Feore) and Sûreté du Québec detective David Bouchard (Patrick Huard) must overcome cultural and linguistic differences in order to solve the murder. Although *Bon Cop Bad Cop* is often referred to as the most financially successful Canadian film of all time, this national success must be mitigated by the difference in revenues between the Francophone province of Québec ($11.3 million in a population of eight million) and the rest of Canada (only $1.3 million in a population of twenty-six million). This disparity illustrates the discrepancy between English Canadian and French Canadian film production and exhibition. While French theaters see a 10 to 20 percent market share of domestic box office attendance (depending on the year), English cinemas see only a 1 to 4 percent share. The struggle for audience attendance facing Canadian cinema is really the struggle of English Canadian cinema.

The producer and writer of *Bon Cop,* Kevin Tierney, states that there are fundamental differences between English and French Canadian cinemas:

> The Canadian [English] film scene cannot get to where Quebec is already. ... It is not physically, spiritually, culturally, historically, or geographically possible. If Quebec shared a border with France, we could compare Canada and Quebec. We don't. What we have here in Quebec is fantastic, but it is utterly unique—for once a pleasant aberration in cultural terms.[7]

In essence, *Bon Cop Bad Cop* stands as a testament to the historical debates between English and French Canadian cinema and society.

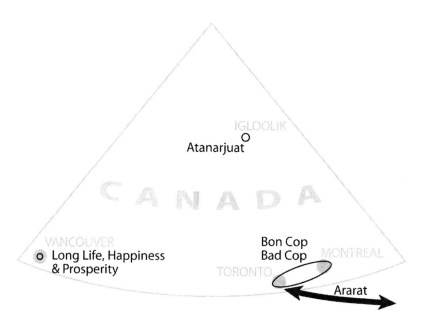

FIGURE 6.1. Localization and spatial extent of the cinematographic territories of the four selected films (in dark).

Although discourse about national identity in Canada has been traditionally focused on the complex relationships between Francophone and Anglophone cultures, it has recently been displaced by multiculturalism. In July 1988, Canada became the first nation to pass legislation to reaffirm multiculturalism as a fundamental national value. The Multiculturalism Act (Bill C-93) was the culmination of a series of laws meant to increase awareness of Canada's ethnic diversity as well as eliminate cultural discrimination and pressure to assimilate. The recognition of this diversity has been associated with the emergence of new cinematographic voices and discourses as illustrated by the following three films.

Based on a tale told to Zacharias Kunuk by his mother, *Atanarjuat* is a feature-length Inuit community effort of self-determined storytelling. Constructed as an exciting thriller that takes place in ancient Igloolik, in Northern Canada (see figure 6.1), *Atanarjuat* gives "a more authentic view of Inuit culture and oral tradition than ever before, from the inside and through Inuit eyes."[8] Contrary to previous films showcasing Canada's Inuit culture from an outsider colonial perspective—such as *Nanook of the North* (dir. Robert Flaherty, 1922)—*Atanarjuat* is the "first feature-length fiction film written, produced, directed, and acted by Inuit."[9]

Atanarjuat's close attention to Inuit storytelling and narration highlight Kunuk's sociopolitical motivation and goal of self-representation. Kunuk has said that when his family spent winters at Kapuivik, storytelling provided one way of reconnecting with his ancestors who had inhabited the Canadian Arctic for generations. According to Huhndorf, Kunuk's adherence to the modes of Inuit storytelling resists the assimilationist influence of Western media by emphasizing the continued importance and relevance of ancient tradition.[10] Indeed, the cultural impact of *Atanarjuat* transcends the historical bipolarity, as neatly captured by Monika Siebert:

> Kunuk's film delivers multicultural Canada to Canadians precisely when it offers to the Inuit the story of their origins and of their modernity in Inuktitut rather than in English (or French).[11]

As emphasized by Atom Egoyan—one of Canada's premier English-language filmmakers—in 2006, the multicultural reality of Canadian society is reflected in its cinematographic productions and aims to reassess not only the historical duality between Anglophones and Francophones, but the tripartite schema, Anglophone /Francophone /Aboriginal,[12] to take into account the emergence of multiculturalism and of its multiple forms of expression, as illustrated by the two following films.

First we will look at *Ararat,* by Atom Egoyan, which focuses on the notions of exile and the trauma of his own Armenian heritage. *Ararat* unfolds in Toronto, Armenia, and Turkey, as well as between past and present in a complex spatiotemporal structure characteristic of Egoyan's previous work. As Egoyan has stated, *Ararat* is less about the fact of the genocide than "about living with the effects of the denial of the event into the present";[13] *Ararat* not only addresses the complicated nature of exile and trauma, but is also deeply geographic since it deals with issues around "home, homeland, spatial displacement, borders and geographic restriction,"[14] as well as about transnationality and contemporary Canada. According to Tom McSorely, *Ararat*

> is as much about Canada now as it is about the Armenian genocide . . . concerned with the processes by which such gnarled matters as identity, history and ethnicity are negotiated. It also explores the specific cultural context within which these negotiations occur: Canada.[15]

Finally, Mina Shum offers another perspective on multicultural Canadian society with her film *Long Life, Happiness & Prosperity*. While Mina Shum is known primarily for her first feature, *Double Happiness* (1994), *Long Life* continues her reflections on Canadian Chinese culture in Vancouver. Although Mina Shum describes *Long Life* as "a love letter to Vancouver," the film's cultural ambience could allude to any North American Chinatown.[16] Within the canon of Canadian filmmaking, the work of Mina Shum is important as it gives light to the experiences of the Chinese Canadian communities in Canada. Shum's choice of subject, a minority group of which she herself is a member, is evidence of a shift in Canadian perspective toward celebrating its cultural diversity.

These four examples illustrate how Canadian cinema has embraced the multiple hyphenated identities that constitute contemporary Canadian society and culture. Although such a small selection cannot pretend to accurately capture the diversity of Canadian identities, it certainly captures some of its main characteristics, such as (1) the recurrent tensions between Francophone and Anglophone; (2) the recent emergence of voices from minorities such as Aboriginal groups and the Chinese community; and (3) the transnational roots of this emerging multicultural society. These films also reflect the idea that Canadian filmmakers are currently "engaged in the search for this newly forming, constantly shifting 'Canadianness' in an open-ended set of narrative possibilities and cinematic expression."[17] These narratives and cinematic expressions propose novel avenues to a conflicted nation that was thought of as monolithic for a large part of its cinematographic history.[18] These narratives define the scope in which the nation's people can address their contemporary problems. We now turn to look at the audiences of these four films to see how these films have not only captured this Canadianness, but also contributed to its production.

MAPPING AUDIENCES

From a cartographic perspective, mapping film audiences involves a multistep process: defining what an audience is, collecting the relevant data, structuring the database, and representing the data in an accurate manner. In this project we have restricted the notion of an "audience" to movie theater audiences in order for the data collection to be manageable. Although movie theaters are no longer the only venues for film viewing (e.g., in Canada, revenues from movie theaters represent only 13 percent of the overall revenues of a given film[19]), they remain at the center of the cinematographic consumption process[20] and represent a key indicator of the overall success of a film. Furthermore, with time, patience, and determination, revenue figures for films in movie theaters can be made available for study. Alliance Atlantis, the distributor of the four selected films in Canada, was willing to provide us with the revenues per day and per movie theater for each of these films.

Mapping revenues was then a question of formatting and linking the data to movie theaters. This last step was slightly more complex than originally imagined. Indeed, there were no comprehensive geographic databases of movie theaters across Canada available, so we had to develop one.[21] Compiling such a geographic database (about seven hundred movie theaters across Canada) was more challenging than expected given the fragmentary nature of existing data.[22] After a long process of gathering and formatting data, we produced a geographic database of the movie theaters in Canada. This database was then linked to the revenues of each film provided by Alliance Atlantis, and the results were mapped within the Cybercartographic Atlas of Canadian Cinema.

The Cybercartographic Atlas of Canadian Cinema is part of a larger project that was developed at Carleton University (Ottawa) on Cybercartography.[23] This project aimed to explore the changing nature of maps under the influence of technology and society. The outcomes of this project were both conceptual and technical, including the development of open source software called Nunallit, designed to create cybercartographic atlases, such as the Cybercartographic Atlas of Canadian Cinema.[24]

To visually explore the weekly revenues of each film in Canadian movie theaters, an interactive map was designed within the framework of the atlas (see figure 6.2). This map made visible some general trends. Some of them were expected, such as the overall decrease of revenues over time, the higher revenues in major Canadian cities such as Toronto and Montréal, and the higher revenues in the more populated provinces of Ontario and Quebec. Beyond these general trends, some particularities started to emerge. For instance, *Bon Cop Bad Cop*, which takes place between Montréal and Toronto, was much more successful in the area between these two cities (and mostly in the province of Québec) than in the rest of Canada. The success of *Atanarjuat* was lower overall in

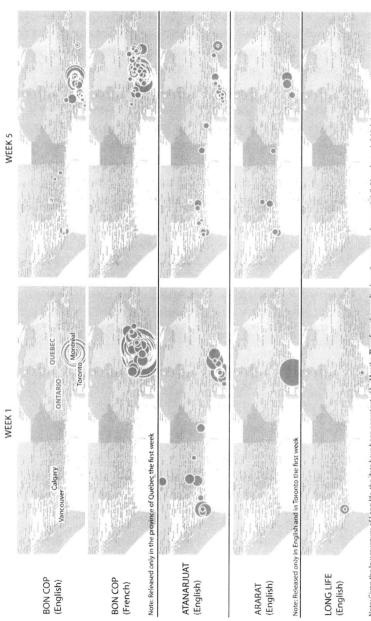

WEEK 1 · WEEK 5

BON COP (English)

BON COP (French)

Note: Released only in the province of Quebec the first week

ATANARJUAT (English)

ARARAT (English)

Note: Released only in English and in Toronto the first week

LONG LIFE (English)

QUEBEC
Montréal
ONTARIO
Toronto
Vancouver Calgary

Note: Given the low revenues of Long life, the data have been aggregated by Months. Therefore, the results show the revenues for month 1 (left) and month 5 (right)

FIGURE 6.2. Screen shots comparing the revenues of each film between week 1 and week 5. Each circle represents a movie theater and the size of the circle represents the revenue of a given film for a given week. The original online interactive map is available at www.atlascine.org.

terms of revenue, but spatially much more balanced across the country. Furthermore, over time the revenues from *Atanarjuat* decreased slower (in relative terms) than those of *Bon Cop Bad Cop*. *Atanarjuat* had a more balanced spatiotemporal presence on screens across Canada. *Ararat* appeared slightly different, with high revenues in Toronto during the first weeks (it was only released in Toronto during the first week), and only a slight presence in a few venues across Canada, mainly in Toronto and Montréal. Finally, *Long Life, Happiness & Prosperity,* which was the only film in the survey that takes place on the west coast (i.e., Vancouver), was also the only film that saw greater success in this part of the country. These initial results emphasize some levels of spatial overlapping between cinematographic territories and audiences that we wanted to further explore.

MAPPING SOCIODEMOGRAPHIC PROFILES OF AUDIENCES

METHODOLOGY

To further explore the overlapping boundaries between cinematographic territories and audiences, another criterion was taken into consideration: the sociodemographic profile of these audiences. The problem is that sociodemographic profiles of past audiences are impossible to define precisely for all theaters across Canada; they can only be assessed. In the Canadian context it has been demonstrated that there is a strong relationship between the revenues of a movie theater and the density of population living nearby.[25] Venkataraman and Chintagunta have gone further by arguing that the sociodemographic profile of an American population living near a movie theater is the main criterion defining the overall revenues of a movie theater.[26] In other words, there is a direct relationship between those who live near a movie theater and who is going to that movie theater. If we can define the sociodemographic profile of the population living near a movie theater, then we can assess the overall profile of its audience.

According to an econometric study led by Davis in the United States, a distance of five miles is the threshold above which the attraction of a movie theater decreases quickly.[27] The problem with this Euclidean distance is that it does not take into account the time required to access a movie theater. A neighborhood could be less than a mile away from a movie theater, but on the other bank of a river without a bridge nearby. Distance-time provides a much more relevant metric since it takes into account the transportation time required to reach a destination. In order to define a proper distance-time that characterizes the accessibility of a movie theater we have done different analyses and surveys.[28]

Based on the results, we have defined that in optimal conditions, a five-minute car ride would be appropriate to determine the service area of each movie theater in Canada. This optimal time-distance does not take into account time constraints such as red lights, traffic jams, poor weather, and time to park the car. Therefore, the five-minute time-distance corresponds more likely to a fifteen- to thirty-minute travel time in real-life conditions. This threshold has been applied to calculate the area served by each movie theater across Canada using the Canadian road network (DMTI Spatial Inc. 2001) and the Network Analyst extension of ArcGIS (ESRI 2001). Each movie theater was then associated with an area from which the large majority of its audience was coming.

The sociodemographic profiles of these service areas were then defined using an "areal" interpolation, which is the process of transferring known data from one set of polygons (e.g., census data from Statistics Canada) to another set of polygons (e.g., services areas defined previously), based on the proportion of the overlap between these two layers. For instance, if the service area of a given movie theater covers 40 percent of a census tract in which the total population is one thousand people, it is estimated that the population of the service area will be four hundred people. This principle was applied systematically to all service areas across Canada using ArcGIS. This process can be seen as a simple way to transfer the original sociodemographic data from one set of geographic features (i.e., census tracts) to another one (i.e., previously defined service areas). Although the outcome remains an estimate, it provides a good sense of the characteristics of the population living near each movie theater (e.g., average income, age, origins, language). It was then possible to compare the revenues of each of the four films in each movie theater across Canada with the sociodemographic profile of the area served by each movie theater. This was first done visually using a specific geovisualization tool called "graphomap."

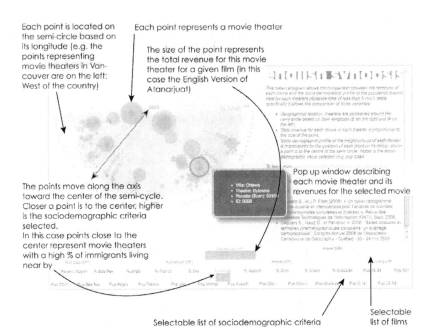

Each point is located on the semi-circle based on its longitude (e.g. the points representing movie theaters in Vancouver are on the left: West of the country)

Each point represents a movie theater

The size of the point represents the total revenue for this movie theater for a given film (in this case the English Version of Atanarjuat)

Pop up window describing each movie theater and its revenues for the selected movie

The points move along the axis toward the center of the semi-cycle. Closer a point is to the center, higher is the sociodemographic criteria selected.
In this case points close to the center represent movie theaters with a high % of immigrants living near by

Selectable list of sociodemographic criteria

Selectable list of films

FIGURE 6.3. Screen capture of the graphomap showing the relationship between revenues of *Atanarjuat* (English version) for each movie theater across Canada and the percentage of immigrants living in the area served by each movie theater.

GRAPHOMAP

"Graphomap" is a hybrid form of visualization between a graph and a map. It has been developed previously in the context of the Cybercartographic Atlas of Canadian Trade with the World.[29] This graphomap reduces the geographic space into one dimension (e.g., longitude) instead of two (i.e., latitude and longitude): it is a one-dimensional spatial representation on which movie theaters across Canada are organized based on their longitude (east/west). The second spatial dimension that has been removed can then be replaced to represent other information. This approach allows mapping of two variables simultaneously: for instance, the overall revenues of a given movie in a given movie theater (size of the point), and the sociodemographic profile of the area served by this movie theater (position of each point on the radius of the circle) (see figure 6.3). Although with this type of representation we lose some spatial information about

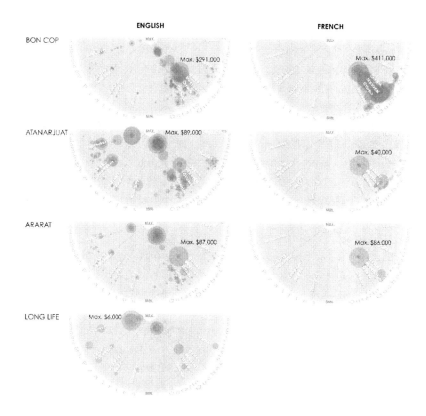

FIGURE 6.4. Comparing the revenues for the selected films in every theater across Canada (size of the circles) with the percentage of immigrants living near the theaters. Larger points reflect higher revenues for the selected film in a particular theater; the closer the point is to the center of the semicircle, the higher is the percentage of immigrants living near the theater. In other words, if bigger points tend to be closer to the center and smaller points to the outskirts (e.g., English version of *Atanarjuat*), the film was proportionally more successful in movie theaters located in neighborhoods with a high percentage of immigrants, and vice versa.

how far north each theater is located, this flaw has been considered minor given that most of the movie theaters are concentrated in the southern-most part of the country.

The visual exploration of the data along with the graphomap confirms the general overlap described previously between cinematographic territories and audiences. *Bon Cop Bad Cop* was clearly much more successful in the eastern part of the country and much less successful in the rest of Canada. *Ararat* was successful only in a few movie theaters across the country, mainly in Toronto and Montréal, while the success of *Atanarjuat* was much more consistent across Canada. Laying these data on the graphomap reveals some other relationships between revenues and sociodemographic profiles.

A major correlation appears between the revenues of *Atanarjuat* and the percentage of immigrants living near movie theaters. This correlation is illustrated by the fact that the bigger points (i.e., higher revenues) are closer to the center of the semicircle (i.e., higher percentage of immigrants) and the small points are on its outskirt (see figure 6.4). A similar correlation between revenues and percentage of immigrants can also be noticed for *Ararat* and *Long Life,* but certainly not for *Bon Cop Bad Cop.* From this perspective, there is a clear distinction between *Bon Cop* and the three other films. With regards to *Bon Cop,* one trend that emerges is the success of the English version of the film in areas with a low percentage of English-only speakers. This reflects the lack of interest in the film in the western part of the country, where the rates of English-only speakers are higher. Another interesting link that emerged from this visualization is the relationship between *Long Life, Happiness & Prosperity* and the Chinese population: The higher the percentage of Chinese population in a theater's area, the higher the revenue seems to be for the film. These relationships (as well as others) were further explored through a more conventional statistical analysis using the Pearson correlation coefficient (r).

STATISTICAL ANALYSIS AND DISCUSSION

Pearson's r ranges from (–)1 to 1. The closer the coefficient is to 1 or (–)1, the stronger the correlation between factors (a negative coefficient means a negative correlation). In social sciences, a coefficient superior or equal to 0.500 is often considered representative of a strong correlation,[30] while 0.300 and 0.100 will show moderate and weak correlations, respectively. The retained correlations should be at least significant at the 0.05 level, which corresponds to the accuracy of the measure that can be interpreted as follows: there is a 5 percent maximum probability that the observed correlation is caused by a random effect. Another way to interpret the Pearson's r is to square it to obtain the coefficient of determination (r^2). An r value of 0.483 gives an r^2 of 0.23, which is a measure of the association

Coefficient of determination (r2) between sociodemographic characteristics (per capita, 2001) and revenues

	n	English	French	Both	None	Can_citizen	Immig	China	Visible	NA_Ind	Unemp	Univ	Low_inc
Ararat English	95	-1%	0%	5%	10%	-14%	13%	4%	12%	-2%	0%	10%	14%
Ararat French	24	8%	-12%	11%	23%	-24%	19%	22%	19%	-2%	-1%	20%	16%
Ararat total	119	-1%	0%	5%	10%	-14%	13%	4%	12%	-2%	0%	10%	14%
Atanarjuat English	162	-3%	5%	1%	17%	-10%	20%	14%	19%	-1%	0%	15%	10%
Atanarjuat French	32	2%	-9%	11%	19%	-4%	17%	20%	17%	-1%	0%	25%	17%
Atanarjuat total	194	0%	-1%	0%	18%	-10%	20%	15%	20%	-1%	0%	16%	9%
BCBC English	134	-23%	12%	24%	1%	-3%	3%	0%	2%	-2%	0%	5%	5%
BCBC French	243	-1%	-5%	11%	14%	-1%	16%	18%	16%	-2%	-11%	23%	-4%
BCBC total	377	-21%	10%	23%	0%	0%	-1%	-1%	0%	-3%	0%	0%	6%
Longlife	16	-2%	0%	1%	31%	26%	23%		24%	-10%	10%	22%	14%

Grey cells are significant at the 0.05 level.
Negative sign corresponds to the r and serves only to show the relation's direction.

Legend
Pop96	Population, 1996
Pop01	Population, 2001
English	English only, population by knowledge of official languages
French	French only, population by knowledge of official languages
Both	English and French, population by knowledge of official languages
None	Neither English nor French, population by knowledge of official languages
Can_citizen	Canadian citizenship population
Immig	Total immigrant population
China	Number of immigrants from China, People's Republic of
Visible	Total visible minority population
NA_Ind	North American Indian
Univ	University, population 20 years and over by highest level of schooling
Aver_inc	Average employment income $, population 15 years and over with employment income
Med_inc	Median employment income $, population 15 years and over with employment income
Low_inc	Low income - economic families
Density	Population density (by service area), 2001

TABLE 6.1. Coefficient of determination ($r2$) between sociodemographic profiles of the service areas of each theater and the overall revenues for each of the four selected films (note: n represents the number of movie theaters across Canada in which each film has been screened).

between two variables and can be interpreted as follows: 23 percent of the variation in the dependent variable (*Bon Cop Bad Cop* revenues) can be explained by the independent variable (the relative bilingual population), with no discretion about the direction of the relation.[31] Since the r^2 is easier to explain and understand, we have used it to show the results of the different analysis (we have also kept the negative signs in order to give a sense of the relation's direction).

Although we need to keep in mind that our sociodemographic profiles were only assessed, the results allow some of the correlations to be emphasized using the graphomap. First, the correlation between the revenues of *Bon Cop Bad Cop* and the spoken language of the audiences is confirmed. Even if this relationship is not extremely strong, it is much stronger than for any of the other films. The stronger relationship appears for the English version (r^2 = 24 percent). This supports the hypothesis that the English version of *Bon Cop Bad Cop* was mostly successful in bilingual neighborhoods, which are mainly located in eastern Ontario and in

Quebec. This is confirmed by the fact that the correlation between the revenues of the English version and the percentage of Anglophones only is also strong, but negative ($r^2 = (-)23$ percent) as already emphasized with the graphomap. The relatively low correlation between the French version and the percentage of Francophones ($r^2 = (-)5$ percent) can be explained by the fact that the film was mainly successful between Montréal and Toronto, where the percentage of bilingualism is high. Finally, it is important to emphasize that *Bon Cop Bad Cop* receives the lower coefficient of determination for criteria relative to immigration and urbanity (e.g., Canadian citizen population, total immigrant population, immigrants from China, total visible minority) (table 6.1). In comparison to the three other films, *Bon Cop Bad Cop* has been successful in neighborhoods that are less multicultural and more suburban.

These results confirm the perfect overlap between the cinematographic territories of the movie and the geography of its audience, both spatially (between Montréal and Toronto) and thematically (in bilingual environments). *Bon Cop Bad Cop* conveys a stereotypical perspective on the relationships between Anglophones and Francophones. In this representation, visible minorities are made invisible. While visible minorities represent 17 percent of the population in Montréal and 43 percent in Toronto,[32] only three non-Caucasian individuals appear in the film, and they only appear for a few seconds. This absence resonates with the overall lack of success of the film in multicultural neighborhoods. *Bon Cop Bad Cop* talks about white characters living in a bilingual environment to a white audience living in the same environment.

Atanarjuat offers a very different perspective on Canada, as mentioned previously. Given its nature, the first hypothesis is that the film was highly successful with Aboriginal people. When comparing the revenues with the percentage of North American Indians—which is the official Statistics Canada category for Aboriginal people, including Inuit people—the result was insignificant ($r^2 = (-)1$ percent). This can be explained by the low percentage of Aboriginal people in the Canadian population, which makes it difficult to identify any meaningful correlations. What appeared more clearly was the success of *Atanarjuat* in multicultural neighborhoods, where neither of the two official languages is spoken ($r^2 = 18$ percent) and there is a high presence of immigrants ($r^2 = 20$ percent) and of visible minorities ($r^2 = 20$ percent).

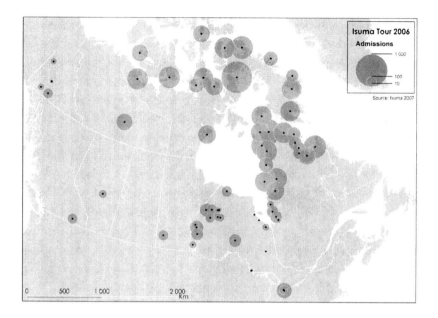

FIGURE 6.5. Isuma Tour 2006 showing places where films (including *Atanarjuat*) were screened as well as the number of admissions.

What is missing in these results is that the revenues provided by Alliance Atlantis did not include the revenues of the films in non-conventional screening venues such as schools or community centers, which are extremely important in more northern Aboriginal communities. When the film was screened in a gymnasium in Igloolik (Nunavut) over three days, 1,500 tickets were sold in the community of only 1,200 people. As the director Richard Kunuk states, "When the credits rolled, people were clapping and crying and shaking our hands. . . . Inuit loved it. Kids were even playing Atanarjuat in the street. Every household in Igloolik had a copy of the video."[33]

This success of *Atanarjuat* in Inuit communities is confirmed by the figures of the Isuma Tour 2006. During 2006, Isuma—an Inuit community-based production company cofounded by Zacharias Kunuk—was touring in northern communities in Canada showing a couple of films every night, including *Atanarjuat* (*Atanarjuat* was often screened during this tour, although we don't know exactly when and where). This alternative way of screening the film reached a high percentage of the population living in these communities, as illustrated by the number of tickets sold in each community (see figure 6.5).

Obviously there is a strong relationship between the territories of the action and the excitement of the communities portrayed, but what made *Atanarjuat* unique in terms of audiences was its capacity to reach audiences beyond its cinematographic territory. Indeed, the core audience for *Atanarjuat* lived in urban areas located far from Igloolik. *Atanarjuat* also received recognition and won multiple awards from film festivals around the world. In this sense, *Atanarjuat* can be seen as contributing to the production of a Canadian postnational identity, not only because of its own existence, but because of its success largely in multicultural neighborhoods across the country, and because of the transnational dimension of its success within Canada and abroad.

While the cinematographic territories of *Ararat* are quite different than those of *Atanarjuat*, their audiences share some similarities. The audience of *Ararat* was mostly located in multicultural urban neighborhoods, as illustrated by the strong negative relationship with Canadian citizens ($r^2 = (-)24$ percent), the strong correlation with Chinese immigrants ($r^2 = 27$ percent), and the very strong correlation with population density ($r^2 = 36$ percent). (This information does not appear in table 6.1.) These results can be explained largely by the success of the film in four movie theaters: two in Toronto and two in Montréal (one in French and one in English). These results seem to indicate an overlap between the cinematographic territories and the audience in Toronto. Although the nature of this overlap is extremely difficult to define given that we don't have any accurate information about the geography of Armenian immigrants in Canada, it is important to emphasize that many Armenian immigrants have settled in Toronto, as well as in the province of Quebec (see Embassy of the Republic of Armenia).

Finally, with regard to *Long Life, Happiness & Prosperity*, it was expected that the revenues of the film would be higher in movie theaters located in neighborhoods with a high percentage of Chinese immigrants, which happened to be confirmed ($r^2 = 29$ percent). Overall this film was successful in urban areas, as illustrated by the strong correlation with the percentage of allophones ($r^2 = 31$ percent) and the negative correlation with Canadian citizen ($r^2 = (-26$ percent). These results emphasize not only the geographic overlap between the fictional geography and the audience of the film in Vancouver, but also the sociodemographic overlap with the Chinese communities across Canada. In this sense, *Long Life* shares many of the characteristics of *Bon Cop*. Although these two films represent the opposite in terms of box office revenues and locations, their main audience shares many of the characteristics of the places and communities depicted in each movie. These films talk about a given community to members of this community, without really reaching other communities. Just like *Bon Cop Bad Cop,* but of a different magnitude, *Long Life* can be considered as contributing to the reinforcement of the identity associated with these places and communities without really crossing any cultural borders.

CONCLUSION

The process of mapping film audiences on a national scale is a complex process that entails a series of approximations and interpolations. Although the results cannot be taken at face value given the level of approximation inherent in the process, they nonetheless bring to the fore some original differences and similarities across the territories of these films. The stories of these four films unfold at different places and at different scales: locale for *Atanarjuat* and *Long Life,* regional for *Bon Cop,* and transnational for *Ararat.* Some of the audiences overlap perfectly in terms of scale and sociodemographic profiles with the territories portrayed in the selected films. This is the case for *Bon Cop Bad Cop* as well as for *Long Life, Happiness & Prosperity.* With regards to *Ararat,* the overlap is not as obvious, but the pattern looks somehow similar. The film that is the most unique in this perspective is certainly *Atanarjuat.* Although *Atanarjuat* has been extremely successful in the Inuit community, its success went well beyond the limits of its cinematographic territories to reach a broader audience in Canada and abroad. In Canada, the film was popular in urban and multicultural neighborhoods. In geographic terms, this success was homogeneous across the country in comparison to the other films studied. In other words, *Atanarjuat* reached audiences from different communities, contributing to a broad recognition of the indigeneity of Canadian society. The mapping of its audiences clearly confirms the impact of *Atanarjuat* in the Canadian postnational identity recreation process, and it demonstrates the relevance of mapping films' viewers while studying the relationships between cinema and identity.

ACKNOWLEDGMENTS

The work presented in this paper was supported by the Social Science Research Council of Canada (SSHRC). We would also like to thank all the people involved in developing the Cybercartographic Atlas of Canadian Cinema and more specifically D. R. Fraser Taylor, Jean-Pierre Fiset, and Victor Perichon.

NOTES

1. See S. Mackenzie, *Screening Québec* (Manchester: Manchester University Press, 2004); J. Leach and J. Sloniowski, *Candid Eyes: Essays on Canadian Documentaries* (Toronto: University of Toronto Press, 2003).

2. B. Anderson, *Imagined Communities: Reflections on the Origin and Spread of Nationalism* (London: Verso, 1991); E. Shohat and R. Stam, *Unthinking Eurocentrism: Multiculturalism and the Media* (London: Routledge, 1994).

3. A. Higson, "The Concept of National Cinema," in *Film and Nationalism*, ed. A. Williams (Piscataway, N.J.: Rutgers University Press, 2002).

4. D. Naud, *Le cinéma québécois: synopsis de l'organisation des espaces ruraux, urbains et périurbains* (Thèse de doctorat, Département de Géographie, Université de Montréal, Montréal, forthcoming); G. Rose, *Visual Methodologies: An Introduction to the Interpretation of Visual Materials* (London and Thousand Oaks, Calif.: Sage Publications, 2001).

5. N. Frye, *The Bush Garden: Essays on the Canadian Imagination* (Toronto: Anansi, 1971), cited here at 222.

6. G. Melnyk, *One Hundred Years of Canadian Cinema* (Toronto: University of Toronto Press, 2004).

7. M. Hays, "Producer of the Year: *Bon Cop*'s Kevin Tierney," *Playback*, 2006.

8. Igloolik Isuma Productions in M. Siebert, "*Atanarjuat* and the Ideological Work of Contemporary Indigenous Filmmaking," *Public Culture* 18(3) (2006): 531–49. Cited here at 533.

9. Igloolik Isuma Production, 2007.

10. S. Huhndorf, "*Atanarjuat, The Fast Runner*: Culture, History, and Politics in Inuit Media," *American Anthropologist* 105(4) (2003): 822–26.

11. Siebert, "*Atanarjuat* and the Ideological Work of Contemporary Indigenous Filmmaking," cited at 547.

12. J. White, *The Cinema of Canada* (London and New York: Wallflower Press, 2006).

13. J. Romney, *Atom Egoyan* (London: BFI Publishing, 2003), cited here at 173.

14. B. Wright, *Film Report: Ararat* (Ottawa: Carleton University, 2007), cited here at 3.

15. T. McSorely, "Faraway So Close: Atom Egoyan Returns Home with Ararat," *Take One,* September 2002.

16. A. Hinshaw and A. Lee, "Long Life, Happiness & Prosperity," press kit (New York: FilmMovement, 2002).

17. T. McSorely "Faraway So Close," cited at xiv.

18. C. Gittings, *Canadian National Cinema* (London: Routledge, 2002).

19. Statistics Canada, *Profil cumulatif, 2006—Provinces et Territoires du Canada (tableau), 'Recensement de la population de 2006,'* (Ottawa: Recensement Canada, 2006).

20. C. Acland, *Screen Traffic: Movies, Multiplexes, and Global Culture* (London: Duke University Press, 2003).

21. Statistics Canada has compiled a similar database but was not willing to release it for confidentiality reasons.

22. For more details about this process, see S. Caquard, D. Naud, and V. Perichon, "La répartition des salles obscures canadiennes: un éclairage géographique," *Cahiers de Géographie du Québec* 53 (2009): 221–41.

23. For more details see D. R. F. Taylor, "The Concept of Cybercartography," in *Maps and the Internet,* ed. M. P. Peterson (Amsterdam: Elsevier, 2003); D. R. F. Taylor and S. Caquard, eds., Special Issue on Cybercartography, Cartographica 41(1) (2006).

24. See, for example, G. Brauen, S. Pyne, A. Hayes, J. P. Fiset, and D. R. F. Taylor, "Encouraging Transdisciplinary Participation using an Open Source Cybercartographic Toolkit: The Atlas of the Lake Huron Treaty Relationship Process," *Geomatica* 65(1) (2011): 27–45.

25. D. Coish, *Régions métropolitaines de recensement constituant des grappes culturelles* (Statistique Canada, 2004); D. Farré, "Entretien à propos des facteurs d'implantation de cinema" (Daniel Naud, personal communication, Montréal, 2009).

26. S. Venkataraman and P. K. Chintagunta, "Investigating the Role of Local Market and Exhibitor Characteristics on Box-Office Performance," in Haas School of Business, Summer Institute in Competitive Strategy Berkeley University of California, 2008.

27. P. Davis, *Spatial Competition in Retail Markets: Movie Theaters* (Cambridge: MIT Sloan, 2001).

28. Caquard, Naud, and Perichon, "La répartition des salles obscures canadiennes."

29. For more details about this tool see S. Caquard and J. P. Fiset, "Un cyber cartogramme source ouverte et interopérable pour l'analyse de données spatiotemporelles complexes et diverses," *Revue des Nouvelles Technologies de l'Information* E13 (2008): 2–18.

30. J. Cohen, *Statistical Power Analysis for the Behavioral Sciences* (Hillsdale, N.J.: Lawrence Erlbaum, 1988).

31. P. Rogerson, *Statistical Methods for Geography* (London and Thousand Oaks, Calif.: Sage Publications, 2001).

32. Statistics Canada, 2006.

33. Z. Kunuk, "The Public Art of Inuit Storytelling," Montréal: Spry Memorial Lecture, University of Montréal, 2002.

SEVEN

The Geography of Film Production in Italy: A Spatial Analysis Using GIS

ELISA RAVAZZOLI

The use of cartographic techniques and geographical principles for the study of cultural phenomena has recently started to be evaluated by scholars as a compelling instrument of analysis. New areas of scholarly concern are emerging that are examining the potential role of mapping technologies in the study of cultural processes; among these are questions about how geographical information systems (GIS) can open up new ways of interpreting the spatial dimension of social and cultural practices and a growing recognition of the need to interrogate and integrate methodologies and approaches. This suggests that in the coming years, web-based maps, GIS analyses, and the various forms of cultural mapping stimulated by these technological encounters will become key instruments of investigation in the humanities, aiding the development of a more nuanced understanding of relationship between culture, spatiality, and place than has hitherto been undertaken.

Today, although the term "mapping" continues to be prominent in these debates, concrete examples of studies of cultural phenomena where cartographical practices have been applied in real terms continue to be relatively rare. In the field of film studies, although some scholars such as Conley, Castro, Lefebvre, and Harper and Rayner are striving to landscape the aesthetic terrain between cartography and cinema with a reinvigorated conceptual apparatus, the words "geography" and "cartography," as well as "mapping," are frequently used as metaphorical terms. The use of cartographic instruments and techniques to analyze film texts and production practices or patterns of distribution and exhibition remains underdeveloped essentially due to an underutilization of empirical methods. Geographies of film production are perhaps an exception to the rule, with maps being used with increasing frequency to explain the geographical patterns of film as an industrial practice.[1] The potential of using maps for the study of film, film practices, and film production, distribution, and exhibition relates to the spatial dimension of the film text, which shares with geography a similar conception of space. Geographically speaking, any film that is shot on location captures a space-time image of the physical landscape, thus it exists as a document of a specific historical time and space.[2] Space in film is semiotically dialogic, signifying the textual diegesis and the pro-filmic space. While the "space in the film" refers to the space of the narrative setting and relates to the film's representation,[3] the "film in space" refers to the real, physical urban space where the film is shot and to the spatial organization of its industries at the level of production, distribution, and exhibition. By considering both of these aspects of the film in space, this chapter seeks to illustrate the advantages of using a practical mapping technology such as GIS for the analysis of the filmmaking process as a specialized cultural practice. In so doing, it investigates the spatial organization of Italian film businesses and the spatial dynamics of film production as an industrial and cultural process, illustrating how geographic tools can be applied concretely to film and media studies, thus strengthening and exploring new relations between the two.

MAPS, MAPPING, GIS, AND SPATIAL ANALYSIS

Maps have always been significant tools for societies; the art of making maps and geographic tables has been part of human history since the Iron Age. From then until now maps have been used for a vast range of purposes and have appeared in many different forms. Conceived as abstract representations of reality, maps not only have the power to describe and represent the world and its multiple facets using the eyes of the mapmaker, but over the years maps have imposed new ways of observing it. With the evolution of printed maps into digital maps, and the growing importance of GIS as an innovative instrument of analysis in many fields of knowledge, the value of maps and the use of mapping have increased considerably. GIS is a powerful instrument of analysis across a variety of fields; it has the capacity to integrate and visualize different types of information, to detect spatial patterns, and to disclose relationships hidden in texts and in statistical information. The compound database that forms the GIS is able to store, manage, model, and select a feature's multiple characters, enhancing the performance of geoanalysis as well as investigating simultaneously different geographical data in either vector or raster format.

Using GIS, an analyst can explore numerous innovative uses of cartography. For example, cultural, social, and environmental data can be visually represented, showing where features are (geographical location) and what they are like (attribute data); digital maps can be created where infinite data layers are analyzed simultaneously; spatial phenomena can be mapped and a dynamic interpretation of multifaceted phenomena performed. Among the numerous applications, investigating the spatial distribution of data that occur in space represents a new opportunity for the explanation of phenomena in many areas of knowledge.

The visualization of the spatial character of phenomena (i.e., mapping) is significant for their comprehension; nevertheless, the process of transforming existing patterns into measurable objects (e.g., areas, point, lines) and analyzing data and phenomena systematically through the use of accurate tools remains challenging. By using procedures based on inferential models, the central idea of spatial analysis is to incorporate space into the analysis and to transform textual information into numbers, points, lines, or polygons (e.g., to transform an address into a point). This allows the relationships that occur between the patterns to be measured, studying the spatial distribution of the measurable objects and the spatial connotations of the data as well as testing hypotheses about dispersion, concentration, correlation, dependency, and spatial regression.

Mapping, if used together with GIS, is not just about studying cartographic maps. It captures the processes that underlie the understanding of space, it characterizes the spatial manifestation of phenomena, it offers a critical interpretation of the cultural processes that manifest the phenomena, encouraging a new thinking about their character.[4] The simple act of locating objects on a space, giving them a geographical reference, does not automatically reveal the spatial correlation between phenomena; it is the use of GIS and spatial analysis that enables us to go beyond metaphorical applications of maps and analyze the different degrees to which cultural phenomena are spatially embedded in local practices. In this respect, GIS-based spatial analysis can be considered part of the "spatial turn" that is shaping developments in the humanities and in the social sciences.[5]

In film and cultural studies research, spatial analysis can be used for the investigation of many aspects related to film: It enables the study of the intrinsic spatial relations between the elements within the film, the analysis of the relationship between the space of the film and the real space, and the investigation of film production as an expression of an interconnected network of film businesses and spatial cultural practices. Various approaches have been used to analyze systems of film production.[6] In general, research that has investigated filmmaking as a cultural industry or a system of production has focused less on consumers and more on how films are made, how the industry works, and how it is spatially distributed within a territory, but without applying an intensive GIS spatial analysis of these phenomena, which remains a new form of examination. In this chapter, GIS spatial analysis is used to study the geography of film production, creating a distinctive focus on the spatial dimension of the film industry with its network of film businesses, and to examine the cultural implications of the filmmaking process in respect of particular locations. Three GIS spatial tools were used: geocoding, density kernel for point features, and the nearest-neighborhood analysis.

1. Geocoding is a process that allows objects to be converted into points on a map. In this chapter, geocoding is used to localize film production companies and films produced on the territory and explore their geographic distribution.

2. Density kernel for point features (sometimes referred to as kernel smoothing) is a spatial statistical method that generates a map of density values from point data. It enables the creation of a density surface that is a raster image created from points, transforming a set of discrete features into a continuous phenomenon dataset. GIS tools process the mapped phenomena into pixels of a size specified by the user; it then sets a specified radius and starts counting all the features that fall within the search radius of each feature, dividing that by the total area where the features are present and creating a pixel with that value. A large radius will give the surface a more generalized look, while a small one will reflect more local variations. In this research a density map was generated to create a smoother distribution of values and to visualize more precisely how the film industry is distributed over the geographic surface.

3. The average nearest neighborhood calculates a nearest-neighbor index based on the average distance from each feature to its nearest neighboring feature, identifying whether data are clustered or dispersed. The index measures the distance between each feature and its nearest neighbor, and then calculates the average. The index is expressed as the ratio of the observed distance, which is the average distance from each feature and its nearest neighbor, divided by the expected distance, which is the average distance between neighbors in a hypothetical random distribution. If the index is less than 1, the pattern exhibits clustering; if the index is greater than 1, the trend is toward dispersion or competition. This technique is used to identify clusters in the film industry dataset.

By combining the GIS spatial techniques to open datasets such as Annuario del Cinema Italiano & Audiovisivi and the Internet Movie Database (IMDb), this chapter illustrates the intensity of film businesses and film production in Italy in two different time periods by using circle graduated symbols (as in, for example, figure 7.2); visualizations such as these help to reveal the relationship between filmmaking as a cultural practice and industrial system of production, as well as a creator of site-specific cultural milieux.

ITALIAN FILM PRODUCTION SYSTEM: A SPATIAL THINKING

If it is true that in the world movie system the successful and exemplary model is the Hollywood one, a model that breaks into the film distribution market in any continent at any latitude and speaks a comprehensible language that many people seem to embrace, it is also true that in Italy we are witnessing a revival of national films in terms of narratives and indigenous production. Instead of opening up the borders and setting its sights on transnational practices (i.e., the interrelationship between local, national, and global in both textual and industrial terms), Italian cinema is promoting national content and local production contexts, refusing the "Babel model," recognized as a quintessential attribute of transnational films.[7]

During the past few years, Italian filmmakers have developed a desire to identify the "self" of the spectator with situations, stories, common senses, and landscapes that are recognizable and familiar, that belong to the national culture, and that bring cinema back into the realm of the personal knowledge and experiences of many Italian viewers. Italian cinema is challenging the universal schemas commonly used to interpret and represent the contemporary world and is sponsoring a local rather than a global approach. This does not signify that Italian cinema is closing down its global market potential or rejecting coproduction partnerships, but comparing Italian film production with European production and considering the new trends in transnational practice that characterize filmmaking in both textual and industrial terms, film production in Italy appears to be more autarkic than in any other country in Europe. In fact, the financial support from the regional film commissions[8] and private investments, product placement, and the new tax credit and tax shelter incentives have spurred a renewed interest in national film production, especially during the past twenty years.[9] These films are not simply cultural products and artifacts; a popular storytelling medium is being used to call attention to the beauty of the Italian landscape, its history and special traditions, with the aim of promoting local and regional identities as well as Italian historical patrimony in general.

At a time when film paradigms internationally are shifting from national to transnational productions, in 2010 Italian national cinema produced 141 films, the highest performance since 2008, when 154 were made by national producers; of the 141 films made in 2010, 114 were produced with Italian funding, while the others were coproduced and financed with the participation of international producers.[10] This testifies to the existence of a consolidated mode of national film production. In the past thirty years the structure of the Italian film industry has expanded noticeably throughout the country. It does not rely only on a major, internationally recognized studio such as Cinecittà,[11] but involves new actors and new nodes of production. Other cities besides Rome have started to play an important role both as homes for film companies and popular film locations. In 2011 the number of film businesses registered at the National Chamber of Commerce was 11,749.[12] Of these, most are localized in Lazio, Rome, Lombardia, Piemonte, Emilia Romagna, and Campania. Referring to the 2009 data (the only data available by categories), it is noticeable that Lazio hosts 47.20 percent of the businesses operating in production and 62 percent of the those working in distribution; Lombardia and the

TABLE 7.1. The Italian Film Industry: Number of Film Businesses in the Italian Regions

REGION	2011			2009		
	TOTAL ASSESSED VALUE	TOTAL %	TOTAL %	PRODUCTION %	DISTRIBUTION %	EXHIBITION %
Abruzzo	203	1.73	1.60	1.80	0.30	1.60
Basilicata	53	0.45	0.40	0.40	0.00	0.50
Calabria	176	1.50	1.50	1.60	0.50	1.50
Campania	743	6.32	5.30	4.40	6.20	7.20
Emilia Romagna	844	7.18	7.00	5.80	1.90	11.70
Friuli Venezia Giulia	133	1.13	1.30	1.30	0.50	1.50
Lazio	3,841	32.69	32.30	37.20	62.00	9.60
Liguria	236	2.01	2.40	1.90	1.20	4.40
Lombardia	2,050	17.45	18.00	19.40	12	16
Marche	243	2.07	2.40	1.70	1.10	4.50
Molise	34	0.29	0.30	0.30	0.00	0.30
Piemonte	625	5.32	5.80	5.20	1	8
Puglia	416	3.54	3.20	2.50	3.80	5.40
Sardegna	194	1.65	1.80	2.00	0.10	1.80
Sicilia	491	4.18	4.40	3.20	3.20	8.00
Toscana	606	5.16	5.30	4.40	2.60	8.80
Trentino-Alto Adige	175	1.49	1.40	2	0	1
Umbria	138	1.17	1.10	1.10	0.00	1.60
Valle d'Aosta	19	0.16	0.20	0	0	0
Veneto	529	4.50	4.30	4.00	3.10	5.80
Total	11,749	100.00	100.00	100.00	100.00	100.00

Source: National Chamber of Commerce, Business Register, December 2009, August 2011.

province of Milan is home to 19 percent of producers and 12 percent of distributors; Emilia Romagna hosts 11.70 percent of exhibitors and 6 percent of producers; while in Sicilia and in Puglia the concentration is smaller but still consistent (table 7.1).[13]

What these numbers really mean is very difficult to understand without a visual representation of them: statistics alone are not able to explain the relationship between the patterns or to unveil the spatial dimension of phenomena. To explain the peculiar nature of Italian film production and its network of small independent businesses, GIS analyses need to be applied to these datasets to capture the spatial character of the industry.

The problem with many institutional datasets (such as the Chamber of Commerce economic data) is their static nature, which does not allow a detailed spatial investigation. Annuario del Cinema Italiano & Audiovisivi and IMDb enable a spatial analysis to be performed because their data have a spatial reference such as an address or a geographic location, allowing the investigation of the spatial dimension of film production as an industrial practice. Annuario del Cinema Italiano & Audiovisivi (2008–2009), published by the Centro Studi di Cultura, Promozione e Diffusione del Cinema and directed by the journalist Emanuele Masini, collects information on Italian film businesses at the postcode level and by category (i.e., preproduction, production, and postproduction), while the use of the IMDb enables an investigation of Italian filming locations, gathering information on the year a film was shot and the exact place of the shooting. Given the dispersed nature of the filming process, which involves different filming locations, data on film locations were gathered at the provincial level rather than at the postcode level, enabling the capture of both the spatial dimension of filmmaking and its relationship to the network of film-specific businesses.

By using these two datasets, each company was given a specific location on the map. Businesses operating in the film industry were classified by category (production, preproduction, etc.) and place of company registration, while films produced were mapped by their locations and put in a comparative perspective. The limitation of using Annuario del Cinema Italiano & Audiovisivi is that it does not recognize every business operating in the film industry; rather, it catalogues only businesses that choose to appear on the online database and in the paper volume of the Annuario. Similarly, the limitation of the IMDb is that a film must meet certain qualification standards to be listed on the database and must be considered of interest to the general public. IMDb therefore credits only "well-known films" and not all the films produced during a certain period in a particular location. Despite their limitations, these databases are valuable for the purpose of this study as they enable an investigation of the spatial dimension of film production and the interrelations between both the network of businesses and the filming stage on location. To-

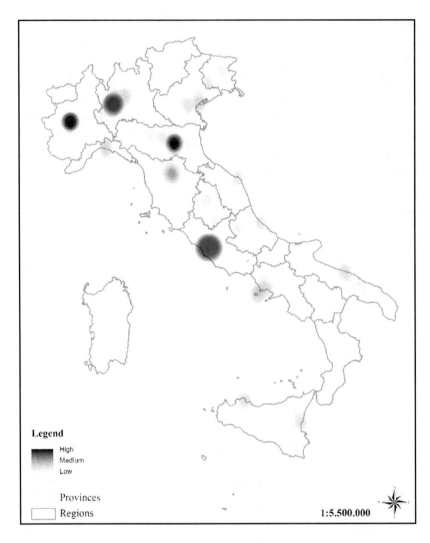

FIGURE 7.1. Film industry density map.

gether with these two databases, information was also gathered from the database of the regional film commission and used to investigate spatial patterns within selected regions (e.g., Emilia Romagna and Rome) that are of particular interest to this study.

Starting from a rigid monocentric structure dominated by the cinema capitals,[14] the Italian industry has moved to a more complex, flexible, and

TABLE 7.2. GIS Spatial Analysis: Near-Distant-Neighborhood Index

FILM STAGE	OBSERVED VALUES	ZSCORE
Post-production	0.12	−23.73
Pre-production	0.19	−13.48
Production	0.07	−41.45
Distribution	0.03	−24.73
Event	0.15	−24.87
Marketing	0.13	−21.93

Source: Annuario del Cinema Italiano & Audiovisivi, 2008–2009.

multicentric configuration, characterized by many small independent film enterprises scattered around the territory and regional clans operating mainly at the local level. From the rudimentary companies developed in the early years of the twentieth century, Cines in Rome, Ambrosio, Itala Film, Unitas in Turin, Milano Film in Milan, and Troncone Brothers in Naples, the film industry expanded rapidly, with periods of ups and downs, shifting over the years from a relatively simple capitalist model of production to an increasingly fragmented and complex model made of majors, mini-majors, and indie.[15] The analyses of the geocoding results and of the density kernel for point data illustrates that at a national level, the concentration of film companies is predominant in northern and central Italy, where firms can be traced in almost every city, in contrast to south Italy, where the density is much smaller. The density map, created by using the density kernel for point feature tool, clearly illustrates this phenomenon (see figure 7.1).

The spatial dynamic of film production shows that Lazio, along with Rome, is the more specialized Italian region, recognized by Gilda Mazzarelli (2008) as a filming district.[16] Other film businesses are localized in Lombardia, Emilia Romagna, Piemonte, Toscana, Puglia, Sicilia, and in other cities where a small cluster of firms can be identified (see table 7.1). Sicilia and Puglia are growing as independent regions within the production system with more than four hundred businesses based there, and immense investments are being made to promote these regions as filming locations. Within each region, film businesses show different patterns and a different tendency to cluster and co-cluster.[17] According to the value of the near-distant-neighborhood index (table 7.2), production and distribution enterprises are the ones that cluster more; in the chief cities of Rome, Milan, Turin, and Bologna they also co-cluster, indicating that there is a link between the sectors.

According to each region's historical specialization in film, such as Rome's association with Cinecittà, Naples's with Troncone Brothers and Turin's with Ambrosio, film companies display diverse spatial forms (patterns) of clustering: (1) concentric, where film businesses are localized within the chief municipal boundaries of the creative production center (e.g., Rome, Naples, and Turin); (2) linear, where companies are spread throughout the region along the major transportation system (e.g., in Emilia Romagna and Veneto); and (3) dispersed, where firms scatter within the region (e.g., Sicilia). Although a spatial cluster of firms based on the distance between points is not enough to define a Region or a city as a "film district," it is however true that the film industry does not operate in a vacuum; independent production companies, film commissions, actors, producers, filmmakers and film related services collaborate in a network environment that, as well enabling the filmmaking process to occur, spurs knowledge exchange and cultural innovation.[18]

The rise of new nodes of film production in addition to the cinema capitals and the appearance of regional clusters of independent firms has fostered films to be shot in the well-established cities (e.g. Rome, Milan, Turin) as well as in unknown locations (e.g. Sicilia, Puglia and Basilicata). In the period 1990–1999, more than 500 films were produced in regions such as Veneto, Lombardia, Toscana, Sicilia, Puglia, and Campania; in the decade 2000–2009 the number reached 1,188 and new filming locations appeared on the map. Campania, Piemonte, Toscana, Friuli Venezia Giulia, and Puglia have been the fastest growing regions in the last two decades, as table 7.1 and figure 7.2 show.

The data display the density of film production (represented by graduated symbols) and demonstrate that film production does not simply occur in locations where the creative specialization is high and the available labor pool is large, but it also happens in places that have a unique geography and a variety of landscapes and in locations that are able to represent narratives that are currently popular. Moreover, the ability of the film commissions to promote a unique cultural milieu and brand the image of the territory determines the success of a region as a filming location.

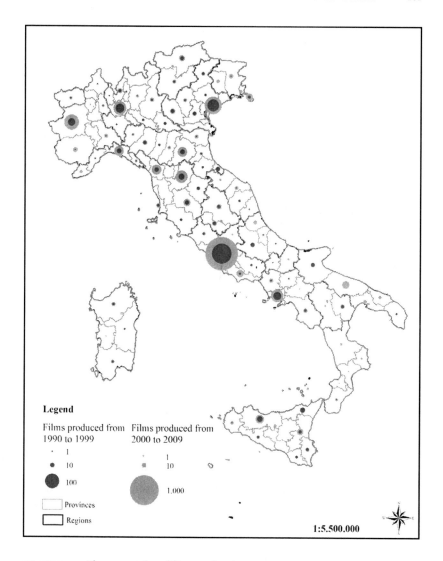

FIGURE 7.2. The geography of film production 1990–2009.

THE NODES OF FILM PRODUCTION

By considering the spatial dynamics of film as a process of cultural production, taking into account the number of films shot during the past twenty years and regional/city specialization in film production, three interconnected nodes of activity can be identified: historical nodes of film production, well-established nodes of film production, and emerging nodes of film production.

1. The historical nodes of film production are Rome, Milan, Turin, and Naples; in the cinema capitals, which are the locations where the most films have been shot and the first movie companies established, film production is vigorous both in economic and cultural terms. The spatial distribution of film companies tells us about three facts: first, it highlights the historical and strategic role played by Cinecittà and the position of Rome as a national hub; second, it shows the importance of Milan, which along with the capital represents more than half of all domestic production; third, it displays the strategic role of Turin as the new capital of cinema.[19] Unlike these three cities, Naples has lost its historical predominance, but its image is still strong in the collective imaginary. At a cultural level, these cities and their locations have historically been chosen by filmmakers for their ability to represent contemporary phenomena (such as industrialization, internal migration), to symbolize the character of the metropolitan areas (such as the contrast between the homes of a wealthy elite and working-class ghettos), to describe the *dolce vita* and ways of enjoying life as well as the problem of the south of Italy, enabling directors to scrutinize the popular imagery of their territory. Over the years a rich legacy of images associated with these cities has appeared that helps to explain their own filmic existence and why they are seen as old nodes of production.

2. Consolidated nodes of film production are Bologna, Venice, and Florence. These cities have a well-established network of film industries operating in the territory, high rates of employment, and a regional sense of place that grounds different types of narratives. What distinguishes these nodes of production is a distinctive "look," which is one of the elements that attracts international filmmakers to these locations. In Veneto, locations are suitable for narratives that foreground the local landscape; in Emilia Romagna producers are attracted by the versatility of the territory located between the Po River, the Adriatic Sea, and the Apennine mountain range. Tuscany has always fascinated filmmakers for its landscape characterized by gentle profiles, hills, and vineyards, and for the

distinctiveness of its cities and towns. Due to the appeal of their surrounding landscapes and their regionally based production infrastructure, Bologna, Venice, and Florence are consolidated nodes of film production.

3. Emerging nodes of film production Sicilia, Puglia, Basilicata, Friuli Venezia Giulia, Marche, and Abruzzo have been chosen by producers for the beauty of their natural and cultural landscapes, but do not yet offer a strong network of film-related services. Within this group, Puglia, Basilicata, and Sicilia are favored by filmmakers mainly for the narrative associations of their rural landscapes and because they mediate perceptions and interpretations of the "southern question of Italy." These sites and cities are frequently used to fulfill the specific needs of the fictional narrative, but their popularity varies from year to year and with the types of narratives that are currently popular. Among the emerging nodes of film production, Sicilia and Puglia are the ones that have shown the most growth, both for the increasing number of small and medium businesses operating in the film sector, and for the number of films that have been shot in the past decade (see table 7.3).

The spatial analysis shows that the Italian film production is characterized by a varied cinematic landscape made up of a polycentric structure and a variety of regional specializations. Besides Rome, which is still the "film hub," many other regional and provincial centers now operate independently in film production, generating what Martini and Morelli have defined as a "patchwork" (figure 7.3).[20]

LOCATIONS, REGIONAL IDENTITIES, AND SITE-SPECIFIC MILIEUX

The peculiarity of the film industry as a cultural industry is that relations between the local film businesses and the motley assemblage of different suppliers who organize themselves geographically on the filming location are economic relations rooted in interpersonal relations that generate an industrial but also a cultural and creative atmosphere. Local interaction, face-to-face communication, or buzz among the members of the troupe stimulates creative knowledge and the rise of creative and cultural mi-

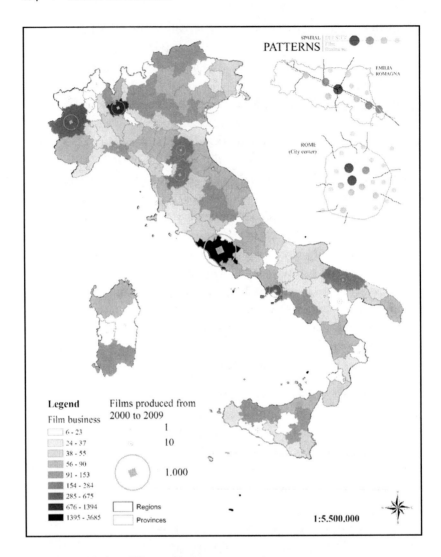

FIGURE 7.3. Nodes of film production.

lieux. When the film industry localizes in a region or city, it spurs the emergence of a community of creative people, the circulation of culture, communication among cultural institutions, and a network of interpersonal exchanges.[21] In industries mediating symbolic knowledge such as the film industry that are based on short, creative projects, interactions among people, buzz, and face-to-face communication are crucial to the

TABLE 7.3. The Filming Locations: The Number of Films Produced
at the Regional Level

	1990	2000	2009	1990–1999	2000–2009	INCREASE ASS. VALUE
Abruzzo	1	1	4	11	22	11
Basilicata	1	—	1	5	14	9
Calabria	—	—	—	1	12	11
Campania	1	5	11	39	100	61
Emilia Romagna	2	7	7	39	96	57
Friuli V. Giulia	1	2	2	5	46	41
Lazio	19	29	58	195	552	357
Liguria	1	3	3	14	45	31
Lombardia	7	7	11	59	128	69
Marche	—	2	1	5	17	12
Molise	—	—	1	1	3	2
Piemonte	6	11	14	32	135	103
Puglia	1	10	6	9	48	39
Sardegna	1	—	—	11	24	13
Sicilia	6	8	6	51	85	34
Toscana	3	13	13	51	166	115
Trentino Alto Adige	—	1	2	11	26	15
Umbria	1	—	5	12	26	14
Valle d'Aosta	1	1	2	3	7	4
Veneto	8	16	19	90	188	98
Total	60	116	166	644	1740	1096

Source: Internet Movie Database, 1990–2009.

development of the cultural product.[22] It should not be taken to imply that there is face-to-face communication all the time, nor that all face-to-face communications are equally important for all participants in the projects, but personal interactions play a vital role. The ability to mobilize relations, to network, and develop face-to-face connections between actors, agents, and suppliers are peculiar characteristics of the film industry. This is particularly true for the shooting stage, where a wide range of highly specialized and skilled artistic talent and technical expertise are involved in assembling all the resources required for the creation of each individual film product. It is at this stage of the production process where the creative industries, the institutions, and the film commissions build relationships and a network of powerful communications appears.

This process of socialization is not only important with regard to training in know-how, but also for acquiring it. The city or region, through the organization of its spaces, gives material support to the complex internal and external relations, direct and undirected, and becomes a node of knowledge and cultural exchange where people can share common languages, uses, and conventions. Moreover, the cluster of creative industries (including companies involved in advertising, marketing, and promotion) at the municipal or regional level enriches the circulation of culture, reinforcing the image of the city and attracting new talents on locations.

Within these nodes of cultural production and especially within established filming sites, the close spatial relations between people working on the shooting phase, the network of film businesses operating in the territory, the creative industries, the cultural institutions together with the citizens' involvement, and the distinctive cultural elements of the location produce a uniquely localized social and cultural legacy and stimulate the rise of site-specific cultural milieux. The concept of milieu was introduced in the geographical literature to identify those "unique characteristics" of places that have been shaped by the spatial and historical relationship between space and society.[23] In this case, the unique characteristics of places are related to the industrial, social, and cultural relations generated by the film industry as a cultural production system in certain locations. Milieux indicate exclusive locations where the specialization in film production is well developed, the social atmosphere generated by the work of creative individuals spurs innovation and knowledge exchange, and the local characteristics of places, natural and social, symbolize the common patrimony of a community and the territorial base of its identity, all of which are vital both for the economic development of the location and at level of the collective imaginary.

So far we have conceived culture as a "product of art" and investigated the film and the filmmaking process as a process of cultural production, considering the regional specializations and the interconnected network of businesses, external expertise, all of which are factors that work together to create the "film product." Culture, however, is also about sharing meanings, values, and beliefs as well as assigning significance to the existing objects.[24] The film text, through sounds, images, and languages, is one of the most, if not *the* most, powerful tools for the production of meaning; the local screening of a film made in a particular place produces meanings and images of that place that have effects on local society and at the level of collective memory. Given that the national cinema of Italy is becoming a regional cinema, it is relevant for the purposes of this chapter to investigate the cultural significance of this spatial configuration in terms of representation and to investigate how the uses of certain locations (at the regional level) generate new meanings and distinctive regional identities.

The existence of different nodes of film production within site-specific cultural milieux and the promotion of regional cinema as an emerging model of film production creates a fragmentary image of Italian national cinema that has implications at the national and the regional scale. At a national level, this spatial conformation deprives the national cinema of its common meaning and images, ascribing new significances to regional identities through narratives and symbols of identification. Today, the images that are being chosen to represent Italy as a film location are numerous and extremely diverse. The ability to promote a region through images and to link those images to specific locations and cultural values is heavily exploited by the regional film commissions, which are "creating" very different Italian landscapes and branding their regional characteristics. At a regional level, the appearance of culturally related film milieux generates directly positive effects on local groups and institutions involved in the creation of culture, meaning, images, and new representations. They reinforce local values and the sense of identification with both Italian culture and the regional traditions, reinforcing the relationship between society, culture, and these ideals. Moreover, at the level of imagination, this produces new regional images of identity and place. The capacity of film to inspire new local imaginaries and the work of the film commission in "selling" it plays a crucial role in the attribution of meaning. On reflection, it is worth noting how the use of certain locations can change the image of an entire region, shaping people's collective imaginary.

During the past twenty years films have been shot both in well-known locations and in lesser-known locations. The well-known locations were chosen for their landmarks and for the ability to symbolize contemporary issues and cities' dynamics, while unknown locations have attracted producers for the beauty of their landscape, for the peculiarities of their places, and for distinct cultural phenomena.[25] Selecting certain locations over others can have important implications at the regional level. The location and the image that the film is representing can become part of the history of a location or part of an image of national identity, or it could be used for tourist promotion, favoring movie tourism development.[26] In the history of cinema, feature films are recognized as unquestioned sources of radical redefinition of the collective imaginary.[27] Film locations play a strategic role in this process.

Without pretending to be exhaustive, this chapter uses Basilicata, a region in the southern Italy, to explain how the films and the regional film commission have reinvented the common image of the region by filming specific locations and attaching precise meaning to them. A location for many films since the early years of the twentieth century, Basilicata has changed its face more than twice. Four main orientations can be discerned in the construction of the image of the region: those of the earthquake disasters in the 1960s that destroyed the city of Craco; those of underdevelopment and of the problems of southern Italy, as in the documentary *Viaggio a Sud* (Carlo Lizzari, 1949), shot in Matera; those of the life story of Christ, depicted by Pier Paolo Pasolini in *Il Vangelo Secondo Matteo* (1964) and by Mel Gibson in *The Passion of the Christ* (2004), which were set in Matera and in Craco; and exotic ethnographic images emerging from the film *Basilicata Coast to Coast* (Rocco Papaleo, 2010), where the natural landscape was the real protagonist of the film. These four orientations refer to different ideological and cultural matrixes that, by ascribing different meaning to places, have identified Basilicata as a "terrible," "Christian," "poor and backward," and "magic and impenetrable" land. Due to these multiple levels of representation, the image that comes out of the region is multifaceted, constantly shifting between what is imaginary and what is symbolic, between the old and the new. These levels of interpretation and representation have produced and continue to produce countless narratives about the territory and its population. Besides the classical elements used to read the southern Italian contexts, new aspects have been added that generate contemporary representations mainly associated with the natural beauty of its landscape.

To summarize, the spatial conformation of film production operates at the level of the film as a cultural product by developing site-specific milieu and at the level of the filmmaking process as a representational practice by generating new collective imagery. In both cases, the geography (i.e., the space), together with the filmmaking, is the real protagonist in this discourse. Geographic elements influence the decision to shoot the film in special locations, which have a certain character; on the other hand the act of filming on location influences the perception of certain spaces, generating new images of the territory and offering new interpretations of the landscape that can either redefine or solidify common values, ideals, and stereotypes.

CONCLUSION

In this chapter, new instruments of analysis have been presented that show how maps, mapping, and GIS spatial analysis can be used for the explanation of cultural phenomena that are spatially embedded in local practices, such as those related to cinema. What distinguishes this study was the attempt to spatially analyze Italian film production and the film industry with its interconnected network of small businesses as a cultural and social process, exploring the association between the two. The results have shown the existence of a varied cinematic landscape characterized by a polycentric structure and a variety of regional specializations. Besides Rome, which still plays a dominant role, many other regional and provincial centers now operate independently in the film-production sector, such as Basilicata, Puglia, and Calabria, which demonstrates the rise of a regional cinema. According to the degree to which the film production is embedded in the local production system and is able to generate new images of the territory, three types of film production centers were detected: historical centers, consolidated nodes, and emerging nodes of film production. Within these national nodes of production and especially within filming locations, the social relations between the members of the production crew and the local businesses, the exchange of knowledge, the promotion of events related to culture, and the buzz created by the creative artists foster the rise of a creative atmosphere. Together with the uniqueness of the landscape and the economic specialization, this social environment generates site-specific cultural milieux, within which the film product was studied both as an industrial process of cultural production and a means of reframing the image of the region and perceptions of local identity.

These aspects have been discussed by studying the geography of film production, by showing the importance of face-to-face interactions and personal communication in generating singular milieux, and by examining how the image of a particular region, Basilicata, has changed as new films were produced. The cultural significance of the spatial dimension of Italian film production was considered too, but this could be further contextualized by comparing these developments with similar developments in other European countries such as Germany, France, or the United Kingdom. Moreover, the concept of a production milieu applied to the locations where a film is shot can open up new ways of thinking about the film as a spatial phenomenon.

Finally, what emerges from this analysis is that film production, like other cultural phenomena, cannot be explained by statistics only, although statistics are essential in every study. Spatial analysis, using maps as well as other cartographic instruments, can offer new interpretations of cultural and industrial phenomena and explain aspects that pure data does not show immediately, strengthening the relationship between cinema and geography and opening up new reflections on the spatial nature of film.

NOTES

1. K. Bassett, R. Griffiths, and I. Smith, "Cultural Industries, Cultural Clusters and the City: The Example of Natural History Film-Making in Bristol," *Geoforum* 33 (2002): 165–77; C. Lukinbeal, "The Rise of Regional Film Production Centers in North America, 1984–1997," *GeoJournal* 59 (2004): 307–21; M. Dahlström and B. Hermelin, "Creative Industries, Spatiality and Flexibility: The Example of Film Production," *Norwegian Journal of Geography* 61 (2007): 111–21; A. Scott, "A New Map of Hollywood: The Production and Distribution of American Motion Pictures," *Regional Studies* 36 (2002): 957–75; J. Boter and C. Pafort-Overduin, "Compartmentalization and its Influence on Film Distribution and Exhibition in the Netherlands, 1934–1936," in *Digital Tools in Media Studies,* ed. M. Ross, M. Grauer, and B. Freisleben, 55–69 (Piscataway, N.J.: Transaction Publisher, 2009).

2. C. Lukinbeal and S. Zimmermann, *The Geography of Cinema: A Cinematic World* (Stuttgart: Franz Steiner Verlag, 2008).

3. C. Lukinbeal, "Geography in Film, Geography of Film" (unpublished PhD thesis, California State University, 1995).

4. T. Castro, "Cinema's Mapping Impulse: Questioning Visual Culture," *The Cartographic Journal* 46 (2009): 9–15.

5. D. J. Bodenhamer, *The Spatial Humanities: GIS and the Future of Humanities Scholarship* (Bloomington: Indiana University Press, 2010).

6. P. M. Hirsh, "Fads and Fashion: An Organization Set Analysis of Cultural Industry System," *The American Journal of Sociology* 77 (1972): 639–59; M. Storper, "The Transition to Flexible Specialization in the U.S. Film Industry: External Economies, the Divi-

sion of Labor, and the Crossing of Industrial Divides," *Cambridge Journal of Economics* 13 (1989): 273–305; M. S. Storper and A. J. Venables, "Buzz: Face-to-Face Contact and the Urban Economy," *Journal of Economic Geography* 4 (2004): 351–70; B. Asheim, L. Coenen, and J. L. Vang, "Face-to-Face, Buzz, and Knowledge Bases: Socio-spatial Implications for Learning, Innovation, and Innovation Policy," *Environment and Planning C: Government and Policy* 25 (2007); 655–70; A. Scott, *Hollywood: The Place, the Industry* (Princeton, N.J.: Princeton University Press, 2005); S. Christopherson and M. Storper, "The City as Studio: The World as Back Lot: The Impact of Vertical Disintegration on the Location of the Modern Picture Industry," *Environment and Planning D: Society and Space* 4 (1986): 305–20; J. L. Vang and C. Chaminade, "Cultural Clusters, Global-Local Linkages and Spillovers: Theoretical and Empirical Insights from an Exploratory Study of Toronto's Film Cluster," *Industry and Innovation* 14 (2007): 401–20; C. Beaudry and S. Breschi, "Are Firms in Clusters Really More Innovative?" *Economics of Innovation and New Technology* 12 (2003): 325–42; N. M. Coe, "A Hybrid Agglomeration? The Development of a Satellite-Marshallian Industrial District in Vancouver's Film Industry," *Urban Studies* 38 (2001): 1753–75.

7. D. Shaw and A. D. L. Garza, "Introducing Transnational Cinema," *Transnational Cinema* 1 (2010): 3–6.

8. Film commissions appeared for the first time in Italy in 1997 as means of promoting the territory and a city's image. They have three roles. First they create connections among different parts of the film division and art-related industries, provide liaison services, keep a local labor pool register, and ensure a film-friendly milieu critical to facilitating the "traveling circus." Second, through a list of available locations, they brand and sell the territory by suggesting interesting locations. Third, they sell "new images" of the city or district, moving away from the traditional ones.

9. The increase in film production from the 1990s onwards is related to the appearance of new laws such as the Law n. 153 (1994), the Legislative Decree n. 28 (2004), and the Ministerial Decree (2007) which reformed aspects of the film industry and allocated more public funding for the production of films. Besides the Special Fund for Performance (FUS), and grants sponsored by public institutions, financial support was also received by the two major private television firms, RAI Cinema and Mediaset-Medusa, which invested 10 percent of their capital in the production of films. In 2010, a tax credit and tax shelter were introduced with the aim of supporting producers and distributors.

10. Fondazione Ente dello Spettacolo, *Il Mercato e l'Industria del Cinema in Italia 2010* (Roma: Fondazione Ente dello Spettacolo, 2011), 123.

11. Cinecittà is a cinema studio located in Rome, opened in 1937. It has been making films for more than seventy years and is the setting for many well-known films. The complex was designed as a complete center of production, offering every type of facility from training through the production of films to postproduction and completion.

12. National Chamber of Commerce Business Register (August 2011).

13. National Chamber of Commerce Business Register (December 2009).

14. G. P. Brunetta, *Cent'anni di Cinema Italiano. Dalle Origini fino alla Seconda Guerra Mondiale* (Bari: Laterza, 1995), 26–40.

15. The Italian film system consists of three types of operators: majors, international holdings such as Universal and 20th Century Fox; mini-majors, national groups, such as RAI Distribution or Mediaset-Medusa; and indie, small to medium-sized Italian independent businesses. Fondazione Ente dello Spettacolo, Il Mercato e l'Industria del

Cinema in Italia (Roma: Fondazione Ente dello Spettacolo, 2009); M. P. Wood, *Italian Cinema* (Oxford: Berg, 2005), 1–34; M. Macchitella and A. Abruzzese, *Cinemitalia 2005: Sogni, Industria, Tecnologie* (Venezia: Marsilio, 2005).

16. G. Mazzarelli, *l'Industria Culturale: il Distretto Audiovisivo nel Lazio,* Quaderni di Economia Regionale. Collana del Servizio Studi di Sviluppo Lazio, n. 9 Anno II, Roma (2008).

17. Cluster is defined as a geographical concentration of interconnected companies, specialized suppliers, and associated institutions in a particular field that compete but that also cooperate. M. E. Porter, "Location, Competition, and Economic Development: Local Clusters in a Global Economy," *Economic Development Quarterly* 14 (2000): 115–34; L. Lazzeretti, R. Boix, and F. Capone, "Do Creative Industries Cluster? Mapping Creative Local Production Systems in Italy and Spain," *Industry and Innovation* 15 (2008): 549–67.

18. P. L. Sacco and S. Pedrini, *Il Distretto Culturale: Mito o Opportunità?* (Torino: Department of Economics, International Centre for Research on the Economics of Culture, Institutions, and Creativity, 2003); I. Gordon and P. McCann, "Industrial Clusters: Complexes, Agglomeration and/or Social Networks?" *Urban Studies* 37 (2000): 513–32.

19. Fondazione Ente dello Spettacolo, *Il Mercato e l'Industria del Cinema in Italia 2008* (Roma: Fondazione Ente dello Spettacolo, 2009).

20. G. Martini and G. Morelli, *Patchwork due: geografia del nuovo cinema italiano* (Milano: Editrice Il Castoro, 1997).

21. R. Florida, *The Rise of the Creative Class: And How It's Transforming Work, Leisure, Community and Everyday Life*(New York: Basic Books, 2002); L. De Propris and L. Hypponen, "Creative Clusters and Governance: The Dominance of the Hollywood Film Cluster," in *Creative Cities, Cultural Cluster and Local Economic Development,* ed. P. Cooke and L. Lazzeretti, 258–86 (Edward Elgar Publishing: Northampton, 2008); S. Christopherson and M. Storper, "The City as Studio, "*Environment and Planning D: Society and Space* 4 (1986): 305–20.

22. E. Currid and S. Williams, "The Geography of Buzz: Art, Culture and the Social Milieu in Los Angeles and New York," *Journal of Economic Geography* 10 (2010): 423–51.

23. F. Governa, "*La Dimensione Territoriale dello Sviluppo Socio-Economico Locale: dalle Economie Esterne Distrettuali alle Componenti del Milieu,"* in *Rappresentare i luoghi. Metodi e tecniche,* ed. A. Magnaghi (Firenze: ALINEA, 2001).

24. N. Garnham, "Concept of Culture: Public Policy and the Cultural Industries," in *The Film Studies Reader,* ed. J. Hollows, P. Hutchings and M. Jancovich, 19–22 (London: Arnold, 2000); G. Harper and J. Rayner, *Cinema and Landscape: Film, Nation and Cultural Geography* (Bristol: Intellect, 2010).

25. M. L. Fagiani, *Città, Cinema, Società. Immaginari Urbani negli USA e in Italia* (Milano: Franco Angeli, 2008), 167–268.

26. Movie tourism is the kind of tourism that results from the popularity of film. It encourages sightseeing in the film locations and aims to develop specific marketing strategies and products for movie fans. Film commissions play an important role in developing movie tourism through branding a territory's exceptional natural, artistic, and cultural characters, using the shooting as a further element of attraction.

27. R. Cheung and D. H. Fleming, *Cinemas, Identities and Beyond* (Cambridge: Cambridge Scholar Publishing, 2009).

EIGHT

Mapping the "City" Film 1930–1980

JULIA HALLAM

This chapter develops ideas about cartography and filmmaking as two kinds of visual practice that share a number of similarities in the ways they describe the surface of an area or territory. As Les Roberts and I discussed in chapter 1, the term "mapping" is now subject to a wide range of interpretive processes and applications in relation to film; here I am interested in exploring the notion of what Teresa Castro has described as film's "mapping impulse," a way of seeing the world that has close affinities with cartography's perceptual processes. In her discussion of mapping as a function that facilitates a spatial understanding of "things, concepts, conditions, processes, or events in the human world," Castro draws on the work of renowned historian of cartography John Brian Harley to argue that the careful "coupling of eye and instrument that distinguishes cartography's observation of space is not so different from the one that determines cinema's careful coding and scaling of the world."[1] Focusing on what she describes as "cartographic shapes," Castro shows how panoramas (viewpoints shaping synoptic and spatially coherent landscapes and vistas), aerial views ("gods-eye" or "birds-eye" perspectives from planes or hot-air balloons), and atlases (spatiovisual assemblies and visual archives) define a cinematic topography in which the mapping impulse is a central cognitive element.[2] Drawing attention to the broad and complex theoretical terrain within which mapping and cartographic practices are embedded, Castro notes that "mapping can therefore refer to a multitude of processes, from the cognitive operations implied in the structuring of spatial knowledge to the discursive implications of a particular visual regime."[3]

Castro identifies three formal phases associated with cinema's mapping of urban space, which are used in this chapter to aid a comparative *well, not exactly*

exploration of the different modes of cinespatial practice found in archive film made in and about cities. The first of these is "topophilia," a love of place in which the idea of mapping refers to processes of self-discovery related to the politics and/or poetics of space. This is accompanied by the descriptive motivation of the images found in camera movements such as panning or tracking and hand-held traveling shots. In this sense, Castro suggests, the second phase of the cinematic mapping process is not dissimilar to conventional mapping procedures, which are a way of graphically describing and cataloguing the surface of the earth. The third formal phase is that of surveying, either by walking and examining the landscape or by scrutinizing it from above. In cinematic mapping procedures such as those noted above, aerial views and traveling shots are often combined during the process of describing and surveying a landscape, although, as Castro points out, such combinations can occur in "surprising and often contradictory ways."[4] By identifying these three phases of mapping activity in archive actuality and factual genres such as documentaries, newsreels, and amateur films, I will suggest that the "view aesthetic" of these films shares with cartography a mapping impulse embedded in the visual regimes of looking, seeing, and recording associated with these different forms of film practice. Focusing on a range of films made about a particular place collated by the *City in Film* project as part of ongoing research into the relationship between film and the urban environment, I will argue that conventional critical and theoretical analysis such as that developed by Castro can be complemented by the use of accurate mapping of location space using geographical information systems (GIS) software.

The use of GIS as a way of analyzing the visual dynamics of filmic space has evolved from the spatial concerns of a project that has created an extensive database of more than 1,700 film and video items that depict a provincial city and its urban environment from the earliest known footage to the present day. The films range across early actualities and travelogues, newsreel footage, amateur and independent productions, promotional material, and campaign videos.[5] Focusing in particular on the period between 1930 and the mid-1980s, when newsreels, documentaries, and amateur films were the most popular genres recording local scenes, this chapter explores the ways these genres have depicted Liverpool's urban landscape, with a view to examining in greater depth both the cross-generic imaginary of depictions of place and the spatial dynamics of the representation of place at particular times in the city's history.

The comprehensive compilation of data relating to films made in and about a particular city, assembled and made accessible in an online catalog as part of the first phase of the City in Film research, has provided the raw material from which the development of a spatial database of the city in film becomes possible. As well as recording conventional filmic data such as title, producer, date, duration, and format, wherever possible films in the catalog were viewed and categorized by their spatial content such as landmark locations and buildings, drawing on criteria developed by Kronenburg for architectural research.[6] The analysis was complemented by an inclusion of the category "spatial use," created to accommodate ethnographic and social engagement with the city's spaces and the changing functions of buildings and spaces over time. Transferring this catalog to a GIS platform, the locations of films listed in the catalog were situated according to their precise geographical coordinates, enabling a more refined process of geohistorical analysis to be developed, as well as the production of a range of associated georeferenced contextual materials including digitized segments of particular films, interviews with filmmakers, amateur cine society programs,[7] company/organizational material, and supporting documentation.

From a methodological standpoint, one of the advantages of using GIS software is that the ability to georeference onscreen locations to precise geographical coordinates lends itself to a specifically spatial mode of historiographical film research. Using a GIS platform (in this particular case ArcGIS) to georeference existing datasets (insofar as these extend to location and geographic data) opens up new directions in archival film practice by privileging processes of navigation through a city's cinematic history *and* geography—through layers of time *and* space—thereby laying the foundations for a spatial historiography of film and the city. The use of GIS enables researchers to create film location maps, enabling recurring patterns and themes to be visualized and assessed. The georeferencing of location points and nodes is digitally mapped in the form of point data; this refers to specific markers of place and location that are recorded on the map as points or nodes: buildings, street names, sites of historical and special interest, place names, points of arrival and departure, and so on. Point data is particularly useful because it corresponds to key features of spatial orientation in what Kevin Lynch has described as the legible sign system of the city.[8] Applying a semiotic understanding to the cognitive processes through which we orient ourselves in urban space, Lynch's notational system of "landmarks," "districts," "edges," "nodes," and "paths" has laid the groundwork for contemporary understandings of the ways people navigate urban space by constructing mental images ("cognitive maps") of their environment, as noted in chapter 1. The importance of particular nodes and landmarks in the construction of cognitive mappings of urban space was observed by Lynch as early as 1960. According to Anthony Raynsford, Lynch drew on an optics of urban design in which the street picture, a development of the picturesque tradition, played a compelling role in the development of his theory; the street picture "generated a stable set of spatial co-ordinates for the viewer, establishing scales and distances between the viewing subject and the perceived urban space" as well as producing "contrast and variety" by allowing the eye to "rest on prominent objects and the mind to make associations between contrasting elements."[9] This populist model of urban aesthetics, although questioned today, informed Lynch's attempts to understand the perceptual processes through which we orient ourselves in our urban surroundings as we walk through and experience them.

Mapping the spaces and places captured in archival film imagery using point data broadly corresponds to Lynch's mapping of topographical cognitive schemata. As well as embedding the images into a perceptual geography of the city's changing landscape, it also provides opportunities to examine the correlations between otherwise unrelated or unevaluated attributes and variables: for example, the relationship between film genre and location (how cinematic geographies are shaped by different film practices and narratives); the ways "landmark" or iconic buildings and vistas are framed by different filmmakers at different moments in time;[10] the filmic mapping of boundaries, gateways, points of transit and connection;[11] the way ideas of the "local" and "regional" have been variously construed in film and the shifting geographies of contested public space, of festivals and parades, sites of leisure and recreation, industry, commerce and civic activities. GIS enables a quantitative visualization of locations that can be usefully complemented by more traditional forms of textual analysis; here, a quantitative account of the characteristic locations found in three different genres, all of which show various forms of topographic fascination in their depictions of urban space, is complemented by comparative critical analysis, revealing the various mapping impulses displayed by each genre. In early cinema, as historians of early cinema Andre Gaudreault and Tom Gunning argue, the aesthetic of the view is primarily descriptive and underpins the dynamic and dialectical interplay of moving image spatial formations;[12] early cinema replicates the pictoralist traditions of landscape painting and photography. The earliest moving images of Liverpool shot by Alexandre Promio in 1897, *Lime Street*, situate his moving subjects against the well-known background of the city's grandest building at that time, the neoclassical St. George's Hall. By analyzing location data such as this, the spatial characteristics of particular visual formations can be identified and the ways in which they implicate their viewers in an urban imaginary of place can be brought into useful dialogic tension with the various forms of amateur, independent, and professional practices that produce them. Here, the focus is on three key moments: the 1930s, when the first amateur cine societies began to make their own newsreels of landmark city events; the 1960s, a period of extensive inner-city demolition and redevelopment that generates both celebrations and critiques of change; and the late 1970s and 1980s, when an emergent radical independent production sector began to challenge officially commissioned accounts of urban life by placing the cameras in the hands of people without other means of access to film and video equipment.

URBAN IMAGINARIES: FILM GENRES

The patterns observable in the mapping of city center locations across various film genres demonstrate the ways in which a city's cinematic geographies reflect what Hallam and Roberts have perhaps more accurately described as *cities* in film: a series of overlapping mosaics of the city's urban landscape that conveys different regimes of meaning and interpretation surrounding the production of films made in and about place.[13] A breakdown by film genre enables a more precise mapping of the shape and form of different production practices over time and of the ways these practices and processes create different cinegeographies. Mapping the location nodes that appear in different genres of urban film highlights the extent to which specific production practices construct and project different spatial perceptions of the city. As discussed in more detail below,

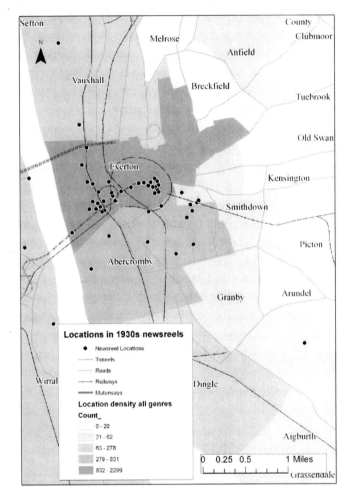

FIGURE 8.1

different genres often use the same range of buildings and locations, but it is the way films in the same genre can share similar spatial formations, suggesting an altogether different urban imaginary and sense of place, that are of particular interest here. Charting the locations featured in newsreels, for example, creates an overall impression of the visual formations commanded by this form of film practice.

The map of newsreel locations shot in the 1930s (figure 8.1) reveals a preponderance of spaces associated with commerce and industry (the docks, waterfront, and business area including insurance buildings, banks, and hotels), transportation links (including tunnels, railway stations, and the route of the "docker's umbrella" [overhead railway[14]]), civic and municipal buildings and monuments (the town hall, art galleries, concert halls), as well as places of worship, education institutions, and associated locations. Strongly reflective of the city's commercial institutions, engineering prowess and proud civic identity, the newsreels depict a city shaped by a vision linked with broader national interests and concerns. The local and vernacular are less prominent in terms of the locations and landmarks represented on screen; there are few images of suburban and residential areas or of local activities and minor civic events.

A closer analysis of newsreel footage in comparison with amateur footage of the same event shot at the same time demonstrates the ways these two modes of production create a very different view aesthetic. Amateur filmmaker and collector Angus Tilston has collated rare amateur footage from the 1930s with newsreel footage to create a montage of the opening of the first road tunnel under the River Mersey in 1934.[15] A major feat of engineering, the tunnel took nine years to construct and at the time was the longest underwater tunnel in the world; its opening was an event of national significance, a chance to show off Britain's engineering prowess to the world. The newsreel footage of the opening ceremony, performed by King George V, is taken from vantage points that are out of the reach of other filmmakers, creating a privileged view of events. A long shot depicts the king arriving by limousine accompanied by a motorcade of local dignitaries and disembarking at a ceremonial platform built in front of the imposing Walker Art Gallery, where he delivers his opening speech.[16] The speech is shot in medium close-up with occasional cutaways to wide-angled long shots that emphasize the size of the vast crowds gathered around the nearby tunnel entrance. Because of their distance from the celebrity figures at the center of these events, the sequences shot by amateur filmmakers can be clearly identified; one of the amateur's shots of the royal visitor are frequently interrupted by people's heads bobbing in front of camera, while another is shot from a high building some distance away. The newsreel cinematographers, briefly picked out in long shots in the amateur footage, are positioned on a specially built platform that affords them an optimal view of events. Vantage point is therefore a key factor in the view aesthetic of newsreel topography; their privileged gaze situates viewers close to the king, as honored guests, witnessing an important event.

Newsreels in general tend to begin with an establishing shot that orients the viewer before moving in to focus on events or newsworthy vistas, and the emphasis is often on celebrity figures of national interest attending important local events such as ship launchings, exhibition opening ceremonies, and, throughout the 1950s in Liverpool, gala film evenings. Frequently, location in newsreels is established by voice-over narration rather than any reliance on potentially recognizable vistas such as landmark buildings, although such buildings are often included in the establishing shots. In spite of the large number of newsreels productions in the City in Film database—some seven hundred films in total—made for regional and local as well national distribution, this spatial and aural formation is a recurring generic trope with little variation. It can be concluded that, combined with the comparatively limited range of other locations in the newsreel density cluster, the view aesthetic of the newsreel serves primarily national, rather than local, interests of identity and belonging.

Turning to films categorized as "documentaries," a different map emerges (figure 8.2). What is immediately apparent is the number and variety of nodal points; more areas of the city are visualized in Liverpool documentaries than in any other genre, with inner-city streets and suburban areas as well as landmark buildings and urban gateways figuring prominently. In addition to many of the customary city views that appear in newsreels, there is also more extensive coverage of the local and everyday (schools, pubs, clubs, sports venues, churches, cafés, and restaurants), with a notable shift toward residential areas, particularly the inner-city tenement housing blocks that became a prominent feature of Liverpool's urban landscape after the 1930s.

A notable example of a 1930s documentary, *Homes for Workers* (National Film Company, 1939), provides a good example of the use of space in the commercially sponsored documentary during this period. *Homes for Workers* is a propaganda vehicle for the Liverpool Gas Company modeled on a similar sponsored documentary, *Housing Problems* (Elton and Anstey, 1935),[17] that promotes the company's modern household appliances through a focus on the city council's slum clearance and redevelopment schemes. The film makes extensive use of aerial shots of the newly built suburban and rebuilt inner-city districts, creating a series of abstract patterned surface images intercut with street-level panoramic panning shots of streets and tenement housing blocks and more intimate close-ups

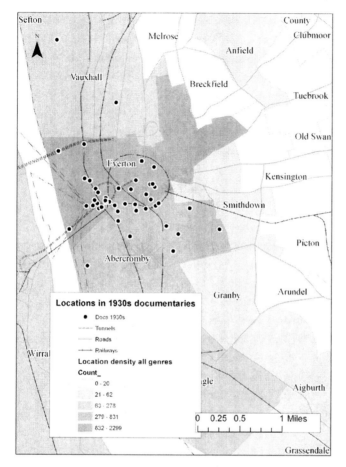

FIGURE 8.2

of women at home in the modern domestic interiors. Castro suggests that the aerial view epitomizes the abstract, documentary look of cartography and shares with it a number of complex and paradoxical traits, given its associative military functions in twentieth-century culture. Following the First World War, aerial imagery was regarded by different avant-gardes "as a means to disrupt and renew one's vision of the world," perhaps because it suggests a dialectic between the act of seeing and surveying the earth from above coupled with the act of walking around (*flânerie*) and recording what is seen with a camera, which evokes cartographic methods: "surveying the earth from above, with the eyes, and scanning it and measuring it by field walking, with the body."[18] Liverpool was one of the first provincial cities in the U.K. to open a commercial airport as part of the planned modernization of the city during the 1920s and 1930s, operating scheduled flights from 1930. In the pre–World War II *Homes for Workers*, it seems likely that the use of aerial photography, made possible by the use of a biplane from the city's airport, is closely linked to the filmmakers' ideas about contemporary visual aesthetics and the city as a place of modernization and progress. Architectural film historian Richard Koeck has pointed out that Liverpool's housing program and the social agenda that underpinned it shared attributes of modernist architectural schemes in Europe.[19] The filmmakers, keen to emphasize the city's modernizing agenda, have updated the view aesthetic in their version of "housing problems" through their extensive use of aerial photography. Castro suggests that this mode of shooting, when combined with more intimate street-level shots, can be seen as part of a broader modernist vision, one that creates "a synthetic vision of a city's social space" that maps and produces urban views and urban identities.[20]

The modernist visions of the city council, articulated in *Homes for Workers* by the then head of the planning department, L. H. Keay, are also found in numerous promotional films made to promote the city and its role in providing for the health and welfare of its citizens. These films are made primarily as marketing devices to raise industrial, commercial, and touristic awareness of Liverpool, but they also serve to justify public spending to the city's ratepayers by projecting an image of a vibrant, well-managed city with excellent infant welfare, library, education, and housing services and support for the elderly.

Locations in these films (figure 8.3) focus on the city's signature buildings and historic monuments, the busy docks, cathedrals, university, railway stations, and the overhead railway, but at the same time they foreground places of leisure, pleasure, and consumption (the central shopping areas, theaters, art galleries, nightclubs, and popular music venues), civic and cultural institutions and heritage sites (Walker Art Gallery, St. George's Hall, Picton Library) as well as Chinatown, acknowledging Liverpool's maritime past and, at least in part, its cultural and ethnic diversity. Typically in the promotional genre, a series of primarily static views of landmark sites and buildings are edited together, often with aerial views, to create an image of the city that is descriptive and flattering in its intentions. In her exploration of what she describes as "cinematographic

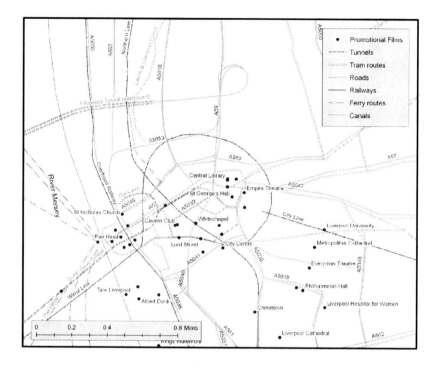

FIGURE 8.3

urban portraits," Castro notes that early travelogues present famous city locations "as a series of views in a seemingly linear manner" where "a succession of shots of emblematic places" seeks to achieve a "totalizing vision."[21] Similarly to early travelogues, promotional films in the 1960s, with their intercutting of static shots of well-known and iconic images accompanied by panning shots of the landscape and aerial views, project an aesthetic in which the series of views is designed to reveal the city's most attractive assets, often accompanied by a persuasive soundtrack.

Turn of the Tide (1966), the first of three promotional films commissioned by the public relations department of Liverpool City Council in the 1960s, exemplifies this technique. Audiences are taken on a virtual tour of the city by well-known television personality Raymond Baxter, presenter of the then popular BBC television science series Tomorrow's World. Arriving in the city by car through the Queensway Tunnel, Baxter emerges to find himself surrounded by Liverpool's nineteenth-century civic grandeur. Before embarking on his journey around the city, he offers a brief historical lesson; early maps and paintings depict the growth of the city from medieval castellated stronghold to enclosed dock. With the camera positioned beside him and looking at the views alongside him, he drives around the city, pointing out notable buildings and landmarks on his way to the new commercial and industrial estates in the suburbs. Arriving at a car factory, tracking sequences of modern production-line processes and fabrication techniques are intercut with a montage of name plaques of well-known banks and insurance companies found in the waterfront business area. Framed by aerial shots of the industrial hinterland that traverse mile upon mile of quays and cranes toward the river mouth where new docks are planned, Baxter's city is a "city on the move," a dynamic, modern environment. This sense of dynamism is replicated by the camera's movement: A series of traveling and panning shots bookended by aerial views map a contemporary "montage of attractions" designed to appeal to business investors, leisure visitors, and residents alike.

A sense of dynamism created by camera movement is also a key feature of some of the amateur films made in the 1960s by filmmakers resident in the Merseyside region. The overwhelming majority of the films in this category are made by filmmakers and cine societies based outside of Liverpool (especially in the neighboring suburbs of the Wirral). The domicile of these filmmakers, and the journeys they undertake, underline the difficulties of determining the finite boundaries of place-based film location studies. For practical purposes, a coherent object of spatial analysis, "the city" was created by using the boundary of a major arterial ring road, Queens Drive, to define the boundary of the city on its eastern and northern side, with the river Mersey forming a natural boundary on the western and southern side.[22] Locations in amateur films display a pattern that parallels the development of Liverpool's new municipal housing estates in the areas beyond Queens Drive in the 1920s and 1930s and the gradual move of the middle classes from the inner suburban areas to the greener environs across the Mersey.

Figure 8.4 shows a selection of locations documented in amateur films that reflect the mobility of these filmmakers. Mapping these more expansive location points highlights the essentially mobile nature of much of the amateur filmmaking practice in the region, demonstrating the extent to which transportation geographies and routes within and

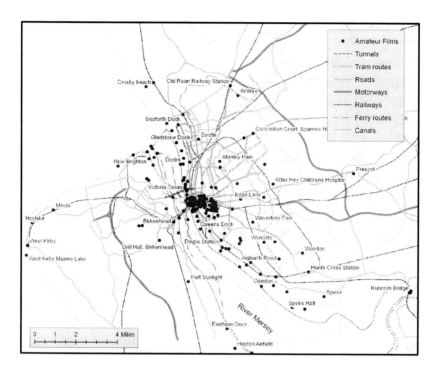

FIGURE 8.4

beyond the city are an important factor in the mapping of Liverpool on film and, by extension, of the feelings expressed about place, locality, and identity. Amateur filmmakers, often traveling from their domestic homes in the suburbs to the center of city, are responsible for some 242 of the films in the catalog made between the late 1920s and mid-1980s; of the 242 films cataloged, 71 are local "journey" and travel films of various kinds, and a further 111 focus on the city's public buildings and spaces. The focus on forms of transportation to and from Liverpool, and within the city center itself, suggests the enduring popularity as an amateur film topic of transportation and the geographical relationship with Liverpool, its transportation routes, and its landmark gateway nodes (ferry terminals, bridges, tunnels, and railway stations) for filmmakers commuting in from the Wirral and the wider Merseyside region, or traveling into the city to participate in (and document) events, festivals, and other activities that have taken place at different times in the city's history.[23]

Films made by Liverpool-based amateur filmmakers and cine societies active from the 1950s (of which, compared to their Merseyside counterparts, there have been comparatively few) are mostly clustered within the central urban area. There is less visible evidence that these filmmakers were interested in filming the wider region, other than perhaps anticipated popular destinations such as Aintree Racecourse to the north or the nearby seaside resort of New Brighton across the Mersey. By contrast, as indicated in figure 8.4, films made by amateur filmmakers operating across the region display a more far-reaching geographical spread in terms of the distance traveled between place of domicile and filmic destination, highlighting the close association between filmmaking and leisure practices such as travel, tourism, and sightseeing. Numerous films from the 1950s onwards document the changes wrought upon the physical and material urban fabric of the city by the ongoing process of decay, modernization, and redevelopment; of the eighty-two amateur films made in the 1960s, for example, fourteen feature reconstruction scenes of the city center. This sense of engagement with the detail of environmental change and modernization is more pronounced in amateur films than in any other genre, perhaps because, as Ryan Shand suggests, amateur filmmakers enjoy "a particular intimacy with geographies close to home," which has made them particularly active "in the exploration of both actual and imagined local worlds."[24]

The notion of an intimate film geography created by an attachment to place and locality such as that implied here has been explored by the cultural theorist Giuliana Bruno, who uses the term "topophilia" in a way similar to Castro to describe the ways in which "the landscape of travel culture" engages with the act of filmmaking, with an added emphasis on the emotional aspect of that engagement.[25] In the following paragraphs, the films of two filmmakers who have created city portraits reveal contrasting emotions to modernization and change. Shot for the most part on 8 mm film stock and assembled without soundtracks, these amateur journeys around the city record their expeditions silently, without distraction from ambient sound, music, or voice-over narration. The footage appears raw in that the camera, often handheld, is sometimes unsteady, absorbing the physical movement of the body. Much of the footage appears to be edited in the camera rather than subsequently, the immediacy of these methods enhancing its visual affect.

Four 8 mm color films made by amateur filmmaker George Cregeen provide an exemplary demonstration of this technique. Some eighty-eight minutes of Cregeen's footage survives intact; although the films are undated, analysis of their content indicates a roughly chronological series beginning with *Liverpool: City of Change* (1963), *Liverpool: The Pace Quickens* (c. 1963–1965), *Liverpool: The Shapes of Future* (c. 1965–1966), and *The Changing Face of Liverpool* (c. 1966).[26] Together, they provide an in-depth survey of the city's central area as it underwent extensive modernization between 1963 and 1966. Each title contains material from various years, suggesting that rather than presenting a historical trajectory, the films were edited after shooting around the four themes of the titles.

In the early films, the shots are mostly static and steady, implying the use of a tripod, although some experimentation is apparent. *Liverpool: City of Change* opens with an image of a street parade, the floats and carriages passing in front of a stationary camera. Subsequent shots cut between discontinuous spaces and places: a new shopping precinct in the suburbs, gardens in the city center, cranes looming over the construction site of the new central market. Sighting his camera solely for the purpose of recording sites of urban change, typically Cregeen finds a vantage point with a good view and films the surrounding vista. The shooting process seems analogous to the view aesthetic in Gunning's accounts of early cinema; the view (of a building, a landscape, an event, an industrial process, an activity) is presented as if the subject filmed would have taken place even if the camera had not been there.[27] The montage sequences, through their juxtaposition of views, imply a journey from the outer suburbs (Bootle) to the center and onwards through the Mersey tunnel to the Wirral, but this impression is contradicted by a subsequent series of shots taken around the development of the new road network behind the Walker Art Gallery, culminating in a trip across the recently opened overpass, the car traveling back toward the Mersey through an empty landscape cleared to make way for new roads and buildings.

In *Liverpool: The Shapes of the Future*, the filmmaker is more ambitious. Opening shots from a biplane depict the nearly completed St. John's Tower, surrounded by the foundations for the new market. Spectacular panoramic shots of the city and the waterfront taken from the incomplete platform at the top of the tower emphasize the scale and extent of the new buildings in the central area around the Three Graces at the Pier Head (the Liver Building, Cunard, and Port Authority buildings) as the camera pans from the half-built steel "wigwam" of the Metropolitan Cathedral in the south to the new office blocks rising high above the surrounding buildings in the north. Static ground-level shots pointedly frame modern high-rise apartments and offices emerging between rows of terraced housing, their steel frameworks and concrete and glass exteriors rising from the dilapidated fabric of the old city. Here the sequencing of panorama and street-level shots creates a total, synoptic view, one that maps a vision of the "new Jerusalem" emerging from the Victorian city.

Cregeen's films map the everyday streets and public spaces of the city, pointing to an essentially mobile form of practice in the documenting of urban space, an intimate geography embodied in the perceptual processes of filmmaking in which his excitement about change and renewal is palpable. Bruno describes this process as one in which the feeling for the landscape is imprinted in its representation: "geography holds remnants of what has been projected onto it at every *transito,* including the emotions . . . cinematically, the affect is rewritten on the land as on a palimpsest, and the moving landscape returns a sign of affect."[28] These positive feelings of anticipation in Cregeen's films, conveyed through dynamic combinations of panoramas, aerial views, and static shots, stand in stark contrast to the atmosphere of loss, mourning, and regret that pervades the films of Jim Gonzales.

Gonzales's films are walking tours of the city center undertaken with a purpose, that of recording the city's markets, streets, and public spaces before they are demolished or irreversibly changed by redevelopment. It is tempting to try to situate these films amidst the wide-ranging literature on film, *flânerie,* and city; the term is used, for example, by Anke Gleber to describe the ways the camera's eye in silent cinema is parallel to that of the *flâneur*'s gaze. Gleber argues that the camera, as it moves through the city streets, transforms exterior public space into interior (subjective) space.[29] Gonzales's experience of walking around the city is, however, different from that of his early twentieth-century counterparts in 1920s Germany, and the camera, although silent, is carried with him rather than fixed to a track or positioned on a tripod. The streets he walks are not the busy, chaotic streets associated with the frenetic modernity of Weimar Berlin, but the empty streets of a postwar, post-industrial provincial city uncertain of its future.

Gonzales made ten films between the early 1960s and mid-1970s that focus on capturing street scenes, shot for the most part in black and white and edited in camera with no soundtrack. One such film, *Old St John's Market and Town Scenes* (c. 1960), begins with footage shot around the ferry terminal at the Pier Head and moves uphill toward the Dale Street area, as if arriving in Liverpool by ferry and strolling up through the city toward the main station. As Gonzales walks through the streets, his feelings for the landscape are imprinted upon the visual record of his journey. Initially, he shoots a lighthearted view of the iconic Liver Buildings with a medium shot of a pigeon artfully placed between the twin birds on the towers captured in the foreground. Walking up Water Street past the former shipping offices, he pauses to record the frontage of the historic Georgian town hall before plunging into the network of alleys that surrounds the old business area, the camera pausing again to focus on the architectural details of buildings and street names.

The pace of the film slows as the camera arrives in the old market area around Queen Square, spending more time noting the details of streets and buildings. Retracing his steps around the cobbled streets, Gonzales gives particular emphasis to the detail of fruit and fish market gateways, to street names, to building frontages, the repetitive camerawork changing the forward trajectory of the journey into a cyclical form of reverie or contemplation. The repetitive mapping of detail is analogous to a survey, the act of walking creating a mobile, peripatetic view dense with visual information that in Bruno's terms could be "driven by a passion for mapping that is itself topophilically routed."[30] Shot shortly before the old markets were demolished to make way for a new shopping and market complex, the repetitive, cyclical detailed looking in this film implies a deep attachment to place, an intimate geography that I have described elsewhere as a "memorializing gaze."[31]

MAPPING PRODUCTION PRACTICES IN THE 1970S

The cinematic geographies of local production practices in the 1970s show marked changes from earlier decades, in part a consequence of technological change and the growing availability of cheaper video production equipment to a new generation of media workers, independent producers that use film and video practice as a social and political tool. By the 1970s, documentary is the most prevalent film genre; of 129 films in the catalog, 54 are documentaries, 37 are newsreels, and 33 are amateur films. Figure 8.5 shows the different ways these documentaries are spatially embedded. As well as being the most prolific genre, documentary continues to have the greatest spatial variation, both in numbers of locations found in individual films and in the range of these locations.

Typically, landmark buildings and sites such as the waterfront, heritage areas, and sporting venues continue to feature, alongside newer attractions such as the Cavern Club and the city center shopping areas. There is also a focus on inner-city areas traditionally associated with poor housing conditions, with particular attention paid to the city's housing action areas in Toxteth and Dingle, as well as in the new town of Kirkby, where many former inner-city dwellers have been rehoused to make way for a second Mersey tunnel. Turning to spatial use, twenty-one films feature sites of leisure and recreation, while carnival and festival sites in the central areas of Mathew Street and Hope Street and the inner-city districts of Toxteth and Old Swan appear as locations for the first time. There is a marked decline in films with ostensibly civic interests and an increase in films about social issues, most of which are focused on poor environmental living conditions in the housing areas designated for slum clearance.

An analysis of documentaries by producer reveals a further layer of geographical attributes. The BBC is responsible for twenty-four of the documentaries, many of which were made for regional magazine and topical current affairs programs such as *Look North* and *Decisions*, while fourteen are made by the regional independent broadcaster Granada. Local independent producers Narrow Gauge Productions and Merseyside Visual Communications Unit (sometimes working in tandem) are responsible for seven productions in the 1970s, all of which focus on heritage and community themes such as carnivals and arts events; some, such as *Super Swan*, are an implicit critique of the cramped and crowded inner-city living conditions in which many working people are living. Others feature explicitly left-wing political views: *Occupy* (Gael Dohaney, 1976) depicts workers' struggles against layoffs in factories in Liverpool and Kirkby, while Nick Broomfield's pioneering early films *Who Cares* (1970) and *Behind the Rent Strike* (1974) continue the invective against the city council's inner motorway (expressway) plan initiated by *Us and*

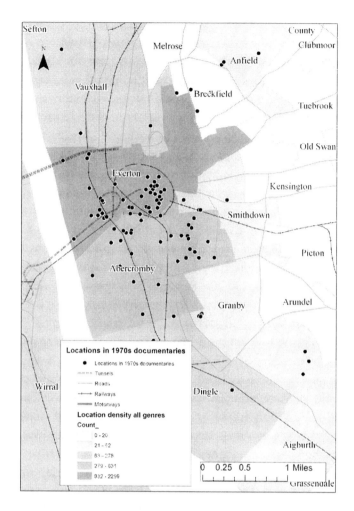

FIGURE 8.5

Them (Peter Leeson, 1969).[32] New video technology was enabling community activists to represent their campaigns to their communities for the first time: *Homes not Roads*, commissioned by Vauxhall Neighbourhood Council, testifies to growing media awareness among working-class activist groups in the city.

By way of contrast, newsreels in the 1970s, although still relatively numerous, have a much narrower spread of locations than do documentaries. Coverage is restricted to major sporting venues, civic and religious spaces, and particular events such as the opening of the second Mersey tunnel and the inauguration of the Anglican Cathedral, with some attention paid to the flourishing music scene in and around the Mathew Street area. With British Pathe (until 1970) and British Movietone News the only two companies producing newsreels by this time, the spatial distribution of coverage testifies to the genre's continuing adherence to a national agenda that covers only the most prestigious and well-known regional events in the interests of entertaining a widely dispersed national audience. Similarly, the visual maps created by amateur filmmakers on their journeys to and from the city reflect ongoing concerns with transportation, leisure, and recreation, with visits to the central area featuring heavily alongside journeys to and from the city and around the suburbs. The spatial documentary practices of the amateurs continues into the 1970s in numerous short films such as *Church Street* (Jim Gonzales, c. 1975),[33] and more considered, constructed pieces such as *This Is Liverpool* (George Gregory, 1974) and *The Pool of Life* (Angus Tilston, c. 1978), complemented by "mood" films such as *Pleasures Past* (Swan Cine Club, 1974) and an increase in the number of short narrative films using actors shot in urban locations, such as *Silent Witness* (Swan Cine Club, 1981).

The development of a nascent independent production sector on Merseyside is represented by seven films in the catalog. These films use, for the most part, 16 mm color sound film with voice-over narration added to ground a particular viewpoint. The political project of these films is implicitly revealed by a topophilia that emphasizes the detail of communal spaces and shared activities such as local arts events and carnivals rather than iconic buildings and landmarks. Films such as *Granby Festival* (Narrow Gauge Productions) and *Super Swan* are miniature portraits of inner-city districts that depict local street festivals. *Super Swan* maps an inner-city area of small terraced houses and tenement blocks straddling a main thoroughfare into the city described by its narrator as "a dirty mucky place . . . a place people pass through"; the streets are cheerfully decorated for the festival, partly masking the poverty, pollution, and overcrowding that typifies the area. Narrated by a local resident and activist, the film guides us around the streets during the course of the festival through a form of *verite* documentary that tries to catch people unawares as they gather to make street bunting from cutting up old clothes and to prepare food for the local carnival celebrations. Wandering around the streets and capturing events as they happen, the filmmakers focus less on the detail of the environment than on the events they are recording, yet it is this mapping of the spaces where time is being lived in the everyday streets, pubs, and open spaces of the city that typifies independent productions during this period.

By the mid-1980s, a fully fledged independent production sector had emerged on Merseyside, focused around Open Eye film and photography workshop, a community facility developed with the support of Granada and Channel 4 Television.[34] During the 1980s, a number of films were produced that present a different map of Liverpool, one with a specifically political inflection and vision. The principal production company, Community Productions Group,[35] was a cooperative of member organizations that employed a small team of media workers to deliver workshops in film, video, and photography to the members, with the aim of enabling them to represent themselves and talk back to official media. Membership was open to all community and neighborhood groups across the city, as well as activist organizations such as trade unions and voluntary groups. Other groups, such as the Women's Independent Cinema House (Witch) had a more specific agenda, primarily serving women's groups and black women's interests. Closely associated with Witch, Liverpool Black Media Workers were also producing films such as *They Haven't Done Nothin* (Bea Freeman, c. 1985), a response to the official accounts of the Toxteth riots in Liverpool in 1981.

These filmmakers, many of them amateurs in local communities or members of activist organizations, produce a map of the city focused on shared spaces and public amenities such as hospitals, wash houses, centers for physically disabled and elderly people, community buildings, youth centers, and workers co-ops. Oral histories such as *Disappearing Communities* (1989) focused on the Italian and Jewish communities in a rundown inner-city area, campaign videos such as *A Tax on Existence* (1989) about people's experiences of the controversial Poll Tax pilot scheme in the crowded inner-city Scotland Road area, and *Speke Enterprises* (1986), a promotional film featuring the community's self-help scheme to teach young people skills and generate employment, are typical of these productions, each of which creates a mini urban portrait. Taken together, this series of films, with their focus on local activities in particular buildings, communities, and territories, reveals a new politics of filmic space in which "the little tactics of the habitat"[36] begin to remap the city's urban spaces and identities.

TOWARD AN ARCHEOLOGY OF CINEMATIC GEOGRAPHIES

The use of Castro's strategies of topophilia, description, and surveying to discuss a range of archive films made in and about a particular city points toward some suggestive ways in which mapping, as a form of communication about space and as a practice that visualizes spatial relationships, can begin to open up new ways of exploring urban identities and feelings about place. This chapter has attempted to begin that process in both a figurative and literal sense by exploring how such a project might develop using contemporary cartographic tools such as GIS to add a quantitative, empirical dimension to what has until now been primarily a critical and theoretical exercise. Taken together, the films in the City in Film catalog constitute a cinematic atlas of a city, one that with the aid of GIS tools can be navigated through both time and space. By tracing cinema's mapping impulse as it is seen at work in a selective range of films made in and about a particular place compiled from various institutional and private archives, it is possible to distinguish parallel, conterminal, and divergent characteristics that mark specific spatial figurations at particular points in time.

The quantitative analysis enables broad generic trends to be identified, such as the focus on sites of commercial, economic, and civic importance that are central to the newsreels' mapping of national space within local territories, or amateur filmmaking's focus on geographies close to home including personal responses to urban redevelopment and change. Qualitative analysis indicates the ways these films share with cartography certain practices such as describing and surveying the surface of an area through the careful coordination of instrument and eye, using a similar range of shared movements and viewpoints such as walking (tracking), panning, panoramas, and aerial views to create graphic representations. The use of GIS in tandem with qualitative analysis has started the process of mapping the intimate geographies of locally produced factual and actuality films as lived, embodied experiences of the urban environment, experiences that are engraved and expressed in the ghostly traces of archive film.

NOTES

1. T. Castro, "Mapping the City through Film: From 'Topophilia' to Urban Mapscapes," in *Urban Projections: Cities, Space and the Moving Image,* ed. R. Koeck and L. Roberts, 144–55, cited here at 145 (Basingstoke: Palgrave, 2010).

2. T. Castro, "Mapping the City through Film," in *Cities in Film: Architecture, Urban Space and the Moving Image*, ed. J. Hallam, R. Koeck, R. Kronenburg, and L. Roberts, 35–40 (Conference Proceedings, Liverpool: Liverpool School of Architecture, 2008).

3. T. Castro, "Cinema's Mapping Impulse: Questioning Visual Culture," in "Cinematic Cartography," ed. S. Caquard and D. R. F. Taylor. Special Issue of *The Cartographic Journal* 46(1) (2009): 9–15, cited here at 10.

4. T. Castro "Mapping the City through Film: From 'Topophilia' to Urban Mapscapes," 145–46.

5. City in Film, http://www.liv.ac.uk/lsa/cityinfilm/html.

6. R. Kronenburg, *Houses in Motion: The Genesis, History and Development of the Portable Building*, 2nd expanded edition. (London: John Wiley, 2002).

7. The cine societies are amateur film clubs established on Merseyside in the 1930s to enable cooperative production ventures. For a more detailed account of their development and their activities, see J. Hallam, "City of Change and Challenge: The Cine Societies Response to the Redevelopment of Liverpool in the 1960s," in *The City and the Moving Image: Urban Projections*, ed. R. Koeck and L. Roberts, 69–87 (Basingstoke: Palgrave MacMillan, 2010).

8. K. Lynch, *The Image of the City* (Cambridge, Mass.: MIT Press, 1992).

9. A. Raynsford, "Civic Art in an Age of Cultural Relativism: The Aesthetic Origins of Kevin Lynch's Image of the City, *Journal of Urban Design* 16(1) (2011): 43–65, cited here at 48.

10. J. Hallam, "Civic Visions: Mapping the 'City' Film 1900–1960," *Culture, Theory and Critique* 53(1) (2012): 37–58.

11. L. Roberts, "Making Connections: Crossing Boundaries of Place and Identity in Liverpool and Merseyside Amateur Transport Films," *Mobilities* 5(1) (2010): 83–109.

12. See, for example, A. Gaudreault, "From 'Primitive Cinema' to 'Kine-Attractography'," in *The Cinema of Attractions Reloaded: Film Culture in Transition*, ed. W. Strauven, 85–104 (Amsterdam: Amsterdam University Press, 2006); and T. Gunning, "Attractions: How They Came into the World," in *The Cinema of Attractions Reloaded: Film Culture in Transition*, ed. W. Strauven, 31–39 (Amsterdam: Amsterdam University Press, 2006).

13. J. Hallam and L. Roberts, "Mapping the City in Film," in *Towards Spatial Humanities: Historical GIS and Spatial History*, ed. I. Gregory and A. Geddes (Bloomington: Indiana University Press, 2014).

14. The electric overhead railway, known locally as the "dockers' umbrella," opened in 1893; it ran the length of the docks from Dingle in the south to Seaforth in the north. Bomb damage in World War II led to its eventual demolition in 1957.

15. *The Mersey Tunnels: 60 Years 1934–1994* (Angus Tilston, Pleasures Past, 1994).

16. The Walker Art Gallery, World Museum Liverpool, and St. George's Hall now constitute the historic cultural quarter, part of the city's world heritage site. See http://www.liverpoolworldheritage.com/map/detail.asp?location=williambrownstreet, accessed January 2012.

17. This film was sponsored by the British Commercial Gas Association.

18. T. Castro, "Mapping the City through Film: From 'Topophilia' to Urban Mapscapes," 153.

19. R. Koeck, *Homes For Workers* (National Film Company, 1939), BFI Screenonline, http://www.screenonline.org.uk/film/id/1305711/, accessed August 2012. This entry was made as part of Liverpool: A City on Screen, developed in collaboration with

the North West Film Archive, University of Liverpool City in Film project, Liverpool Libraries, and Record Office and North West Vision and Media to celebrate Liverpool's tenure as European City of Culture in 2008, a year after the city celebrated its 800th anniversary.

20. T. Castro, "Mapping the City through Film: From 'Topophilia' to Urban Mapscapes," 153.

21. Ibid., 148.

22. For a more detailed analytical account of the changing shape of the city and the challenges this raises for spatial analysis see Hallam and Roberts, "Mapping the City in Film."

23. For a more detailed discussion of the ways transportation features in amateur films, see Roberts, "Making Connections."

24. R. Shand, "Amateur Cinema Re-Located: Localism in Fact and Fiction," in *Movies on Home Ground: Explorations in Amateur Cinema*, ed. I. Craven, 156–81 (Newcastle upon Tyne: Cambridge Scholars Publishing, 2009).

25. Similarly to Castro, Bruno draws on the work of geographer Yi-Fu Tuan, *Topophilia: A Study of Environmental Perception, Attitudes and Values* (New York: Columbia University Press, 1990), new edition with a new preface. See G. Bruno, *Atlas of Emotion: Journeys in Art, Architecture and Film* (New York: Verso, 2002), cited here at 354.

26. These films form part of a private collection and were viewed courtesy of Angus Tilston.

27. T. Gunning, "Before Documentary: Early Nonfiction Film and the 'View' Aesthetic," in *Uncharted Territory: Essays on Early Nonfiction Film*, ed. Daan Hertogs and Nico de Klerk, 9–24 (Amsterdam: Stichting Nederlands Filmmuseum, 1997), cited here at 14.

28. Bruno, *Atlas of Emotion*, 355–56.

29. A. Gleber, *The Art of Taking a Walk: Flânerie, Literature and Film in Weimar Culture* (Princeton, N.J.: Princeton University Press, 1999).

30. Bruno, *Atlas of Emotion*, 354.

31. J. Hallam, "Mapping Urban Space: Independent Filmmakers as Urban Gazetteers," *Journal of British Cinema and Television* 4(2) (2007): 272–84.

32. For a more detailed account of these films and urban regeneration in the 1960s, see L. Roberts, *Film, Mobility and Urban Space: A Cinematic Geography of Liverpool* (Liverpool: Liverpool University Press, 2012).

33. On *Church Street*, see Ryan Shand in this volume.

34. For an account of the UK film and video workshop sector, see, for example, J. Newsinger, "The 'Cultural Burden': Regional Film Policy and Practice in England," *Journal of Media Practice* 10(1) (2009): 39–56; and http://alt-fv-distribution.net/index .html (visited September 2, 2012).

35. This group was known later in the decade as Community Productions Merseyside.

36. M. Foucault, "The Eye of Power," in *Power/Knowledge: Selected Interviews and Other Writings 1972–1977 by Michel Foucault*, ed. C. Gordon (London: Harvester Wheatsheaf, 1980), cited here at 149.

NINE

Retracing the Local: Amateur Cine Culture and Oral Histories

RYAN SHAND

Oral history and moving images have considerable potential synergy.

While amateur films/footage of landscapes and sociocultural practices often account for the majority of regional film collections, accompanying materials such as scrapbooks and interview transcripts can take up more physical space than an archive can reasonably be expected to store in the long term. As a result, the thought processes behind the making of these productions can be difficult to discern for the visiting scholar who does not have the local knowledge required to assess the significance of the films. This problem is compounded by the lack of synchronized sound in many amateur cine productions, meaning that they have now effectively become silent films even if an accompanying soundtrack once existed. In particular, *non-fiction* films/footage that documented local events, buildings, and spaces are available to view, yet their significance often lies outside the boundaries of the frame.

The necessary turn toward local history that results from these problems can be facilitated by interviews with the amateur filmmakers themselves, a research methodology that was developed in the project Mapping the City in Film: A Geohistorical Analysis at the University of Liverpool (2008–2010) and continues in Children and Amateur Media in Scotland at the University of Glasgow (2010–2014).[1] The added benefit of these oral histories is that they are stored digitally, which requires less physical space in the archive itself. Therefore this chapter will seek to provide reflections on adopting the methods of oral history to increase our understanding of amateur cine culture and the potential difficulties faced by both archivists and scholars in this activity. To do this I will provide a comparison between two films from the collection of the Merseyside-based collector and filmmaker Angus Tilston, namely *Church Street* (c. 1975, Jim Gonzales/Liver Cine Group) and *A Pool of Life* (1976–1978, Angus Tilston/Swan Cine Club). Both films were shot in central Liverpool at around the same time, but this comparison will be used to illustrate epistemological problems as well as to explore possible solutions.

After this opening section, attention will turn to examining how the problems previously identified are routinely solved by staff members working in film and television archives using established protocol at the acquisitions stage, but also to exploring how the use of the Internet is changing the ease and scope of the cataloging process itself. Building on the groundwork provided by these film and television archivists, the next section explores why scholars might be drawn to digital mapping platforms such as GIS in order to organize the wealth of empirical data that can now be gathered from various disparate sources. The use of GIS software allows the researcher to organize and analyze this combination of geographical and historical information, incorporating it into layers on digital maps that can be navigated, compared, and used to determine new patterns and data correlations. As Jeffrey Klenotic has suggested:

> In addition to offering powerful tools for researching and representing cinema history, GIS opens new opportunities for interdisciplinary engagement across cinema studies, ethnography, oral history, architecture, economics, geography, historical geography, historical GIS and other fields and disciplines with potentially mutual interests in the socio-spatial history of cinema and everyday life.[2]

Therefore, this chapter details how GIS software offers various contextual solutions to many of the problems that have been identified by both archivists and scholars relating to the appreciation and study of amateur non-fiction films. While these technologies do not solve all the potential difficulties encountered by viewers of this material, I argue that in combination with the practice of oral history these developments make possible a practical means of bringing previously "local" cultures into the wider public space. Indeed, archivists, scholars, and museum curators have various mutual interests in helping to facilitate the circulation of archival film into display and dialogue with contemporary audiences, those who often have both personal and sociocultural investment in images and sounds from their (and our) localized past.

First of all, this chapter will highlight one of the main problems facing researchers of amateur films/footage that are held in public archives. These are issues that archivists face on a daily basis; it is therefore useful to draw attention to these problems for the benefit of future researchers so they can become more aware of the best approaches to archival material.

AMATEUR FOOTAGE AS AN INCOMPLETE OBJECT

If a film scholar discovers an old feature film, either in an archive or on television, it is usually fairly easy to discern what the filmmaker intended to accomplish. If the film is a comedy the filmmaker was trying to make the audience laugh. If it is an action film the filmmaker was usually attempting to thrill the viewers with spectacular scenes. If the film is a documentary the filmmaker is often shining light on a topic that has passed most people by. This is also the case for most amateur *fiction* films, which tend to follow generic patterns similar to the professional cinema. If it is amateur non-fiction *footage*, however, things can be much less clear-cut.

To illustrate this problem, a brief description of a very short piece of amateur footage that shows an anonymous street will suffice. Shot with a single 16 mm camera, the silent footage records various cars, buses, and pedestrians as they pass by. With a running time of just under a minute and a half, nothing else of real significance happens, nor do you get the impression that something will. This is a slice-of-life scene similar to those of the earliest filmmakers, only this footage is in color, so its relatively contemporary nature suggests that it would not have been made as a visual novelty. The film mostly consists of either pedestrians or vehicles moving horizontally through the static frame, with the camera positioned at various points, looking both up and down the street.

There are just two exceptions. First, early on the inclusion of a short shot with the camera held sideways (clearly a mistake or outtake) indicates that this footage was probably not shown publicly. Second, at the end of a later shot the camera pans to center on the storefront of a

FIGURE 9.1. Location in film by Jim Gonzales.

large Woolworth's store. Other than this reframing, there is little other evidence of any artistry or indeed intention behind these series of eleven shots.

This is obviously footage of a street, but which street? If you had seen this footage in a national film archive could you be sure which city this film was made in? If you were sharp-eyed and worked out that it must be Liverpool, could you narrow it down to a particular street? Even if you knew the city well today could you spot that this was in fact Church Street? It looks very different now. If you spotted that this was Church Street could you tell what decade this was from? Finally, even if you could do all this, how would you know who made this film (there are no opening or closing credits after all) and perhaps more fundamentally: *why* did he or she make it? Was it, for instance, made by an employee of a company that was thinking about opening a new shop in this street? Out of all the possible subjects in the world, why did this filmmaker choose to expose film on this seemingly ordinary city center street?

It is questions like these that face the film archivist every day. In 2006–2008 researchers working on the University of Liverpool's City in Film project faced similar questions. In many ways I had it easy. After watching this film and wondering what I had just seen, I just looked it up on the City in Film database (which is now publicly available on the website[3]) and most of my questions were answered instantly. I found out that this was a film called *Church Street,* which was probably made sometime in the 1970s before that area became a pedestrian zone. Very usefully, the catalog entry also told me that it was made by a Liverpool-based amateur filmmaker named Jim Gonzales, who was also a member of the Liver Cine Group. Things start to become a little clearer. If I did not have access to this information it would have been difficult to know how to start researching the history of this film. In a similar vein, Mark Neumann and Janna Jones note that:

> amateur films often come to us with a minimal amount of contextual information regarding their production. That an amateur film has survived at all does not guarantee that a corpus of historical or contextual information regarding its production is available. In most cases, analysing such films requires piecing together any available information about the circumstances of their production. A great deal of ambiguity surrounds such films.[4]

It is this ambiguity that is important; therefore I want to explore its resulting problems for the rest of this chapter. Films made within what Richard Chalfen called the "home mode" tend to focus on family events and the people who are closest to the filmmaker.[5] This was clearly not the case with *Church Street,* which takes as its subject an anonymous stretch of road featuring many passersby with no direct connection to the filmmaker. Therefore, the main stumbling block to understanding this film is not tracing genealogical histories, but rather to become more familiar with *local* knowledge.

This is an issue that has become a recurring concern in a number of articles recently published in the journal *The Moving Image.* For example, while discussing itinerant filmmakers in the United States, Martin Johnson noted that:

> Though local film is often described as a historical record of people and places otherwise undocumented, it is also the product of chance encounters between filmmakers and the particular people and places filmed. These

fleeting encounters between a person and a camera that appear in a local film make for compelling viewing but are difficult to analyze because so much of the knowledge contained in that moment was only available to the audiences who saw the film at the time of its initial exhibition. Nevertheless, a broader historical view may reveal information that is not obvious from researching the immediate reception of the film.[6]

Although the analysis here was centered on films made for commercial purposes, the above quote has resonance with historical research methods into amateur cinema. In my *The Moving Image* article from 2008, I argued that one of the dominant ways to study amateur film was to examine it from what I called the *evidential* perspective:

> In this way, film almost becomes a scientific tool for the recording of moving images and objects that will be of interest to the retrospective viewer in years to come. However, this method requires supplementary material for the visual evidence to become historical knowledge. Without knowledgeable commentaries from people who can interpret the images, the film in itself can become relatively meaningless.[7]

While the article overall was an attempt to encourage scholars to consider researching amateur *films* (i.e., crafted and edited works that often included either a soundtrack or intertitles in order for the audience to understand what they were being shown onscreen) in addition to amateur *footage*, these contextual problems overlap considerably, whether it is a short piece of amateur footage or an amateur documentary without explanatory intertitles or an accompanying soundtrack. Indeed, when writing on home movies that have been sold as secondhand goods, Devin Orgeron points out that:

> The object, in other words, is stripped of its aura, its temporal, geographical, and personal specificity that, of course, was tenuous to begin with. Typically only semi-articulate in the best of conditions, in their often mildew-ridden boxes or vinegaring cans, on other people's projectors, on the Internet, these films are even further "removed," are rendered increasingly opaque.[8]

This is one of the main problems with viewing material in an archive rather than through a private collector; you are viewing material that is "removed" from its original context. It is a necessary removal to be sure, but one that often then requires the researcher to *retrace* the movement of the film in order to make sense of it. One of the main stumbling blocks in retracing this journey is that the filmmaker may no longer be alive. By removing amateur filmed material from its original context, archivists and researchers have to bridge the resulting gap in local knowledge in order for it to be comprehended by non-local viewers.

In order to illustrate this, another amateur film stands in relief in many ways to *Church Street*. *The Pool of Life* (1976–1978, color, sound, 13 minutes), made by the amateur filmmaker Angus Tilston, is a documentary which appears to tell a "day in the life" of a square in Liverpool's city center. Williamson Square, located just a few minutes' walk from Church Street, is a busy retail area that now also features a computer-controlled fountain. Tilston's film opens with a shot of the statue of Carl Jung in nearby Mathew Street before cutting to an aerial view of Williamson Square looking down sharply from an extreme high angle, which makes the people far below seem tiny. Next a shot of St. John's Beacon tower confirms how the preceding vantage point was made possible, before Tilston pans down to the people at ground level in Williamson Square. A motif running throughout this film is the constant cutting to signs, both those indicating locations and advertising businesses and more temporary placards held by people. In this sense *The Pool of Life* is similar to an untitled Jim Gonzales film described by Julia Hallam in which the camera movement stops "to focus on the details of buildings and street names."[9] This technique finds early expression in a closeup of the Richmond Street sign, locating the images within the area before the shot zooms out and pans to the right, settling on a view with the Liverpool Playhouse theater in the background. A commentary informs us that "[i]n 1927 Carl Gustav Jung, Swiss philosopher, had a dream that represented the culmination of his psychological development. He found himself in Liverpool and eventually came upon a square in which there was a pool, which only he could see, and in this pool he saw that Liverpool was the pool of life." This quotation, "Liverpool is the pool of life," is locally famous and helps to bring context to Tilston's film in a way that is quite different from *Church Street*. While he does not locate the square on a map of Liverpool for the benefit of non-local viewers, the shots of street signs and buildings, as well as the music and commentary, helps the spectator to form general impressions of where and what we are seeing.

The film itself could be said to be loosely structured by sequences indicated by the soundtrack choices, but it is also visually based around

FIGURE 9.2. Still from *The Pool of Life*.

contrasting images and recurring themes. For example, early shots of young creative people with guitars or selling their art, as well as an accordion player, are immediately followed by a man searching through a litter bin and older people sitting watching the world go by. The solemn nature of a choir singing is cut against a sleeping baby and young boys sliding down a set of stairs. There is a brief quiet interlude following pigeons, then a sequence following a number of activists as they use the square to help spread their message, before the documentary draws to a close with shots of various people packing up and leaving for the evening.

In this way the illusion that the film represents a day in the life of the square is confirmed. Yet despite the various groups of people, waiting in lines for buses or taxis, interestingly while the soundtrack plays an instrumental version of the Beatles "Eleanor Rigby," Tilston includes a number of shots of a man sitting alone reading and then eating while music implies the missing lyrics "All the lonely people, where do they all come from? All the lonely people, where do they all belong?" This feeling of being alone while surrounded by crowds is a common part of the urban experience, one that this film manages to convey particularly well using visual contrasts combined with a carefully chosen musical accompaniment. Like a series of waves, the gentle, meandering, unhurried rhythm of the piece allows individuals to enter and leave the frame without focusing on anyone in particular. Here the star of the film is the location; the people are just passing through. Finishing with a return to a shot of the Carl Jung statue before the closing credits inform the viewer that the film they have just seen is "Produced by Angus Tilston: and a production of 'Swan Cine Club Wirral.'" Despite being the work of one man, the fact that it was then also credited to his cine club suggests that Tilston did not see his own filmmaking as separate from the group's activities. The existence of credits, unlike *Church Street,* also suggests that the film was intended to be seen in public screenings.

This idea of building an amateur film around a specific micro-geography is also in evidence in other titles from the Merseyside region, including *Fair Play* (George Gregory, 1960s), *Years of Change* (Jim Wood/ Hoylake Moviemakers, 1960–1990), *Chester, City of Charm* (Les Holloway/Swan Cine Club, 1971), *Pleasures Past* (Graham Kay/Swan Cine Club, 1974), and *Walk a Gentle Mile* (Southport Movie Makers, 1985). What *The Pool of Life* makes clear is that in the amateur sound era a filmmaker did not need someone to explain or lecture during film screenings; this information could be integrated onto the soundtrack itself. As the example of *Church Street* demonstrates, however, providing the contextual information necessary to understand some amateur footage is now the preserve of others, often without personal connections to the subject matter, as the next section details.

INDEXING IN THE AGE OF THE INTERNET

The staff working at a film archive would encounter the problems described above on a daily basis. This process is managed by a series of well-developed protocols and specialties, which aim to quickly gather and synthesize the maximum amount of information relating to film collections. At the time of deposit, the acquisition staff records related contextual information from the donor (who is not always the filmmaker, but often a friend or relative) using written correspondence, diaries, letters, and any notes of conversation they have had about the collection. As Snowden Becker points out:

> More often, a donor will present a handful of unidentified reels as part of a larger, attic-clearing bequest following the demise of the one remaining person who *could* have identified all the participants, locations, and activities. Collections managers and curators should not despair under these circumstances; given that they are the rule rather than the exception, it is possible to examine these materials and to work out a set of standards to improve the quality of the information a museum gathers about each item and thereby improve access.[10]

This quotation resonates with conversations I have had with archival staff in regards to the acquisition and subsequent cataloging of amateur films from donors. To understand more fully how an archive deals with new material I asked Ann Cameron and Liam Paterson, who work at the Scottish Screen Archive, to complete a written questionnaire.[11] The following section is therefore a reflection on this information, which they helpfully provided.

Once the collection is in the care of the archive, it is only when viewing copies have been made of the original prints and most importantly for the issues under discussion, details about the film has been entered into the film and video records database by one of the archive's catalogers, that this material is available to researchers. As Ann Cameron noted, "The cataloguer will judge where best to site the information in the catalogue record." These records provide context to the collection as a whole (for example with cross-references to paper archive records) and also shot lists of individual films. These catalog records, which are often not available to the general public in their complete form, allow the researcher to navigate information on entire collections, to search for titles with specific affinities using keywords, or to simply learn more about one title of special interest. As Cameron acknowledged, the cataloger must make a series of judgments about what is the most important information in relation to each and every entry in the database. In some ways it is analogous to archaeology or detective work in that all available information is used to make a "best educated guess" as to what is depicted in each film. This is an interpretive activity to be sure, but one that can be verified to some degree by reference to various extra-textual sources. As we have seen, this contextual information is often more important in understanding amateur film collections, since, unlike commercially released films, data on production and exhibition often lies outside the realm of easily accessible public records.

This cataloging process is not confined to new acquisitions, however, as one of the most challenging issues facing the contemporary film cataloger is how much time to allocate to recataloging older entries in light of newly accessible information. In response to my question as to what extent are older catalog entries now being updated, Cameron wrote, "Regularly, I'd say on a weekly basis. I receive e-mails and occasionally letters on a drip-feed basis offering information about films. I will then judge the accuracy of the information based on things like the reliability of the source and update the catalogue or the paper archive accordingly." In addition to these correspondences, new books of historical interest are published that might cause an older entry to be amended, but both this sort of research and correspondence with donors can be excessively time-consuming and impractical. This is where new technologies have aided contemporary cataloging and have an added advantage over older techniques. For example, text files written by donors can be pasted directly into the catalog records, which is especially useful in covering a large body of films perhaps made by a disparate group of people, as is often the case for cine clubs that have been in operation for a number of decades. Arguably the most significant technological change affecting the gathering of such contextual information, however, is the wealth of material and speed of access provided by the Internet.

While Cameron was keen to stress that "The catalogue records are written primarily from a real-time viewing of the moving image itself and described as the cataloguer watches the moving image—so I'd say the catalogue records are not really written using the Internet in the main." She also added that the Internet does have some real practical benefits, in that it "has enabled a quick visual reference source that was not available before without spending time looking up books etc." Therefore, it is within this context of technological change and the new possibilities emerging from these developments that we can explore the consequences of this recataloging of amateur film collections using the Internet as an extra aid to information.

Much like certain cultural commentators, film archivists may be skeptical about the reliability of user-generated websites, yet such caveats tend to be balanced by the need to collect information quickly and easily, so sites like Wikipedia have their uses for cataloging purposes.[12] Other well-known, more "officially" sanctioned sites like Google Maps, Ordnance Survey, and Scotland's Places, allow the cataloger to map the amateur footage onto recorded data of places and locations already in the public domain. This is to be expected, but it is perhaps less well understood how the growing number of local community and history websites have transformed the possibilities of organizations such as film archives to "place" previously idiosyncratic material into localized contexts. This relatively recent wave of do-it-yourself websites effectively means that previously localized cultures are becoming accessible to wider demographics in the age of the Internet. Being able to verify that an event depicted in an amateur film happened on a certain day in a particular place by cross-referencing, say, photo-sharing websites along with written accounts on a local history enthusiast's page is increasingly becoming standard archival practice. Both Cameron and Paterson have described to me how they have used local history websites to better understand what might have otherwise existed in the aforementioned cloud of ambiguity. For example, Cameron was able to recatalog the Bo'ness Children's Fair Festival film collection using detailed information from The Fair Day site.[13] She explained:

> This helped identify people, their role in the proceedings, and date the films accurately, for example. (Information that was not there in the records, before). This really benefited the catalogue and visitors were able then to pick out the particular year they were interested in and see that film.

Newly available resources such as these therefore enable much more specific catalog entries than have been possible previously, which as Cameron acknowledges is of immense benefit to researchers interested in this material. Also, Paterson related that:

> A film in the Templar Collection (*Crane Collapse on Building Site* (1958c)), featured news footage of a construction accident, but with no mention of location or date. The Kodak film box had a return address in Dundee, and a man in the film is seen wearing a jacket with an SSHA (Scottish Special Housing Association) logo. The Canmore website (http://canmore.rcahms

.gov.uk) provided information about postwar SSHA building projects in
Dundee, including photographs of Dryburgh Gardens. Google Streetview
then provided a modern view of a block of flats in Dryburgh Gardens which
matched the camera position in the original film almost exactly, thus providing an approximate date and exact location for the film.

In this case, the Internet provided detailed information in a matter of
minutes that would have been almost impossible to find otherwise. A
future researcher would now be able to use this improved catalog information to facilitate further research of the event in local newspaper
archives.

This web of cross-referencing sites, quickly and easily accessible, is of
great pragmatic value in numerous instances, both to archive catalogers,
but also to scholars working on archival film. Amateur films frequently
focus on more localized topics. They have become more practical to research only in recent years, partly due to the accessibility of key contextual information from the increased digitization of many national and
regional newspapers.

As indicated by the final sentence of Paterson's example above, there
is a limit to the amount of detail that shot lists can reasonably be expected to cover. Therefore, how detailed should they be? This is an ongoing discussion in the archive journals, yet the staff of the Scottish Screen
Archive tends to adhere to general guidelines. To explain this in more
detail, Cameron wrote:

> GENERALLY the shotlist is a matter of judgement, and will vary in length
> according to the type of footage being described. For example, a technically
> detailed 30 min film about mining machinery may only have a 2 line shotlist
> whereas a travel home movie may have a longer shotlist identifying people,
> place, event in greater depth even though it only lasts 5 mins. It is always
> a matter of balancing time and staff resources and making sure every film
> is given the same level of attention, whether it is a subject of interest to the
> cataloguer or not. The shotlist must be an objective, factual account of the
> action of the film and not veer off into 'personal interest' research.

In short, shot lists effectively function as concise pointers, which researchers can then use as the basis for more in-depth contextual research.

Up until now this highly specialized role has been the preserve of
professional catalogers. There is much debate at the moment in archival

journals, however, about the advantages and disadvantages of opening this activity up to amateur enthusiasts. User-generated material is the engine of sites like Wikipedia, and YouTube videos of local interest often contain comments posted by knowledgeable non-professionals. This rush to an open-sourced two-way system, to which people can contribute at their own leisure, is, from the professional archivist's point of view, problematic to say the least. As Cameron notes:

> It can however be a double-edged sword as we need to judge, as cataloguers, what to include and what is relevant to the film record (and not just something that is vaguely "interesting" in relation to the catalogue record.) We have to maintain throughput of cataloguing and not veer into the realms of extra research.

In some ways, these comments echo the passage above in relation to e-mails received from donors, in that the professional's interpretation as to what is significant and what is insignificant should not be bypassed if standards of quality are to be maintained. Developments in technology, however, do have the potential to aid the gathering of extra information without a significant burden being placed on the cataloger. For example, going back to the examples of amateur filmmakers who provided lectures or commentaries during screenings, it is clear that it would represent a huge loss if this kind of detailed local knowledge was lost over time. Therefore, one possible solution would be for the archives to record audio commentaries of amateur filmmakers' memories of their productions at the time of donation. This could also be expanded to include friends or relatives of a filmmaker if they have close knowledge of what the often silent non-fiction film being passed onto the archive depicts and what it meant for the filmmaker. Of course, this is no replacement for the thorough contextual work that a professional cataloger would do; it would merely represent another layer of meaning that could be consulted and interpreted by the researcher at a later date. Becker has outlined an ideal process for films that are to be incorporated into an archival collection:

> The routine cataloging of a home movie within a museum (a process to be completed more or less objectively, by a cataloger who watches the film and describes it basically without additional input, or with the benefit of historical research materials in the case of identifiable events) should be

FIGURE 9.3. Ashby Ball, chairman of Southport Moviemakers,
providing a commentary for the film *Southport* (1958).

accompanied by as much additional material as possible. The ideal scenario
might include a special viewing of the home movie, with curatorial or collections staff and the family of the filmmaker present, in a room with a tape
recorder. Commentary from the audience should be encouraged, especially
identification of people, places, or activities, and the museum staff present
should be able to make follow-up inquiries after the film is over. In this way,
the home movie could be presented in its natural habitat, if you will, and enriched almost as it would be there by a family dialogue, a sort of oral history
that would add dimension and meaning to the elusive characters called up in
the projector's flickering light.[14]

In the absence of this practice in operation at most archives, however,
the role of the scholar in doing such work takes on even greater importance. This task will now be explored in relation to the possible expanded
role for oral history as a tool for scholarly research into the relationship
between amateurism and localism.

LOCATING THE LOCAL THROUGH
ORAL HISTORIES

What can researchers do to shed more light on these films that often exist in this cloud of ambiguity? Thankfully this problem is considerably lessened by the well-researched catalog entries by archivists described above, but one of the main ways film researchers can aid work on amateur film is to conduct interviews with filmmakers themselves. This is the reasoning behind work that was conducted on the project Mapping the City in Film at the University of Liverpool.[15] For a demonstration of the benefits of the interview process, here is a short transcript of the amateur filmmaker Angus Tilston sharing his memories of Jim Gonzales:

> Well Jim Gonzales was a keen member of the cine movement quite early on. He helped to form the Liver Cine Group in about 1968 but he did a lot of filming before that. He was a member of the I.A.C.[16] and the North West Council and he used 16 mm basically. He did a lot of recording in Liverpool and made/ started a film on Liverpool Cathedral; he did, but he did two films. One was called—the film itself has vanished, I don't know what's happened to it since he died—called Silently They Stand Together. It was a story about both cathedrals, linked by Hope Street basically, but all this other stuff he gave to me. One or two he hung on to, but after his death I don't really know what happened to them. It would have been a really nice film to have in the collection really. He was quite a quiet sort of person, but he was always there if you know what I mean. Wherever there was a film-do on he would always be there, sometimes filming it as well actually.[17]

Tilston is a skillful verbal storyteller and this extract would work extremely well in stand-alone form as an audio clip. This is not always the case, but this example shows the potential of this material as an audio-only file that could be usefully employed as a sound file to run at the same time as one of Jim's films. While Angus knew the man himself and talks about him so well, he still did not have knowledge of why Jim made his film about Church Street. These are the kinds of limitations that are frequently run into in trying to unpack the amateur filmmaking process of the past. However, in 1976, C. A. Clyde of the University of Leeds published a report called *The Pedestrianisation of Church Street, Liverpool.*[18] This might offer a clue as to why this film was undertaken in the first place. Perhaps Jim Gonzales heard that proposals were underway to change this road in the near future, and, thinking ahead, he decided to film the street as it was at the time. At the moment this is my best guess as to why Jim Gonzales made his film, but still I have to admit that an ambiguity remains. This would not have been the case had someone interviewed him about his work at an earlier date.

While the literature on oral history has tended to be either historical or practical in nature, some more recent theoretical work, such as Lynn Abrams's Oral History Theory, is beginning to provide frameworks of particular relevance to the activity.[19] The benefits of the use of oral history methods in film studies have been exemplified by at least two major studies, Kevin Brownlow's The Parade's Gone By and Annette Kuhn's An Everyday Magic: Cinema and Cultural Memory,[20] which focus on American silent movies and British audience reception, respectively. It is clear that there are precedents for the use of this research method in the field. Others have noted the potential of combining oral history with the study of amateur film. Stefan Szczelkun writes, "In spite of the general recognition of the importance of film to oral history, very little analysis has yet been made of the home movies now in public archives," but little sustained activity in this regard has emerged since the publication of this article.[21] Interestingly, while later describing a screening of amateur films at the Museum of the Moving Image in London, Szczelkun comments, "At best each movie could do with a historical introduction or commentary by the filmmaker. Is a general audience expected to know the cultural significance of the annual parade to the people of Chingford, Essex?" and further, "The lack of critical discourse on amateur film means that many of the images can easily be dismissed as having little value once they have left the localised context in which they were made."[22] In this regard, the following represents an attempt to address the lack of critical discourse on amateur films and issues of context.

On the Mapping the City in Film project, one of the main priorities of our research was to develop a strong network of contacts with the amateur film community in the Merseyside region. Our initial short list of potential interviewees was made up of people whose contact details we gained through an amateur film evening we held in the School of Architecture in November 2008. Five clubs took part in that event (Hoylake, Warrington, West Cheshire, Southport, and Swan), and we asked each to show a selection of films in their own twenty-minute time slot. As a result of this we became aware of at least twenty filmmakers with whom

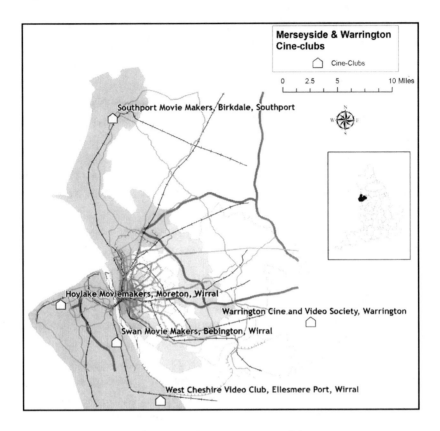

FIGURE 9.4. Map of Merseyside and Warrington cine clubs.

we could then request interviews. Of course, we constantly added to this short list by various means, such as keeping track of what was happening on the amateur film scene through newsletters and attending public screening events put on by the filmmakers themselves, as well as by asking who else they would recommended we should also talk to at the end of each interview.

When we searched for moviemaking clubs that still existed in the local area, we immediately noticed that they were almost all in the suburbs, well outside of the Liverpool city center. It seems that there was at one time a club based near the city center called the Liver Cine Club, but the club, established in 1965, did not last long.

Unlike earlier oral history projects, which tended to focus on working-class and/or female participants,[23] most of our interviewees were male suburban residents who were either retired or approaching retirement. This is not so much because of our own bias, but more because of the demographics that take part in this organised leisure activity. Since most of the people we talked to do not live in or near the city center of Liverpool, they have a different way of looking at the city than they perhaps would if it was more a part of their day-to-day experience. For example, Angus Tilston explained the motivations behind making *The Pool of Life* in the following way:

> I did that because I knew Liverpool was changing and I thought I'd like to record what happens in Williamson Square. I mean I had no idea then how Williamson Square would change anyway. I thought it would be interesting to record a bit. I took a few bits and thought this looks good and it encouraged me to carry on and film some more. So I did it really over a two-year period, bit by bit. It's put together to look like it's all in one day but of course it isn't, I did a little bit at a time. So therefore that's how it came about by putting it all together as one day. One idea was to have a child running through it as like a link; that was Graham Kay's suggestion. I did think about that but then I turned that down because I just wanted what was really happening rather than a mixture of pretend and what was really happening. Maybe his idea might have been better, I don't know. But at least it is a record now of what Williamson Square was like in 1974–5–6, around that time.[24]

The film was therefore inspired by a desire to record an area and a way of life that was about to be altered, and in this way the film itself now functions as a unique relic, a way to re-experience what Williamson Square was once like. Indeed, the fact that most of our interviewees are retired or approaching retirement helps us to have them reflect on how the city of Liverpool has changed over the years. Roland J. Grele has defined oral history as "the interviewing of eye-witness participants in the events of the past for the purposes of historical reconstruction."[25] In this respect at least, the interviewees were ideal for this part of the project's research, which is of a *qualitative* nature, engaging with an inherently subjective approach such as personal memories that do not readily lend themselves to quantitative approaches. For example, Tilston reflected on how the location has changed since he made his film:

> I just wanted to get a sense or a feel about Williamson Square as it's changed so much over the years. To me it's now more clinical than it used to be because there seems to be less going on there now. You've got the odd kid's

roundabout now and again, the odd market now and again, but as a day-to-day place of maximal activity and things going on for interest to wile the time away if you wanted to . . . there were lots of seats there if you notice, you don't get so many there today and so it was a place for people to relax in the summertime. I tried to capture that a little bit, you see the lines of people sitting on their seats watching what was going on.[26]

In this way, amateur film practice facilitates the comparison between places as they once were and how they are now. The historical reconstruction of these memories was particularly well illustrated by an amateur documentary called *Looking Back,* a short history of the now defunct Curzon Cine Club, which used to hold their meetings in the Birkenhead Liberal Club. The filmmaker is former member Frank Baker, and he follows his fellow founding member Les Holloway back to the building where they used to meet, forty years ago. Incorporating clips from films they made with contemporary interview footage shot in the former club meeting area, the film is an example of auto-ethnography documentary filmmaking that will be of great interest to archivists and scholars in the future, replicating as it does the methods and motivations of so much of our research methods and outputs. When inquiring about the back catalog of cine clubs it would certainly be worth asking if documentaries of this kind, often made for screening at club anniversaries or other special events, were ever attempted.

The interviews we conducted with local moviemakers have been passed on to the North West Film Archive in Manchester as a collection of DVDs. These interviews now form part of the archival collection, sitting alongside many of the amateur films that were identified as part of the first City in Film project. The DVDs then represent supplementary material to aid future research into amateur moviemaking in the Merseyside region. Secondly, the locations featured in the films were input into a GIS map of Merseyside. The hard disk of this map is now held by the University of Liverpool; the Museum of Liverpool has used a GIS map as the basis of their History Detectives Gallery to create an interactive display that includes film and other materials. The benefits of using this technology are that audio-visual material is present-linked to the actual locations where it was shot. In effect, digitized clips from the amateur films, as well as the interviews, now function as hyperlinks when they are added to a GIS map. As Klenotic notes, "The geodatabase can also include hypertext that links specific locations on the map to sources of external information such as audio or video files, text or image documents, online archival materials, internet websites or even to other GIS map documents."[27] The locations that the amateur filmmakers choose to shoot can then be compared to the locations that, say, the sponsored filmmakers decided to use. In this regard, it is significant that the surviving amateur moviemaking clubs were located in the suburbs and the outlying towns rather than in the city of Liverpool itself. There were many amateur films made about Liverpool, but they tended to be made by clubs and individuals that do not live there. Therefore, as most amateur filmmakers in the Merseyside region lived in the suburbs, their films on Liverpool tended to be made on day trips. These suburban filmmakers would often travel to Liverpool on a Saturday armed with their cine camera to film anything of interest and to document their journeys. For example, Jim Gonzales lived in Walton, a suburb to the northeast of the city center, while Angus Tilston lives in Bebington, which lies across the River Mersey on the Wirral. Local amateur filmmakers visited the city almost as if they were tourists, on day excursions looking for visually interesting subjects to use in their films. This idea of the filmmaker as a *suburban outsider* to everyday life in the city is certainly true of Gonzales and Tilston, and it also helps us to understand why their films present a certain view of Liverpool that lies somewhere between close familiarity and the tourist's gaze. In short, by focusing on amateur cine culture as a *social* practice, located in particular geographical areas, we can better appreciate the motivations and local cultural resonances behind their resulting filmmaking choices.

THE WIDER CIRCULATION OF AMATEUR FILMS

Throughout this chapter I have been describing the problems with what I have termed "embedded localism."[28] Comparing the circulation of amateur films with that enjoyed (or not) by commercial feature films made in the United Kingdom, I argued, "As a filmmaking strategy, non-fiction reinforces the link between location and representation."[29] In this chapter, it has been shown that this inherent link between location and representation can be fragile and that its subtleties can be easily broken or lost in their movement into archives and public screenings hosted outside the film's original geographical context. Just as it became necessary to adopt the concept of "transnational" cinemas in relation to commercial productions, in this chapter I have indicated that it might become useful to develop what might be called a translocal perspective on amateur cine cultures. As has been noted, in the past embedded localism was transformed into translocalism via knowledgeable commentaries during semipublic film screenings, but today it is achieved through documentaries or museum exhibits that recover a context to this material for potentially non-local or uninformed audiences. By adding layers of meaning[30] to visual material that has an uncertain status, information that is not available from print sources can be passed onto future generations via short audio-visual clips. These documentary materials can then be shown at specially organized screenings, on websites, and as featured content on interactive museum exhibits. Activities such as these are ways of mediating the journey of films produced almost exclusively for community exhibition in small suburban screenings into wider public dissemination and discussion using new digital technology and software formats such as GIS mapping software. This supplementary contextual data helps make amateur films that focus unapologetically on local topics available and understandable to *translocal* audiences. Our pursuit of primary empirical evidence as part of the Mapping the City in Film project has taken many forms, from newspapers and journals to maps and interviews. In essence, we were attempting to combine the cartographic with the ethnographic, providing new perspectives on the role filmmakers have had in preserving and reflecting on changes in Merseyside's urban landscape. This enabled us to negotiate the gap between mapping and memory in various practical ways, which could be similarly replicated in geographic areas around the world.

NOTES

Epigraph: S. Szczelkun, "The Value of Home Movies," *Oral History* 28(2) (2000): 94–98, cited here at 94.

1. See the project websites for more information; Mapping the City in Film: A Geohistorical Analysis (http://www.liv.ac.uk/lsa/cityinfilm/index.html) and Children and Amateur Media in Scotland (http://www.gla.ac.uk/cams), accessed December 12, 2011.

2. J. Klenotic, "Putting Cinema History on the Map: Using GIS to Explore the Spatiality of Cinema," in *Explorations in New Cinema History: Approaches and Case Studies*, ed. R. Maltby, D. Biltereyst, and P. Meers, 58–84, cited here at 66 (Oxford: Blackwell, 2011).

3. The City in Film online catalog is available at www.liv.ac.uk/lsa/cityinfilm/catalogue.html, accessed December 12, 2011.

4. M. Neumann and J. Jones, "Amateur Film and the Rural Imagination," in *Cinematic Countrysides*, ed. R. Fish, 231–48, cited here at 233 (Manchester: Manchester University Press, 2007).

5. R. Chalfen, "Cinema Naïveté: A Study of Home Moviemaking as Visual Communication," *Studies in the Anthropology of Visual Communication* 2(2) (1975): 87–103.

6. M. L. Johnson, "The Places You'll Know: From Self-Recognition to Place Recognition in the Local Film," *The Moving Image: The Journal of the Association of Moving Image Archivists* 10(1) (2010): 23–50, cited here at 41.

7. R. Shand, "Theorizing Amateur Cinema: Limitations and Possibilities," *The Moving Image: The Journal of the Association of Moving Image Archivists* 8(2) (2008): 36–60, cited here at 47.

8. D. Orgeron, "Mobile Home Movies: Travel and *le Politique des Amateurs*," *The Moving Image: The Journal of the Association of Moving Image Archivists* 6(2) (2006): 74–100, cited here at 79.

9. J. Hallam, "Mapping City Space: Independent Film-makers as Urban Gazetteers," *Journal of British Cinema and Television* 4(2) (2007): 272–84, cited here at 279.

10. S. Becker, "Family in a Can: The Presentation and Preservation of Home Movies in Museums," *The Moving Image: The Journal of the Association of Moving Image Archivists* 1(2) (2001): 88–106, cited here at 94–95.

11. Scottish Screen Archive, c/o: National Library of Scotland, 39–41 Montrose Avenue, Hillington Park, Glasgow G52 4LA, United Kingdom; tel.: 0845 366 4600; http://www.nls.uk/ssa/; email: ssaenquiries@nls.uk. Answers received July 21, 2011.

12. For a critical perspective on the current proliferation of user-generated content, see A. Keen, *The Cult of the Amateur: How Today's Internet Is Killing our Culture and Assaulting our Economy* (Boston and London: Nicholas Brealey Publishing, 2007).

13. http://www.thefairday.com/former_characters.htm, accessed December 12, 2011.

14. Becker, "Family in a Can," 97–98.

15. The project team consisted of Dr. Julia Hallam (principal investigator), Professor Robert Kronenburg (co-investigator), Dr. Les Roberts (research associate), and Dr. Ryan Shand (research associate).

16. I.A.C. is the Institute of Amateur Cinematographers, formed in 1932 by Percy Harris. It is an organization that encourages and supports amateur moviemaking in the United Kingdom. www.theiac.org.uk, accessed December 12, 2011.

17. Angus Tilston, interview with the author and Les Roberts, October 8, 2008.

18. C. A. Clyde, *The Pedestrianisation of Church Street, Liverpool* (University of Leeds, 1976).

19. L. Abrams, *Oral History Theory* (London: Routledge, 2010).

20. K. Brownlow, *The Parade's Gone By* (London: Secker & Warburg, 1968); A. Kuhn, *An Everyday Magic: Cinema and Cultural Memory* (London: I. B. Tauris Publishers, 2002).

21. S. Szczelkun, "The Value of Home Movies," 94.

22. S. Szczelkun, "The Value of Home Movies," 97.

23. Abrams, *Oral History Theory*, 3–9.

24. Angus Tilston, interview with the author and Les Roberts, November 25, 2009.

25. R. J. Grele, "Movement without Aim: Methodological and Theoretical Problems in Oral History," in *The Oral History Reader,* ed. R. Perks and A. Thomson, 38–52, cited here at ix (London: Routledge, 1998).

26. Angus Tilston, interview with the author and Les Roberts, February 24, 2009.

27. Klenotic, "Putting Cinema History on the Map," 67.

28. R. Shand, "Amateur Cinema Re-Located: Localism in Fact and Fiction," in *Movies on Home Ground: Explorations in Amateur Cinema,* ed. Ian Craven 156–81 (Newcastle upon Tyne: Cambridge Scholars Press, 2009).

29. Shand, "Amateur Cinema Re-Located," 172.

30. H. Norris-Nicholson, "Virtuous or Virtual Histories?: Changing Ways of Working with Archival Film Footage," paper presented at the Future Histories of the Moving Image conference, University of Sunderland, November 16–18, 2007.

TEN

Beyond the Boundary: Vernacular Mapping and the Sharing of Historical Authority

KATE BOWLES

It's easy to lose the humanity when you start showcasing tech.

—CHRIS MILK, DIRECTOR, *THE WILDERNESS DOWNTOWN*

We are damned by the arrogance with which we ignore the immensity of the territories we presume to tame with our absurdly precise instruments of measure, and redeemed by a cunning, even courageous naiveté that persuades us to believe that they are approachable, knowable, chartable.

—STEPHEN S. HALL, "I, MERCATOR"

For the past ten years, a substantial international community of cinema historians has been drawing attention to factors that traditional cinema studies had a tendency to overlook: first, that wherever cinema attendance is a social habit, it is not exclusively or even strongly shaped by the content of films themselves, but by the attractions and distractions of public cultural participation; and second, that what is social is also inevitably spatial.[1] Surviving evidence of the mass commercial orchestration of cinema as a cultural practice has offered digital historians a gold-edged invitation to count, to measure, to analyze, to aggregate, and above all to map.[2] Several project teams internationally, some of which are featured in this book, have spent years developing large-scale digital collections of historical data related to cinemagoing and have been doing so in a way that increases the potential to share commonly managed data across collections. The potential of this kind of global collaboration in the humanities is dazzling; it tempts us to imagine an "histoire totale" of cinema attendance founded on rigorous analysis of statistically significant changes to the routines of commercial, political, and social regulation of cinema markets worldwide, over more than a century. The opportunity to build capacity for this kind of panoptic overview is surely equal to those in which we have treated the history of films and their production as matters of industrial scale or presumed wide cultural impact.[3]

But at the heart of the task is a problematic myth that we might describe, misquoting Bazin for a moment, as "the map of total cinema." This map can never be drawn, and yet it haunts discussions of cinema attendance research as an ideal, the gross visualization of historical experience related to cinemagoing to which all smaller projects aspire to contribute. It is a map of unimaginable complexity, both at the level of scale and in its focus on a cultural practice that cannot simply be analyzed as mass spatial behavior. Cinemagoing is highly regulated by programming and scheduling and is easily measured by paid attendance. For this reason it seems exceptionally amenable to predictive trend data analysis, and even rational addiction theory.[4] But the process by which any individual shows up at a theater for a particular screening is in fact a complicated muddle of social, financial, interpersonal, familial, and environmental decision making. People go to the movies—and have always done so—as the consequence of elaborate planning, or out of habit, or on the off chance; they attend both decisively and reluctantly, and sometimes accidentally. Spatial factors are relevant, but the cultural and personal meanings attached to space, place, time, and distance are both volatile and transient. So while we can agree that it matters where movie theaters have been located, and we can see that their location has affected the flow of product through cinema markets as much as it has shaped the experiences of individual moviegoers, it remains difficult to work out exactly how we should try to collect and represent the evidence of this.

The suggestion explored in this chapter is that despite the obvious gains from having developed a productive, stimulating, and dataphilic partnership with empirical geographers, and particularly with geographers with geographical information systems (GIS) expertise, historians of cinema attendance need to be careful not to weaken their appreciation of the idiosyncratic nature of cinema attendance. It is precisely this that makes cinema such a valuable lens on social history; each cinema audience consists of individuals who have made their way somewhat independently to the movie theater on time (or not) through a maze of sociohis-torical circumstances.[5] We cannot diagnose these circumstances from the data generated by their showing up; this is not a matter of information so much as of narrative. In order to understand the social narratives by which communities, families, or individuals came to value or disparage cinema in particular historical contexts, we need to design research that is open to the collection of stories, and we need to think more carefully about the way these stories are told and the best formats in which they can contribute to our research.[6] This in turn requires us to reflect on reasons why our cautious apprenticeship to GIS might have made us so reluctant to share the historical authority to map cinema as part of everyday life experience.[7]

This dilemma is not special to cinema historians. Productive debates on the nature and rigor of qualitative GIS use, particularly involving the use of GIS in public participatory mapping projects (PPGIS), have prompted discussion among professional geographers about the dilemma of quality presented by "volunteer geographic information" (VGI).[8] This has led to the recognition that popular enthusiasm for open-source and web-based mapping has been both politically and technically conducive to the rise of "vernacular mapping." As described by Joe Gerlach, vernacu-lar cartography is a politicized collaboration aligned to other open-source movements that extends the critique initiated by PPGIS of institutionally regulated data collection and analysis, such as those using expensively licensed GIS software and similarly restricted spatial data, and published in formats to which members of the public have very limited access. Ver-nacular mapping champions the potential of open, participatory, and collaborative mapping practices to produce new possibilities, both for knowledge and for mapping itself:

> Vernacular mapping incorporates a cartographic ethics that realizes that the question for increasing precision and accuracy is an unimportant distrac-tion but, at the same time, acknowledges that it is not simply a case of carto-graphic relativism.... Vernacular mapping performs ethically insofar as the orthodox cartographic quest for meaning and certitude is replaced by the multiplication of difference and the production-through-mapping of other worlds, of other spaces.[9]

This is easy, and inspiring, to read. In practice, and in the context of re-search that is accountable to multiple stakeholders and exemplifies the "quest for certitude," the tension between orthodox and vernacular mapping is more difficult to resolve. In particular, it is not clear how or why wide public engagement with the mapping of cinema history might be achieved, and this remains one of the most important problems for cinema historians to address.

The case study on which these reflections are based involves a long-running nationally funded cinema research project in Australia.[10] Our aim has been to come to grips with the history of Australian cinema distribution and exhibition. This history has been difficult to recover for so long as the attention of Australian cinema researchers has been distracted by the parallel story of Australian film production, given that the aspirations of the Australian film industry have foundered on the indifference of the Australian cinema audience. As a result there has been a scholarly history of avoiding, rather than simply overlooking, the audience in Australian cinema research, and the operations of foreign distributors or their partnerships with Australian exhibitors have been doubly erased.[11] The aim of our project has therefore been to try to address this problematic denial and to understand the characteristics of the Australian cinema market in its own terms, not simply through the lens of its failure to sustain the local production industry.

We set out to do this by collecting large samples of the data we believed would best expose the broad trends in Australia's emergence as a distinct national cinema market dominated by the circulation of imported films. The first step was to design a national database for managing historical business data relating to venue location, associated companies and industry personnel, and film screenings. As Ian Gregory and Richard Healey note, the development of the wider field of historical GIS has been characterized by the slow building of substantial databases to "both national and urban scales," and we would certainly support their observation that "results are inevitably lagging behind database creation."[12] Nevertheless, the Cinema and Audiences in Australia Research Project (CAARP) collection has begun the process of recording the professionalization of cinema delivery in Australia, as the early history of speculative and entrepreneurial involvement by forward-looking individuals became an organized trade sector managing complex obligations to both foreign and local stakeholders. It aims to become the national reference collection of data on the ways both purpose-built and non-theatrical cinema venues around the country changed over time and how film product flowed through this network.

GIS scholars working with the first layers of data in the collection have begun to produce maps and diagrams of the distinctive spatial elements to Australian cinema history. Given the scale and low population density of the Australian market, spatial considerations were critical to industry logistics, from the location and development of cinema venues, through the management of film print distribution, to the coordination of multiple individual decisions and journeys that enabled an audience to show up together and on time.[13] Spatial factors further help us to understand how Australian cinema history has been affected by population shift, changes in family and work patterns, neighborhood gentrification, or the topography of television signal reliability. The first maps generated by this project, for example, demonstrated an unexpected role played by Italian and Greek cinemas in predicting the eventual consolidation of an ethnic community in a particular suburban location.[14] More recently, our colleagues have focused on trying to discern significant patterns in the contraction of the cinema exhibition sector during the period in which Australian television broadcasting spread outwards from Sydney and Melbourne.

These are undeniably useful discoveries for researchers interested in the relationship between cinema's business history and its social impact. The more valuable lesson we have drawn from this experience, however, is that cinema research is massively unfinishable. Although Australian cinema admissions records are uncertain before 1976, it is reasonably clear that in the decade prior to the consolidation of television broadcasting, a population of below nine million sustained the habit of attendance at well over one hundred million admissions per year—a remarkable rate of per capita commitment to a cultural product that was at that stage almost exclusively foreign.[15] Taking the scale of this activity seriously, and respecting that each visit would in turn have generated different patterns of repeat behavior that were critical to the viability of Australian cinema, we are forced to admit that our research has only begun to explore the impact of spatial factors on cinema's survival. Indeed, our data collection can only move beyond the demonstration stage if we find appropriate means to keep the database open beyond the immediate capacity and resources of the project that established its design, and it is this challenge that takes us into the territory of vernacular and participatory mapping.

BOUNDARY, SCALE, AND SCOPE:
WHAT ARE WE PROTECTING?

Cinema exhibition studies such as ours that focus on national or state-based cinema markets within narrow time periods have become more common over the past ten years, but they still grapple with elementary problems of scale, scope, and funding that are familiar to geographers. First of all, these projects are shaped by the opportunistic search for a boundary that will make the project substantial and achievable within the relatively short time frame that aligns with typical research funding programs. National funding bodies encourage national studies, in obvious ways, regardless of the contortions that such studies are pressed into in order to enable the aggregated local to speak on behalf of the imaginary national particular. State-based studies might derive either from state-directed funding or the happenstance of institutionally located research archives; nevertheless, as bounded propositions they pass the vetting process on the grounds that territorial generalizations make sense *in general,* overlooking the fact that all generalizations break down at particular localities. The larger the bounded territory, the harder we have to work to convert its aggregations of microhistorical data into a stable, unified account of its overall features. We are not encouraged to question what these scaled-up projects help us to understand, or what they might mask in terms of locality; it seems we are transfixed by the virtue of scale itself.

Second, conformity to high standards of data management that make data efficiently searchable and shareable has diverted substantial thinking, planning, and negotiation with commercial database designers to questions of metadata. While this is often simple taxonomic work, it is also scholarly and ethical, addressing the compromises that must occur at micro levels in order to achieve compatibility at macro levels. This is a straightforward language problem: in any attempt to organize human experience as collectible data, the particularities and nuances of localized vocabularies for places, practices, and ideas about public culture must be subordinated to generalization if they are to function as priorities in any taxonomic system. This flattens the differences between one case and another, promotes the elements that recur and invite comparative analysis, and causes the authority to decide what to call things and where to put them to be conservatively shared. The boundaries we place around the project are also therefore the boundaries we erect around our expertise as scholars in this field. Through the standardization of method and tools, we establish our credentials in terms of rigor; in the same move we determine our tolerance for allowing others authority to collect or interpret data with us, or for their narratives of experience to shed light on what we deduce in relation to the overall profile of a national cinema market. We prioritize our own interpretations and speculations as to which features have been the most important in attracting audiences to cinemas in the past, drawing as much on conversations and disputes with our disciplinary colleagues as on the insights of those who were there. By these means we mark out and prepare to defend the boundary around our research against disruption or contamination.

Sources of contamination might include all kinds of vague, unsubstantiated personal memories that come to us through oral histories and life narratives, or the sudden, almost accidental, glimpses of cinema that flash up in the background of other more purposeful pieces of writing, as in this famous case:

> The bus stop was outside the cathedral. I had been looking at the Mappa Mundi, with its rivers out of Paradise, and at the chained library, where a party of clergymen had got in easily, but where I had waited an hour and cajoled a verger before I even saw the chains. Now, across the street, a cinema advertised the *Six-Five Special* and a cartoon version of *Gulliver's Travels*. The bus arrived, with a driver and a conductress deeply absorbed in each other. We went out of the city, over the old bridge, and on through the orchards and the green meadows and the fields red under the plough.[16]

In context, this moment is part of a carefully assembled narrative designed to service a particular goal. When Raymond Williams goes on to point out that this ordinary bus journey is one "that in one form or another we have all made," he is preparing the ground for one of his most important arguments, that what we define as culture is not found in our singular encounters with specialist forms. Rather, the culture of our everyday navigations and un-self-conscious routines depends entirely on our capacity for rapid, continuous evaluation of the things we see around us, and is then expressed in all the tiny choices that we make to move in one direction or another. Seen in perspective, cinema is one small thread in the overall cultural weave. But by bringing together the revered historic map, the chains around the library where it can be seen, and the bus journey, Williams proposes that culture as a "whole way of life" is grounded in both the symbolic and the practical nature of the spatial—the defining methodological proposition for historians of cinema attendance.

The glimpse of an actual cinema in the background of Williams's argument, however, with its tiny bit of historical programming data, symbolizes the even more acute and practical temptations that Williams's story presents to the dataphile cinema researcher. Couldn't we extract and clean up this data somehow? Could we pin down the very day on which Williams went to the cathedral by triangulating his recollection with local newspaper, or even with the box office ledger of the cinema if it survives, and on that basis couldn't we add this detail to the expanding collection of screening and venue data on which we might base our imaginary total map? But would we then be naïve enough to trust that Williams remembered correctly what was screening when he came out of the library thinking about the Mappa Mundi? What if he confused this with a different year, or a different film, a different bus stop? Does it matter to the credibility of this account that we know who Williams was? What if he embellished his narrative about the ordinariness of culture with this piquant *but entirely made up* detail for strategic reasons?

The case is hypothetical, but the questions are reasonably typical of those asked all the time about popular narratives, oral histories, and in particular about the recollections of elderly informants who are the surviving repositories of cinema's earlier history. This is the familiar dilemma of trust in non-specialist historical actors that frames our approach to the problem of soliciting public contribution to research data. It presents a formidable obstacle to research in an area in which there are few official, verifiable sources. We can interview people, and we can retrieve data from some archival sources, particularly including newspaper advertising, that in the pre-Internet era was consistently the means by which cinema schedules were advertised.[17] But these are labor-intensive methods, and they retain their focus on the expertise and editorial superiority of the small research team. For a national cinema history project to take seriously the problem of scale and detail thrown up by cinema history itself, we must begin to imagine solutions to our resistance to volunteer-contributed information.

RURAL CINEMA HISTORY: A PROBLEM FOR GIS

The anxiety generated by volunteer-contributed data is connected to an important misunderstanding of the value of narrative research. Memory narratives are undeniably a weak source of quantitative data, and they will struggle to be accommodated comfortably in cinema projects that elevate the countable and verifiable (film titles, tickets sold, seating capacities) over the impressionistic, the unreliable, and the variable elements of the cinemagoing experience (planning, catching the bus, eating at interval, driving, parking, buying and bringing food, kissing, crying, throwing lollies). The problem is made more acute when the focus of a project is the generation of a map that depends on precise spatial data. All too quickly, individual stories of cinemagoing become like colored historical postcards of picture theaters: they can be associated as objects with GIS maps and or databases, and they can even be separately interrogated by standard software to generate content and relational analytics,[18] but in themselves they seem to have become second-order forms of data—tiny failures of the empirical project, always slightly suspect in their sentimentality.

This is particularly important as we seek to do justice to the history of rural cinema attendance. As an obvious consequence of population density, the patterns generated by orthodox data collection are most clearly visible in urban areas where competition between nearly colocated venues promoted movie choice as a feature of the cinema attendance experience, and for this reason the urban can too readily become the exemplary motif for the national. There is also more likely to be surviving archival evidence from the more robust commercial enterprises that serviced urban audiences. From the commencement of our project it was clear that Australia's country cinema sector, servicing very small populations scattered over a very wide area, was unlikely to produce data of sufficient quantity, coverage, or reliability to compare with the urban case studies. Competition organized by product differentiation was only an occasional factor, for example in larger regional centers where there might be a choice between a local village picture show run as a part-time operation in the community hall and a trip to a purpose-built picture theater in town bundled with monthly shopping.[19] Rural cinemagoing in Australia has a fragile, intangible heritage much more like rural partici-

pation in other community institutions—churches, sporting organizations, or membership of fraternal and mutual organizations. Its features
are the single weekly screening program, a relative lack of competition,
and a higher degree of grudging acceptance of poor-quality experiences,
specifically including uncomfortable seating and poor picture quality
or sound.

In terms of the quality of archival data, the relative lack of choice in
programming terms, combined with significant distance and travel times
from the metropolitan offices of the distribution companies, lowered the
premium on sophisticated advertising, particularly involving images; village newspapers might include a note about the films to be screened in the
weekly picture show in roughly the same way that the title of a sermon
might be advertised or the boxers in a fight might be arranged on a fight
card. Surviving business records from the rural non-theatrical sector are
relatively rare; a picture show license was often only one aspect of a community organization's operations. Venue details including seating size
may well be unreliable, and critical data concerning individuals involved
in these community business histories often amounts to stories held in
popular memory. The capacity for spatial analysis that is beginning to
animate the study of urban cinema in Australia seems at first sight to be
much weaker in rural contexts, relying on the survival of locally produced
country newspapers or the surprise discovery of a collection of receipts
or correspondence that sheds some light on how these precarious businesses connected with distributors or city-based exhibitors, or how they
exchanged news and tips amongst themselves. Much of this information is either in private hands or tenuously held in volunteer collecting
institutions and local museums, where the history of cinema has not as-
serted itself as an organizational category, and so any surviving materials
concerning buildings, personnel, or memorable events is often found in
files otherwise devoted to agricultural shows, boxing matches, and card
nights.

Nevertheless, the history of rural cinema participation does prompt
questions that might lend themselves to mapping. This creates a challenging opportunity for historical GIS to come to terms with incomplete
data sets and to find ways to make use of community and personal narratives. These are awkward issues for humanists and historians, who are
only just coming to terms with the data-processing capacity of GIS, and

they prompt a return to two fundamental questions: What exactly do we think would benefit from being represented by means of a historical map? And is GIS the best way to generate such a map, or are there alternatives?

In response to this, there are three dimensions to rural cinema history in Australia that seem worth exploring. First, memories of rural cinema attendance coproduced by older narrators have volunteered many details about the impact of weather and transportation on the decision to attend or not. This suggests we may be able to test the hypothesis about the primary impact of film title by analyzing instead seasonal variation in social catchment around local amenities such as rural picture shows, as people living in country areas clearly adjusted their willingness to travel after dark or in bad weather or by moonlight in districts where road quality was poor. The value of being able to see the catchment around particular cinemas in terms of local road conditions and seasonal weather would help counter the explanation that cinemas succeeded or failed primarily because of their distribution contracts and programming strategies; some may simply have failed because of unlucky location or a run of poor weather. There are, however, obvious practical problems with retrieving the appropriate data. It is relatively straightforward to access the history of road surfacing or bridge reconstruction that made rural travel safer over time; likewise, rainfall data and lunar calendars are easy to check.[20] It is much harder to ask people to recall in a specific rather than general sense how their decisions might have been affected by any of these conditions. Again, the capacity of sparse spatial data to be enriched by community and memory narratives is critical, but is the hybridization of GIS the best way to achieve this goal?

A second question that may lend itself to mapping is whether the presence of a local picture show correlated in any way to population stability in very small rural communities. These villages were often trying to copromote other modern enterprises with the arrival of cinema, and their struggles were paired with the effort to secure from state or council authorities a reasonable supply of electricity, sewerage, and other primary amenities. Unlike government-managed or licensed services such as radio, the telephone, or, later, television, rural cinema in Australia was awkwardly located between service categories: at one and the same time a locally owned commercial enterprise, a parochial community amenity, *and* an essential component in the national infrastructure of cultural participation, all the while servicing business interests located elsewhere. This complexity surfaced repeatedly, for example in the 1950s, when arguments in the Australian trade press about the quality of the cinema attendance experience urged the entire industry to boycott the emerging 16 mm sector in order to preserve urban cinemagoing standards as the threat of television became more significant. The rural situation made this far more complicated, however, as for many rural communities the 16 mm non-theatrical community circuit represented the only cinemagoing opportunity, and so could not be considered to constitute either a threat to quality or a rival operation, except in the case where distributors would prefer some parts of the country to miss out on cinema altogether.[21] National histories focused on patterns in metropolitan market competition will naturally overlook such precarious operations, but popular memory asserts their significance to longer-term patterns of rural town sustainability—what is the best way to invite this popular contribution as a form of community history making?

Third, and more sensitively, there is in the Australian situation some potential to draw on indigenous and non-indigenous community memory to try to understand the spatial diffusion of practices of racialized theater segregation. Rural cinema exhibition in Australia enabled a limited and awkward sharing of a new kind of public space and made it possible for proprietors with small or transient populations to maximize their potential market while maintaining the social rules that managed other public spaces in the same community. Specific segregation techniques, from customary practice to the presence of moveable ropes or fixed barriers, varied in different parts of rural Australia and may well have varied at different times according to seasonal migration related to the calendar of, for example, fruit picking employment. But as with the former two examples of ways in which empirical and spatial data analysis could assist, many practices of segregation would have occurred in non-theatrical venues where the standards of historical evidence are fragile. Memory narratives may well be the best way to begin to allow the stories of segregation in Australian cinemas to be told, but at the same time may not be the most apt sources of data on the exact details of when, where, and how such segregation occurred. It is also important to remember that non-indigenous historians are not necessarily either culturally skilled enough or sufficiently trusted within indigenous communities to be invited to hear the stories of those who were subjected to the broad insult of segregation across multiple venues and public spaces. We therefore need to take particular time and care in building strong collaborative partnerships with community researchers in order to enable these accounts to emerge in safety and to be used where they are most needed.[22]

Sensitive cultural experiences such as racial segregation are among the most obvious situations where we would expect the relationship between quantitative and narrative research to be fraught. Writing on the tension between the demands placed on the narrative of former slave Frederick Douglass that he recount the details of his life as facts, leaving the "philosophy"—or the interpretive work—to others, oral historian Alessandro Portelli points out that "persons have an (un?)fortunate reluctance to reduce their lives to data for someone else's interpretations." He goes on to describe the awkward results of attempting to convert traumatic experience into data:

> For instance, Nobel Prize winner Robert Fogel and his colleague Stanley D. Engerman in their classic *Time on the Cross* did not concern themselves with the feelings of those who whipped and were whipped, but concentrated instead on counting the number of lashes. By means of ample documentary sources and sophisticated means of statistical analysis, they reached the conclusion that slaves were likely to be whipped an average of 0.7 times per year.
>
> This is a legitimate, even necessary approach, because it guarantees a degree of abstraction that allows us to formulate general hypotheses, rules, and interpretations. On the other hand, while we are thankful for abstraction, we need to remind ourselves that it also involves a great deal of simplification. After all, it is materially impossible to whip anyone 0.7 times.[23]

Portelli's observation speaks directly to the tensions inherent in projects such as ours, looking to scale up from the multiple stories of singular encounters with a film, a crowd, a date in a cinema (or something like it) to a comprehensive, general, and rigorous history of cinemagoing. Our research has certainly caused us to reflect on the hubris in our original proposition, and our experience has been one of continuous modification as we seek the most appropriate use of GIS while attempting to balance the demands of coverage and compromise, all in ways that will be familiar to professional geographers.

THE AUSTRALIAN CINEMA MAP

We have debated the meaning of these compromises on and off over the life of the project; our discussions have intensified as we have tried to find the most effective source of historic spatial data to build a single national map of the cinema market during the period in which Australia fitfully experienced the transition to television broadcasting. Television was first introduced to parts of Sydney and Melbourne in 1956; our interest in building a time-lapse map of cinema openings and closings after this period lay in testing the assumption that cinema attendance uniformly gave way to television across Australia from this date. If there were significant regional variations in cinema's pattern of adaptation to television's presence, can we use this information to better understand the general conditions that framed their rivalry or cooperation? How long did it take, for example, for television to move outward through the suburbs and begin to affect the viability of cinemas operating across rural Australia? What were the local tipping points that encouraged Australians in different parts of the country to adjust to home-based forms of entertainment? Could a national map help us to connect these tipping points to other cultural trends? This map initially appeared to us to be a more modest proposition than the total map of all cinema experience, by virtue of its tight focus on venue openings and closings in one national market during a bounded time period. It seemed not to tangle with questions of memory or narrative, but with the most straightforward of industrial facts: when cinemas opened, when they changed hands or were remodeled internally (for example, when large single-screen venues were multiplexed), and when they finally succumbed.

The potential of this map lies in its capacity to expose larger patterns of synchronized business activity not visible from a single case study alone. This, we reasoned, would produce the most robust test of the hypothesis that cinema was swept aside nationally by the attraction of audiences to a competing medium. It would in addition provide a platform for subsequent analysis of regional variation in the diffusion of television reception, largely a problem of physical geography, alongside socioeconomic factors including the expansion of postwar suburbanization. In Australia as in other countries, suburbanization drove improvements in local infrastructure while temporarily overstretching transportation networks between outer suburbs and the urban centers where major cinemas were located. Other coevolving factors redirecting leisure and entertainment practices away from public space toward the suburban home included postwar birth rates and changes in patterns of employment. Relevant physical conditions included climate, both in terms of ordinary and local seasonal variations that would have adjusted the opportunity for travel to cinema venues, but also the impact of weather on cinema attendance in the parts of Australia with more extreme climates, including the tropical north, or holiday destinations where smaller cinemas were often sustained by tourist audiences. A map that could show how these factors intersected with the variable footprints of broadcast signal quality expanding around Australia's major capital cities would prompt closer investigation of places where topographical, demographic, or political irregularities provided an air pocket for cinema's survival.

Despite its apparent simplicity, this project has presented a number of practical challenges. The first is one commonly experienced by geographers seeking to capture large-scale patterns of change over time. Australian cinemas opened, closed, opened again, changed hands, changed names, or were internally remodeled throughout the year. Capturing each adjustment that might be relevant to our wish to build a more granular history of television's impact is not feasible. As a result, the map has been built using national census intervals as a standard, and it focuses on aggregate data expressed in five-year time slices. This fairly conventional solution opens onto a more troubling problem, however, in relation to data integrity. *The Film Weekly,* the national trade paper that awarded itself the task of reporting annually on infrastructure in the Australian national exhibition sector, would seem to be an appropriate source of the data we need. To a professional GIS geographer, however, its cinema listings represent spatial data of a poor quality. Cinemas are not always identified by precise street address, and rural postal codes in Australia are very wide; it is therefore genuinely difficult to establish the exact spatial coordinates of a large number of cinemas listed in *The Film Weekly* except by tracking them down on Google Maps or standing outside them with a GPS. The spatial data that can be derived from *The Film Weekly* is by GIS standards of fairly ordinary quality; perhaps its sole virtue is that it is internally consistent, even if this means that it is consistently likely to be slightly unreliable.

Having taken some time to decide whether or not the map should be drawn at all, we are left with questions about whether data of this quality should be retested, or simply quarantined from other apparently more reliable or spatially meticulous data collections, including our own. And what should we do about the fragile web of sporadic, subtheatrical, and perhaps sublegitimate cinema practices that might well have seemed too marginal from the vantage point of the urban exhibition industry to be represented at all in trade paper surveys? It seems a minor issue to omit these, except that in the pursuit of coverage, we need to acknowledge that in rural Australia, venues of this kind are likely to have been the central means by which mainstream cinema was experienced at all. To fail to be able to account for them is to confirm the marginalization of rural cinema from our composition of a national history.

The frequent discussion of data integrity that we have returned to as we have tried to resolve this issue seems to suggest that the only way forward for data-led historical research involves fitting the ephemeral social history of cinema attendance to the rigorous standards of GIS analysis, whose capacity for precision derives from its more common application to the kinds of geophysical research where spatial precision *is* paramount. But we are not mapping flood levels or fire threat; we need not to lose sight of the fact that the opening and closing dates of the solitary cinema in a two-street country town can be mapped with sufficient precision for our purposes even if the exact spatial coordinates are vague. Second, we need to be mindful of the problem discussed earlier of relegating qualitative or narrative accounts of cinema's cultural history to the illustrative margins of the dataset. In summary, our experience has taught us about the risk of distraction by two parallel visions: the potential for coverage and the vision of pristine data. Perfectionist ambitions can only take us, ironically, into the territory of double failure: failure to achieve our own goals and failure to recognize the point at which our goals become perverse.

This question of failure is an important one for researchers drawn to massively unfinishable historical projects, and again geographers have some timely words of comfort for us. Swedish time geographer Torsten Hägerstrand, writing in 1967 in anticipation of the imminent impact on geography of computerized data-processing capacity, reflected on two significant common elements in geography that between them had the ironic effect of expanding geography's capacity for failure: that geographers depended on "information in very large quantities" and had "a habit of depicting on maps the information we have obtained, both for the sake of analysis and for the sake of communication." The consequence of these two factors, he argued, was geographical research condemned by its own aspiration to totality:

> This habit forces us to assemble complete information concerning the area under observation to a degree which can often be avoided in other branches of research. Undoubtedly we have all at times met a situation where mapping or calculation was never accomplished for the simple reason that the amount of work proved to be insuperable.[24]

As we have found ourselves retreating from the daunting task of sorting through the ephemera of everyday cultural practices, having already more than enough to worry about with business data, venue attributes, and spatial coordinates, we can only sympathize with the precomputer geographer—but now because the increased processing power anticipated by Hägerstrand has not solved our own problems with insuperability, and may even have worsened them.

The problem of insuperability relates in unexpected ways to our ongoing ambivalence about user-contributed data. We have become more conservative about allowing direct contribution to our primary database at the very moment that the expanding ambition to know more and more about the history of Australian cinema attendance, particularly in rural and regional areas, should encourage us to turn to the assistance of communities with direct access to their own local historical resources. There is a straightforward tension between institutional taxonomy and open "folksonomy" in any participatory digital data collection, and these problems become acute if the goal is to create a reliable historical dataset on which others can depend, and which is in many cases difficult to check. Our obligations as curators of fragile cultural knowledge, for which much of the archival record has not been preserved, compel us to hoard historical authority over the collection. At the same time by working with (and underusing) the most powerful tools for spatial data analysis, and by accepting the restrictions placed on licensed spatial data that underpins any significant mapping project, we have hardened the layers of institutional protection around this history of the popular experience in public space.

This problem recurs across projects within the emerging field of the digital humanities, where the demanding nature of archival data scraping, metadata management, and spatial data standards have played a dominant role, the invitation to include qualitative research has been more uncertain, and the opportunity to hack and remix data has been seen as a threat. Under these circumstances, what is the least compromising means of using GIS to explore the social or emotional experience of cinema attendance? And what approach could be taken to enable public contribution without compromising the standards of the underlying dataset? A web-based input form for text and photographs is a common and obvious method, and this will certainly be part of the national map we have produced.[25] But this finally causes us to reflect on the nature of this invitation as seen from the perspective of the potential contributor: Why would members of the public be interested in participating in such a conversation with us? What could they gain from contributing to the work of national research institutions and their otherwise cloistered projects—particularly in areas such as the history of popular entertainment rather than in projects that enhance public good outcomes such as improved health?

These problems are familiar to cultural geographers, who have themselves generated significant critique of GIS as a heavy-handed and exclusionary imposition of empiricist techniques and positivist values. Their commitment to qualitative and participatory GIS projects, in which communities and individuals are actively engaged in the development of protocols for codirected research projects, suggest one way forward.[26] Large-scale open-source mapping projects, such as OpenStreetMap, in which professional geographers volunteer mapping time and processing power to document cultural spaces on the basis of user-generated hand-drawn walking maps, offer another.[27] These developments offer potential benefit to cinema historians but do not entirely address the problem of how to recruit and support direct public engagement with non-technical users. Neither do they fully exploit the potential that we now have to use maps to trigger memory and reflection and to open up a dimension in the research process for collaborative creative practices.

In what follows, I suggest that cinema historians looking to develop a more open-ended and imaginative approach to crowd-sourced data might be interested in the philosophy behind an example from an entirely different field, the music industry. This project has drawn directly on the appeal of maps as creative, accessible, social, and mashable digital objects. Its method is technically complex but conceptually simple, and it offers an alternative model for ways we might approach collaborative public participation in institutional research.

VERNACULAR MAPPING: CREATIVITY, MEMORY, AND IMAGINATION

The Wilderness Downtown is a 2010 collaboration between Google, B-Reel, Milk+Koblin, and the Canadian band Arcade Fire, built initially to demonstrate the use of HTML5 through the Google Chrome web browser to generate tailored video content.[28] The project combines recorded video, CGI layers, and satellite mapping synchronized to a music soundtrack—the song "We Used To Wait," about memory, loss, and return home. By entering a street address into a web query form, each viewer creates a video mashup that blends stock footage of a hooded character running down a suburban street with images of their own childhood neighborhood, sourced from Google Maps and Google Street View. At the end of the video, viewers are invited to write a reflection on the memories and associations prompted by the experience, in the form of an online postcard to their childhood self. Late in 2010, when the project site had received thirty-five million hits, a selection of these postcards were subsequently re-rendered as material objects: printed and impregnated with seeds to be planted in reference to the closing frames of the video in which new trees sprout and grow through the urban streetscape of the viewer's remembered childhood. The Wilderness Downtown is a highly engaging project that has more to do with massively open web-based creative projects such as PostSecret than it does with specialist and professionalized mapping services involving GIS. It involves the participant in a complex act of networked creativity that is at once social and intensely private, a horizon of possibility for other participatory mapping projects seeking to engage contribution through imagination and play, offering a reflective experience in return for user-contributed data.

To understand how effectively this project models the capacity for cinema historians to generate high levels of engagement with participatory research, we need to think about the reasons why people are attracted to maps at all. These are the reasons we all search through Google Street View, not only for our own remembered places but also for signs of other people in places we will never visit, as they navigate through the everyday realms of their own ordinary, unspectacular cultural experiences, like Raymond Williams sitting on the bus. The popularity of Google Street View and Google Earth, and the rise of social memory mapping projects such as the Flickr Memory Maps pool, seem to connect to the way our ability to operate within space at all is simultaneously social and intensely private. Seen in this way, culture is a perpetual practice of geosocial sense making, as Stephen S. Hall writes:

> Like memory, geography is associative. In this process I call orientating we all carry a personal atlas in our brains (which obliges this psychic gazetteer- ing because it happens to be the most sophisticated, supple map-making device ever created). We flip through it with synaptic rapidity; we crash just so through a wilderness of neurons primed and aligned by experience, traveling a decade in an instant, traversing hemispheres in the span of a few axons, snagging now and then on the nettles of a sad recollection, exhila- rated by the sheer expanse of territory covered, surprised at how our brains can organize so much information along emotional latitudes, their very architecture a kind of microscopic merging of all the cartography we have acquired and stored.[29]

Hall returns us to the first principle of cinema mapping: that the simplest potential benefit to cinema history lies in being able to imagine the emo- tional and physical calculations about the meaning of space that have structured every single instance of cinema delivery and cinema atten- dance. Like other persuasive miniaturizations—the dollhouse, the min- iature railway, the architect's scale model—maps invite us into the spaces and temporal rhythms of possible worlds. Entering these spaces, we use our own remembered experiences and our imagination to begin to think about what might have mattered in the past, how things might have felt, and how such private feelings about cinema experiences, varying widely over a single lifetime, might together have generated the mass cultural phenomenon of global cinema attendance. The Wilderness Downtown suggests that we can harness these pleasures and intimacies to encour- age public contribution to large-scale historical mapping projects. This opportunity requires us to think less as quantitative researchers driven by the demands of powerful data-processing tools, and to think instead as storytellers interested in the differences between each individual recollection. A creative narrative interface designed for collaborative digital storytelling, rather than a data-collection interface focused on minimum thresholds of tolerance for volunteered data, might be more successful in helping researchers to gather the ephemeral traces of cinema attendance history from all the places where it lies hidden by its own lack of historical consequence: in the folds and gaps of family memory, lost in the cardboard boxes at the local museum, or buried on the back page of suburban newspapers.

The GIS maps that we dreamed of generating as the primary outputs from large-scale research projects cannot represent historical experience, however broad or detailed their coverage, however pristine their data. While they lack the contribution of narrative and reflection that each individual brings to the process of creative remembering, they remain radically incomplete, and we struggle to use them well to explore the complex connections between locality, network, and everyday decision-making practices that constitute cinema's social history. We use them best when we remember that their function was to begin our exploration, not to represent its conclusion. As we begin to seek out more accessible models of social and vernacular mapping, therefore, digital historians will need to create new partnerships with web designers—and perhaps musicians—to explore more fully the potential of the map remix, the mashup, and the vernacular mapping project as exciting models for open historical research.

The project of mapping the ordinary cultural experience of cinema attendance by these means will of course remain deliberately incomplete, and this will require us to learn new modes of humility and even institutional patience in the face of what remains to be mapped. This will take orthodox cinema history a step closer to the realm of the Open Street Map, the ongoing social annotation of Google map data, and other massively open web-based mapping projects. Its unfinishability will not represent insuperability, however, nor will it derive simply from the exhaustion of the formal research resources. Rather, it will suggest a more tactful and mutable approach to professional research into everyday life experience, founded on participatory relationships that are genuinely open, voluntary, and driven by shared historical curiosity.

NOTES

The first epigraph is from M. Castillo, "The Wilderness Downtown's Creator Talks About What Motivated Him, What's Next," *Time Techland* [Sept. 10, 2010], http://techland .time.com/2010/09/10/the-wilderness-downtowns-creator-talks-about-what-motivated -him-whats-next/, accessed June 13, 2011.

The second epigraph is from S. S. Hall, "I, Mercator," in K. Harmon, *Personal Geographies and Other Maps of the Imagination* (New York: Tributary Books, 2004), 15–19, cited here at 16.

1. There are a growing number of publications related to this work, but see in particular K. H. Fuller-Seeley, ed., *Hollywood in the Neighborhood: Historical Case Studies of Local Moviegoing* (Berkeley and Los Angeles: University of California Press, 2008); M. Jancovich and L. Faire with S. Stubbings, *The Place of the Audience: Cultural Geographies of Film Consumption* (London: BFI Publishing, 2003); R. Maltby, D. Biltereyst, and P. Meers, eds., *Explorations in New Cinema History: Approaches and Case Studies* (Chichester, West Sussex; Malden, Mass.: Wiley-Blackwell, 2011); R. Maltby, M. Stokes, and R. C. Allen, eds., *Going to the Movies: The Social Experience of Hollywood Cinema* (Exeter: University of Exeter Press, 2007).

2. See J. Klenotic, "Putting Cinema History on the Map: Using GIS to Explore the Spatiality of Cinema," in Maltby, Biltereyst, and Meers, *Explorations in New Cinema History*, 58–84. For a discussion of the parallel emergence of historical GIS over the same period, see I. N. Gregory and R. G. Healey, "Historical GIS: Structuring, Mapping and Analyzing Geographies of the Past," *Progress in Human Geography* 3(5) (2007): 638–53. Further substantial discussion of this shift is offered by Anne Kelly Knowles in *Placing History: How Maps, Spatial Data, and GIS Are Changing Historical Scholarship* (Redlands: ESRI Press, 2008).

3. K. Bowles and R. Maltby, "What's new about new cinema history?" Remapping Cinema, Remaking History: XIVth Biennial Conference of the Film and History Association of Australia and New Zealand: Conference Proceedings (2009), 7–21.

4. There are many examples of the application of trend analysis to cinema attendance, but see in particular A. Collins, C. Hand, and A. Ryder, "The Lure of the Multiplex? The Interplay of Time, Distance and Cinema Attendance," *Environment and Planning A* 37 (2005): 482–501; A. Sisto and R. Zanola, "Cinema Attendance in Europe," *Applied Economics* 17 (2010): 515–17; E. Yamamura, "Rethinking Rational Addictive Behavior and Demand for Cinema: A Study Using Japanese Panel Data," *Applied Economics* 16 (2009): 693–97.

5. The differentiation between cinema's social and cultural history is discussed in K. Bowles, "Lost Horizon: The Social History of the Cinema Audience," *History Compass* 9(11) (2011): 854–63.

6. Annette Kuhn suggests that even "merely personal or idiosyncratic" memories of cinemagoing can be inspected more closely and made to reveal "shared or collective attributes," although she does not discuss the reasons why this would be a useful thing to do. See A. Kuhn, "What to Do with Cinema Memory?" in Maltby, Biltereyst, and Meers, *Explorations in New Cinema History*, 85–98.

7. This is a phrase now in common usage but that points to a substantial engagement by oral historians with the ethics of research collaboration since the publication of

M. Frisch, *A Shared Authority: Essays on the Craft and Meaning of Oral and Public History* (Albany: State University of New York Press, 1990).

8. S. Elwood, "Grassroots Groups as Stakeholders in Spatial Data Infrastructures: Challenges and Opportunities for Local Data Development and Sharing," *International Journal of Geographical Information Science* 22(1) (2008): 71–90; S. Elwood, "Volunteered Geographic Information: Future Research Directions Motivated by Critical, Participatory, and Feminist GIS," *GeoJournal* 72 (2008): 173–83; S. Elwood, "Integrating Participatory Action Research and GIS Education: Negotiating Methodologies, Politics and Technologies," *Journal of Geography in Higher Education* 33(1) (2009): 51–65; A. J. Flanagin and M. J. Metzger, "The Credibility of Volunteered Geographic Information," *GeoJournal* 72 (2008): 137–48; T. Hawthorne, J. Krygier, and M-P. Kwan, "Mapping Ambivalence: Exploring the Geographies of Community Change and Rails-to-Trails Development Using Photo-Based Q Method and PPGIS," *Geoforum* 39 (2008): 1058–78.

9. See J. Gerlach, "Vernacular Mapping, and the Ethics of What Comes Next," *Cartographica* 45(3) (2010): 165–68, cited here at 166–67.

10. The genesis of this project is briefly discussed in K. Bowles, R. Maltby, D. Verhoeven, and M. Walsh, "More than Ballyhoo?: The Importance of Understanding Film Consumption in Australia," *Metro Magazine* 152 (2007): 96–101.

11. K. Bowles, "'Three Miles of Rough Dirt Road': Towards an Audience-Centred Approach to Cinema Studies in Australia," *Studies in Australasian Cinema* 1(3) (2007): 245–60.

12. Gregory and Healey, "Historical GIS," cited here at 650.

13. K. Bowles, "The Last Bemboka Picture Show: 16 mm Cinema as Rural Community Fundraiser in the 1950s," in Maltby, Bilereyst, and Meers, *Explorations in New Cinema History,* 310–21.

14. D. Verhoeven, K. Bowles, and C. Arrowsmith, "Mapping the Movies: Reflections on the Use of Geospatial Technologies for Historical Cinema Audience Research," in *Digital Tools in Film Studies,* ed. M. Ross, M. Grauer, B. Freisleben, 69–81 (Bielefeld: Transcript Verlag, 2009).

15. For data on cinema admissions, and an explanation of the reason why pre-1976 cinema admissions are partly estimated, see Screen Australia, "Overview of Cinema Admissions and Key Events, 1901–2010," http://www.sa-minihost.com/research/statistics/wchistsince1900.asp, and "'Entertainment Taxes' as a Source of Admissions Data," http://www.sa-minihost.com/research/statistics/wchistsource.asp, accessed September 2, 2011.

16. R. Williams, "Culture Is Ordinary" [1958], in *Resources of Hope* (London: Verso, 1989), cited here at 3.

17. For a discussion of the time frame for mixed archival and interviewing methodology, see L. Fair, "'They stole the show!': Indian Films in Coastal Tanzania, 1950s–1980s," *Journal of African Media Studies* 2(1) (2010): 91–106.

18. For a substantial discussion of technical methods that can be used to integrate storytelling to GIS using a coding editor for interview material, see Kwan and Ding, "Geo-narrative: Extending Geographic Information Systems for Narrative Analysis in Qualitative and Mixed-Method Research," *The Professional Geographer* 60(4) (2008): 443–65.

19. K. Bowles, "'All the evidence is that Cobargo is slipping': An Ecological Approach to Rural Cinema-Going," *Film Studies* 10 (2007): 87–96.

20. For an interesting analysis of the correlation between weather and box office in a metropolitan Scottish cinema, see I. Jeacle, "'Going to the movies': Accounting and Twentieth Century Cinema," *Accounting, Auditing & Accountability Journal* 22(5) (2009): 677–708. For discussion of the impact of both drought and coastal rainfall on precarious rural picture shows in Australia, see K. Bowles, "Limit of Maps? Locality and Cinema-Going in Australia," *Media International Australia* 131 (2009): 83–94.

21. Bowles, "The Last Bemboka Picture Show," 313–15.

22. Nancy Huggett discusses the complexity of conducting oral history research with non-indigenous participants in racially segregated cinemagoing in Australia. See N. Huggett, "'Everyone was watching!' Strategies of Self-Presentation in Oral Histories of Cinema-Going," *Studies in Australasian Cinema* 1(3) (2007): 261–74.

23. Alessandro Portelli, *The Battle of Valle Giulia: Oral History and the Art of Dialogue* (Madison: University of Wisconsin Press, 1997), 81.

24. T. Hägerstrand, "The Computer and the Geographer," *Transactions of the Institute of British Geographers* 42 (1967), 1–19, cited here at 1.

25. For a brief editorial discussion of the opportunities and limitations of web GIS, see S. Carver, "Editorial," *Environment and Planning B: Planning and Design* 28 (2001): 803–804. Carver points out that "many people in positions of power regard developments in on-line PPGIS with some skepticism, doubting the ability of the general public to grasp fully the intricacies of the planning process—and therefore they doubt the ability of the public to make useful contributions." Cited here at 803. See also B. Pedersen, F. Kearns, and M. Kelly, "Methods for Facilitating Web-Based Participatory Research Informatics," *Ecological Informatics* 2 (2007): 33–42, for a practical discussion of input form design in a project designed to solicit large-scale public input to fire safety data.

26. Chris Perkins notes, however, that true community mapping as well as more activist "countermapping" is far less common than PPGIS, particularly in developed countries, and points out that PPGIS still "emphasizes the incorporation of local voices into maps produced and controlled by specialists and articulating their agendas, rather than subverting mapping, or changing what is mapped." See C. Perkins, "Community Mapping," *The Cartographic Journal* 44(2) (2007): 127–37, cited here at 127.

27. The OpenStreetMap project is a large-scale global wiki intitiative; open mapping has also generated the first substantial record of the Kibera "informal settlement," housing more than one million people on the outskirts of Nairobi, Kenya. See http://www.openstreetmap.org and http://mapkiberaproject.yolasite.com/mission.php, accessed June 13, 2011.

28. The Wilderness Downtown, http://thewildernessdowntown.com/, accessed June 13, 2011.

29. S. Hall, "I, Mercator," in K. Harmon, *Personal Geographies and Other Maps of the Imagination* (New York: Tributary Books, 2004), 15–19, cited here at 15–16.

ELEVEN

Afterword: Toward a Spatial History of the Moving Image

JULIA HALLAM AND LES ROBERTS

This book has aimed to provide a preliminary navigational guide through the new and emergent interdisciplinary landscapes that distinguish the ways in which "the spatial turn" in the humanities has generated a new wave of film scholarship in recent years. It has focused in particular on the way mapping technologies such as GIS and Google Maps have been harnessed to map the social experience of film as both a commercial industry, invested in particular sites of production, shooting, and distribution, and a leisure activity, produced and consumed as part of everyday leisure activities in various ways at particular places. To date, the majority of work in this area has focused on developing a history of commercial cinema as a history of social experience, focusing, as Robert C. Allen has succinctly put it in this volume, on understanding cinema "as a set of processes, practices, events, spaces, performances, connections, embodiments, relationships, exchanges, and memories—experiences, in other words, associated with but not reducible to films." Many of the contributors in this book have pioneered work in this area, developing an approach to the study of moviegoing and cinema audiences that Maltby, Biltereyst, and Meers and others have dubbed "the new cinema history,"[1] a history characterized by, in many cases, work that is both collaborative and interdisciplinary, drawing on the skills honed by anthropology, geography, computer science, architecture, and civic design, to name but some of the associations that have led to the development of the approaches that appear in this volume. In this brief endnote, we want to outline some of the tendencies that seem to characterize the development of work in this area, focusing in particular on the ways many of these projects are engaging with cultural memory and vernacular memories of cinemagoing, touching on some of the issues raised by Kate Bowles' experience of working on the Cinema and Audiences in Australia Research Project (CAARP) in her final chapter for this collection.

In many cases, the projects that feature GIS as a linchpin of their methodology are large-scale, national projects that aim to capture a comprehensive picture of a particular phenomenon across a specific period of time. For example, several contributors to this book are researchers on the Australian Research Council–funded CAARP project "Mapping the movies: the changing nature of Australia's cinema circuits and their audiences 1956–1984," which is mapping the social and economic circuits of cinemagoing and identifying with the aid of geovisualization tools the variables that explain cinema diversification, survival, or closure; as part of this there are plans to launch an interactive website that demonstrates many of the project outcomes.[2] By way of contrast, Caquard's Cybercartographic Map of Cinema Territories presents a contemporary rather than a historical analysis of Canadian cinemas and their audiences from a primarily geographic perspective.[3] The focus here has been on the development of cartographic tools such as Google mashups that incorporate data from the researcher's database, using an experimental Cybercartographic Atlas to analyze how a (post)national identity is projected in contemporary Canadian films and assess audience engagement with these films.[4] While large-scale datasets often characterize this research, such as the collation of statistical material held in various industry yearbooks or the gathering of references to film exhibition spaces, at the same time there is also a move away from these large-scale, nationally funded projects to those that have more local concerns, sometimes led by individual researchers rather than a large interdisciplinary team, reflecting the new and varied ways GIS is infiltrating the research agenda in film studies.

Although there are a number of differences in the way these researchers are using maps, they all share a desire to combine the quantitative approaches typical of the social sciences and computing sciences with the qualitative work more typical of that undertaken by humanities researchers. New work in this area is seeking to move beyond visualizing geographical sites of cultural experience that have typified approaches and uses of GIS to investigating the ways arts and humanities researchers might expand the use of the technology by exploring its potential for mapping artistic representations of spaces and places. Cooper and

Gregory in their Mapping the English Lakes project are testing the possibilities of a qualitative, literary GIS by embedding the practice of digital mapmaking within the interpretive process; crucially, this involves a shift toward using GIS as "a tool for critical interpretation rather than mere spatial visualization"[5] that seeks to map subjective experiences and what might be loosely defined as "psychogeographic" understandings of places and landscapes. There is also, as part of this move, a corresponding commitment to a self-reflexive scholarship that seeks to include reader experiences, irrespective of expertise, as part of research design. A user-friendly online interface using Google Earth potentially allows anyone to engage with their maps while reading an annotated copy of the texts that describe the journeys undertaken by Lakeland poets.[6] This commitment to sharing information beyond the usual constituencies of fellow researchers, policymakers, and interested parties with the aim of engaging a wider public, including those who may not be experts in a particular field but who might be interested in the material that has been collected and collated, has led to new projects that have mapping various aspects of personal cultural experience at the heart of their inquiry.

During 2010, Julia Hallam, Ian Gregory, and Les Roberts invited a group of humanities researchers, museum curators, and artists with known interests in exploring digital mapping technologies to a series of workshops to share their work, with a view to developing new associations and collaborative projects;[7] here we will briefly elaborate on two projects that indicate some of the ways researchers and curators attending the workshops are exploring the use of GIS to create "deep memories" of particular places. They are aided by the incremental capacity of GIS to store multiple memories, stories, images, and documents, allowing the different views of engaged participants to give shape and substance to their own vision of local history.

Moving away from the focus on cinemagoing that informed Going to the Show, Robert C. Allen's Main Street, Carolina project can be seen as one way in which a deep mapping of the experience of cinemagoing can be developed. Using the Sanborn maps that form the basis for Going to the Show, Allen, in collaboration with library scientists at the University of North Carolina, has created a free, web-based history resource that enables libraries, museums, and other locally based community organizations with little technical knowledge or expertise to preserve and document their history in the first decades of the twentieth century. Currently, seven pilot projects have been developed to demonstrate the capabilities of the software, which combines built-in features with the option of using existing external social network applications such as Flickr and YouTube. This will provide organizations with a flexible, user-friendly digital platform on which they can add a wide variety of local historical data such as oral history interviews, photographs, newspaper articles, advertisements, and other artifacts, which can be retrieved using place markers on the maps.[8] This work will integrate the history of cinemagoing in North Carolina into the localized social and economic contexts in which personal decisions about "going to the show" were made, creating a landscape of memory in which the social experience of cinemagoing takes shape amidst the attractions of the downtown areas in which it took place.

In contrast to these localized histories of cinemagoing, the Mapping the City in Film project has focused on documenting the locations in films made for local purposes ranging from the promotional to the political, from the factual to the entertaining, using GIS to visualize these locations and assess their relationship to urban change and (re)development. The films, often created by professional and amateur filmmakers who have a close personal relationship with the place they are making films about, constitute a wide range of genres that can be classified as "local," whether their remit is regarded as "regional" or has a distinctively metropolitan perspective. This moving-image record of the events and activities of everyday life, formerly the province of social historians, is increasingly valued by film researchers interested in how the identities of small nations or regions or particular groups of people are mediated by local cultures of film production and consumption.[9]

It is also of interest to museum curators seeking new ways to engage local communities with their collections. The GIS workshops created the opportunity for curators from the new Museum of Liverpool (the first purpose-built museum to open in the U.K. in more than a hundred years) to discuss location-based approaches to organization and accessibility of the museum's collections. Inspired by the theories and practices presented by contributors to the digital mapping workshops, curators explored the practicalities of using ArcGIS software as a springboard for expanding their collections and making them more accessible by geo-

FIGURE 11.1. The History Detectives Gallery of the Museum of Liverpool, 2012.

referencing all the materials and artifacts relating to the Liverpool area in the National Museum's Liverpool collections and developing their existing GIS database to enable public access through a permanent exhibition platform. David Bodenhamer has eloquently described the possibilities of this form of deep mapping in his essay "Creating a Landscape of Memory":

> Each artifact from a place—a letter, memoir, photograph, painting, oral account, video, and so forth—would constitute a separate layer of memory that we could arrange sequentially through time, with as many stacks of layers as the evidence permits. Each layer would represent a memory anchored in time and space, thus allowing us to keep them in relationship, and each stack of layers would contain the unique view over time, the dynamic memory, of an individual, a family, an organization, or some other social unit. The layers could incorporate active and passive memories, the memories generated by intentional recall as well as memories left to us in some fixed form. They also might contain memory accounts from the natural world, such as found in meteorological and geological records.[10]

These ideas underpin the development of the History Detectives gallery, opened in December 2011. Designed as a digital repository that will expand to contain a range of audio-visual materials and digitized artifacts collated through workshops, outreach programs, and online participatory projects, the contents can be accessed in the gallery through a touch screen map of the contemporary Merseyside area. People can excavate the history and archaeology of their area through a series of themes (nature, people, buildings, etc.) or trails (for example a virtual Beatles tour), and access films of particular local interest. The museum has also drawn on the work of the City in Film project[11] to create some of its audio-visual display materials; for example, based on his research at the Lumière archives, Richard Koeck has created a georeferenced animated reconstruction of what it was like to travel on the Liverpool overhead railway in 1897 to accompany the display of one of the original carriages.[12]

The new Museum of Liverpool is situated on the riverbank at the Pier Head close to the newly opened cruise ship terminal amidst the cluster of structures built at the beginning of the twentieth century—the Liver, Cunard, and Port Authority buildings—that contribute to the waterfront's world heritage status. Tagged as the "gateway to Empire" in the nineteenth century due to its domination of the North Atlantic trade routes, the city's wealth and status declined in the twentieth century as the activities of the port changed to accommodate the increasing size of container ships and accompanying mechanization of cargo handling. In common with many port cities in Europe, the city has struggled to reinvent itself for the modern era and has become dependent on past glories as the motor of a new tourist economy. Les Roberts argues that in post-industrial cities such as Liverpool, the cultural economics of the heritage and tourism industries are shaping the ways in which moving image media "provide virtual pathways to and from a city's lived spaces of history and identity."[13] Roberts seeks to reframe filmmaking and film consumption as fundamentally spatial practices in which the dialectical histories that emerge between virtual and material geographies, between the archived past and the lived present, are closely bound up with the questions of mobility and consumption that typify experiences of contemporary life in the postmodern city.[14]

This book demonstrates how mapping technologies and spatial analysis can contribute to new understandings of the ways moving-image media have affected the development of (post)modern, mobilized subjectivities and identities. It also leaves a number of areas unexplored and numerous questions unanswered about how a spatial history and analysis of the moving image might enhance further understandings of film production and consumption as practices both constitutive of and shaped by considerations of place. How might a rigorous georeferencing of early film locations on a GIS map of London, Tokyo, or New York alongside, for example, a register of local film businesses and exhibition venues enhance our knowledge of early film cultures? Such a project might bring together, for example, Ian Christie's research on the early film business in London between 1894 and 1914[15] and aspects of Patrick Keiller's City of the Future project. Keiller analyzed a corpus of more than two thousand films held in the UK National Film and Television Archive dating from the early 1890s to the 1950s to form the basis of an exploration "between the familiarity of old city fabric, the strangeness of the past, and the newness of present-day experience."[16] What might such a map contribute to an expanded interpretive agenda of films made in and about places that currently typifies accounts of film location and cinematic landscape, such as Brunsdon's *London in Cinema?*[17] Evidence of growing scholarly interest in the relationship between film locations and the areas in which film production and shooting takes place as well as in location visiting as a leisure activity undertaken by film fans is found in the proliferating literatures of critical interpretation and movie travel guides in print and online (with some websites such as the Cine-Tourist combining the two).[18] How might online digital mapping platforms that invite public or fan participation begin to alter the ways in which historiographies of moving-image media are conceived and mediated? How might the shift from producer-generated content to user-generated content that typifies contemporary media use aid in the construction of landscapes of film history that more inclusively combine vernacular memories as part of academic discourses of film, place, and space?

In her article for this collection, Kate Bowles cautions against the search for a "map of total cinema" these questions might imply, drawing on her experiences of working on a large-scale national research project that aims to produce the Australian national collection of reference materials relating to the way cinema venues and distribution networks have changed and developed over time. The problems that Bowles outlines, such as the search for boundaries that make projects viable within the time frames granted by research funding and the amount of time spent on metadata design, inevitably shape projects that are creating large databases, particularly when there is a concern to create data that is efficiently searchable and shareable. Such research, she argues, is fenced in by disciplinary expertise and defended against "contamination" from the kinds of sources that might pollute methodological credentials of rigor such as personal memories. These kinds of "fuzzy" data are less easy to integrate into the overall research design and become second-order forms of information, characterized in Bowles' example as not dissimilar to colorful historical postcards of cinema venues, ephemera that supports the research narrative but not the material on which the authority of research outcomes are grounded. Given institutional investments in research and increasing demands that academic research have demonstrable impact value, this situation seems unlikely to change. This is true whether we understand that value in terms of knowledge exchange by making the results of our research available beyond their immediate constituencies of interest to a public eagerly anticipating opportunities to participate, or by seeking to prove that research such as that on cinema memory, for example, has a positive effect on the participants. Bowles advocates that researchers work with web designers to create innovative online platforms that assist in the development of participatory online communities using open-source resources such as Open Street Map. This would free popular memory projects from expensive software licenses and institutional frameworks of collection, analysis, and interpretation and allow people to create their own histories in a shared space where the collective abilities of the members of an online network could be harnessed by the members themselves to create a new kind of historical resource.

Such proposals speak to new horizons of possibility for film history scholars; technological convergence has, as Bodenhamer argues, the potential to "to revolutionize the role of place in the humanities by allowing us to move far beyond the static map, to shift from two dimensions to multidimensional representations, to develop interactive systems, and to explore space and place dynamically—in effect, to create virtual worlds embodying what we know about space and place."[19] The fertile imaginary accompanying this technological convergence has the potential to significantly reshape film history, a history that is, as this collection demonstrates, beginning to explore and advance new understandings of the sociality and experience of cinema in all its diverse forms and to map the complex spatial dynamics that have shaped the production and consumption of localized film cultures and geographies.

NOTES

1. R. Maltby, D. Biltereyst, and P. Meers, *Explorations in New Cinema History: Approaches and Case Studies* (Oxford: Wiley Blackwell, 2011).

2. www.deakin.edu.au/arts-ed/research/arc-2008.php?print_friendly=true, accessed January 3, 2012.

3. www.atlascine.org/iWeb/Site/e/cyber.html, accessed January 3, 2012.

4. "Cybercartography is a new multimedia, multisensory and interactive online cartography" developed by the Geomatics and Cartographic Research Centre at Carleton University; its main products are "cybercartographic atlases using location as a key organizing principle. These atlases create narratives from a variety of different perspectives using both quantitative and qualitative information sources including stories, art, literature and music as well as socio-economic and environmental information." https://gcrc.carleton.ca/confluence/display/GCRCWEB/Overview, accessed January 3, 2012.

5. D. Cooper and I. Gregory, "Mapping the English Lakes: A Literary GIS," *Transactions of the Institute of British Geographers* 36(1) (2011): 90.

6. www.lancs.ac.uk/mappingthelakes/STC.html, accessed January 8, 2012.

7. Landscapes, Memories and Cultural Practices, AHRC/BT AH/H018190/1, May 2009–Jan 2011.

8. http://mainstreet.lib.unc.edu/pilots.htm, accessed January 9, 2012.

9. See, for example, J. Hallam, "Civic Visions: Mapping the City in Film 1900–1960," *Culture, Theory and Critique* 53(1) (2012); M. Jonsson, "Lund: Open City? Swedish Municipal Mediation 1939–1945," in *Regional Aesthetics: Locating Swedish Media,* ed. E. Hedling, O. Hedling and M. Jonsson, 291–306 (Stockholm: Mediehistorist Arkiv 15, 2010); E. Lebas, *Forgotten Futures: British Municipal Cinema 1920–1980* (London: Black Dog Publishing, 2011).

10. D. Bodenhamer, "Creating the Landscapes of Memory: The Potential of Humanities GIS," *International Journal of Humanities and Arts Computing* 1(2) (2007): 105.

11. City in Film: Liverpool's Urban Landscape and the Moving-Image, funded by the UK Arts and Humanities Research Council 2006–2008 to explore the relationship between film and urban space. An online searchable database of more than 1,700 entries was collated as part of the project; see http://www.liv.ac.uk/lsa/cityinfilm/html.

12. R. Koeck, "Liverpool in Film: J. A. L. Promio's Cinematic Urban Space," *Early Popular Visual Culture* 7(1) (2009): 63–81.

13. L. Roberts, *Film, Mobility and Urban Space: A Cinematic Geography of Liverpool* (Liverpool: Liverpool University Press, 2012), 7.

14. Roberts, *Film, Mobility and Urban Space,* 29.

15. See, for example, http://londonfilm.bbk.ac.uk/, accessed January 10, 2012.

16. "Most of the films are included as documents of urban space but the selection also covers transport, communications, oil, electrification and some colonial subjects, including railway and port construction." P. Keiller, Notes on the Database, "The City of the Future, Urban and other Landscapes in the UK's National Film and Television Ar-

chive," Arts and Humanities Data Service, www.vads.ahds.ac.uk/collections/CF.html, accessed April 28, 2007. See J. Hallam, "Mapping Urban Space: Independent Filmmakers as Urban Gazetteers," *Journal of British Cinema and Television* 4(2) (2007): 272–84.

17. C. Brunsdon, *London in Cinema: The Cinematic City since 1945* (London: British Film Institute, 2007).

18. For scholarly examples see, for example, the World Film Locations series (Bristol, Intellect) and http://www.thecinetourist.net/, accessed January 12, 2012. An example of the proliferating print and online film location guides for tourists can be found at http://www.movie-locations.com/, accessed January 12, 2012.

19. Bodenhamer, "Creating the Landscapes of Memory," 101.

Contributors

ROBERT C. ALLEN is James Logan Godfrey Distinguished Professor of American Studies, History and Communication Studies, University of North Carolina. He has written on the history of U.S. radio and television (*Speaking of Soap Operas*, 1985), film history and historiography (*Film History: Theory and Practice*, 1985), and American popular theater of the nineteenth and early twentieth century (*Horrible Prettiness: Burlesque and American Culture*, 1992). He is also the editor of *To Be Continued: Soap Operas around the World* (1995) and of two editions of the widely-used television anthology *Channels of Discourse* and *Channels of Discourse Reassembled* (1987, 1994). He is the co-editor of *The Television Studies Reader* (2004) and *Going to the Movies: Hollywood and the Social Experience of Cinema* (2007). A National Endowment for the Humanities Digital Humanities Fellow for 2008–2009, his digital project Going to the Show documents the history of moviegoing in North Carolina from 1896–1930 (http://docsouth.unc.edu/gtts/). In 2011, Going to the Show received the Roy Rosenweig prize for innovation in digital history, awarded jointly by the American Historical Association and the Centre for History and New Media at George Mason University.

COLIN ARROWSMITH is Associate Professor in the School of Mathematical and Geospatial Sciences at RMIT University. He holds a Doctor of Philosophy from RMIT as well as two master's degrees from the University of Melbourne, and a Graduate Diploma of Education from Hawthorn Institute of Education. Colin has authored more than 40 refereed publications and six book chapters in the fields of GIS, tourism analysis and in film studies. His research interests include the application of geospatial information systems, including geographic information systems (GIS), geospatial science education, investigating the impact of tourism on nature-based tourist destinations, tourist behavior, as well as investigating the issue of managing micro-historical data within GIS utilizing cinema data. Colin is an editor for the *Journal of Spatial Science*, Member of the Surveying and Spatial Science Institute of Australia, and a Fellow of the Royal Geographical Society.

DANIEL BILTEREYST is Professor in film and cultural media studies at Ghent University, Belgium, where he leads the Centre for Cinema and Media Studies (CIMS). His work on film and screen culture as sites of controversy and public debate has been published in many journals and edited volumes. He is the editor, with Richard Maltby and Philippe Meers, of *Explorations in New Cinema History* (2011) and of *Cinema, Audiences and Modernity: New Perspectives on European Cinema History* (2012). He is currently editing *Silencing Cinema: Film Censorship around the World* (with Roel Vande Winkel).

KATE BOWLES is a cinema historian at the University of Wollongong, specializing in the social history of rural cinema attendance in Australia. With colleagues Richard Maltby, Deb Verhoeven, Mike Walsh, Colin Arrowsmith, and Jill Julius Matthews, she is involved in the ongoing collection of data related to Australian cinemagoing history, in particular exploring the use of GIS and oral history methods to examine the social and trade logistics of Australia's country cinemas. She has written widely on the historical process of cinemagoing in journals such as *History Compass* and *Media International Australia* and is currently co-authoring a book with Richard Maltby, Deb Verhoeven, and Mike Walsh titled *The New Cinema History: A Guide for Researchers* (forthcoming).

SÉBASTIEN CAQUARD is Assistant Professor in the Department of Geography, Planning and Environment at Concordia University, Montréal. For the last few years Sébastien has been examining the technological, artistic and scientific frontiers of cybercartography, more specifically in the emerging field of cinematic cartography. In his current research, he seeks to explore further the relationships between places and fictions through the development of new ways of categorizing, visualizing, and analyzing cinematographic territories. Sébastien Caquard is also the chair of the Commission on "Art and Cartography" of the International Cartographic Association (ICA) (http://artcarto.wordpress.com/) and the co-founder of the collective blog (e)space & fiction.

JULIA HALLAM is Reader in film and media and Head of the Department of Communication and Media at the University of Liverpool U.K. She has written on women's representation in the media (*Nursing the Image: Media, Culture and Professional Identity,* 2000), on women writers in the U.K. television industry (*Lynda La Plante,* 2005), on contemporary film aesthetics (*Realism and Popular Cinema,* 2000) and co-edited two collections of essays on popular fiction (*Medical Fictions* 1998, *Consuming for Pleasure* 2001). Her work has been published in journals such as *Screen, Culture Theory and Critique* and *The Journal of British Cinema and Television;* she is a corresponding editor for *Critical Studies in Television.* Julia has contributed to numerous radio broadcasts and television programs including an eight part series celebrating the work of the first generation of writers at Granada Television (*Those Were the Days,* ITV 2005) and a documentary on doctors and nurses in film (*Trust Me, I'm a Doctor: Medics in the Movies* BBC 2007). From 2006–2011 she led three collaborative projects on film and place funded by the U.K. Arts and Humanities Research Council (*City in Film, Mapping the City and Film, Landscapes, Memories and Cultural Practices*); an inter-active map developed from these projects can be seen in the History Detectives gallery at the new Museum of Liverpool which opened in 2011.

JEFFREY KLENOTIC is Associate Professor of Communication Arts at the University of New Hampshire. In 2005 and 2012, he won UNH Faculty Scholars Awards for his pioneering work using Geographic Information Systems to study the history of cinemagoing and everyday life in New Hampshire. His essays have appeared in journals such as *Senses of Cinema, Film History, Communication Review* and *Velvet Light Trap,* as well as in numerous anthologies. Recent publications include "From Mom-and-Pop to Paramount-Publix: Selling the Community on the Benefits of National Theater Chains" in *Watching Films* and "Putting Cinema History on the Map: Using GIS to Explore the Spatiality of Cinema" in *Explorations in New Cinema History.*

PHILIPPE MEERS is Associate Professor in film and media studies at the University of Antwerp, Belgium, where he is Head of Department and deputy director of the Visual Studies and Media Culture research group. He has published widely on historical, contemporary, and ethnic film cultures in journals such as *Screen*, *Critical Studies in Media Communication*, *Javnost/The Public* and in edited collections such as *The Contemporary Hollywood Reader* (2009). With Richard Maltby and Daniel Biltereyst, he edited *Explorations in New Cinema History, Approaches and Case Studies* (2011), and *Audiences, Cinema and Modernity* (2012).

DANIEL NAUD is completing his doctoral thesis in cultural geography at the University of Montreal, which focuses on the representation of urban, rural, and suburban areas in Quebec cinema. Daniel is interested in the creation and evolution of spatial discourses and is a GIS lecturer at Concordia University in Montreal. He is currently collaborating on the *Cartography of Fictional Spaces* (http://www.atlascine.org) project and the *Turcot: The Road Became Architecture* project, mapping an immersive and interactive environment of a modern interchange soon to be dismantled.

ELISA RAVAZZOLI works as a researcher in the Institute for Regional Development and Locational Management at *EURAC research*. She completed her Ph.D. in Economics from the *University of Bologna* in 2011 and was visiting research fellow at Brown University, University of Chicago, and Columbia University. Her main research interests are in urban, social, and cultural geography as well as in spatial data analysis. In particular, her research has focused on studying the socio-spatial dynamics of cities and regions, making the Geographic Information System an essential instrument of investigation.

LES ROBERTS is a research fellow in the School of the Arts at the University of Liverpool. His research interests are in the cultural production of space, place and mobility, with a particular focus on film and popular music cultures. Les's recent projects include a GIS-based geo-historical study of Liverpool's urban landscape in film, and ethnographic research into popular music as cultural heritage. He is author of *Film, Mobility and Urban Space: a Cinematic Geography of Liverpool* (2012), editor of *Mapping*

Cultures: Place, Practice and Performance (2012) and co-editor of *Liminal Landscapes: Travel, Experience and Spaces In-between* (2012) and *The City and the Moving Image: Urban Projections* (2010).

RYAN SHAND is Research Assistant on the A.H.R.C. funded project "Children and Amateur Media in Scotland" based at the University of Glasgow. He has contributed chapters to the anthologies *Movies on Home Ground: Explorations in Amateur Cinema* (2009), *The City and the Moving Image: Urban Projections* (2010), and his article "Theorizing Amateur Cinema: Limitations and Possibilities" was published in *The Moving Image*. Ryan is also the co-editor of *Small-Gauge Storytelling: Discovering the Amateur Fiction Film* (forthcoming).

DEB VERHOEVEN is Professor and Chair of Media and Communication at Deakin University. Her research is principally focused on extending the limits of conventional cinema studies through collaboration with specialists in diverse fields such as geo-spatial science, economics, information management, and the creative arts. She is currently co-authoring a book with Richard Maltby, Kate Bowles, and Mike Walsh titled *The New Cinema History: A Guide for Researchers* (forthcoming) and is the architect of several online cinema research resources. Deb is Project Director of the Humanities Networked Infrastructure (HuNI) Virtual Laboratory: a two-year linked data project that will provide creative arts and humanities researchers around the world with access to the combined resources of Australia's major cultural datasets and information assets.

BENJAMIN WRIGHT is the Provost Postdoctoral Scholar in the Humanities at the School of Cinematic Arts at the University of Southern California. He received his Ph.D. from the Institute of Comparative Studies in Literature, Art and Culture at Carleton University in 2011. His research focuses on the production culture of Hollywood film and television sound professionals.

Index